Modern Politics and Government

Also by Alan R. Ball

British Political Parties (2nd edition)

Pressure Politics in Industrialised Societies (with Frances Millard)

Also by B. Guy Peters

American Public Policy (5th edition)

Comparative Politics

Modern Politics and Government

SIXTH EDITION

Alan R. Ball
and
B. Guy Peters

CHATHAM HOUSE PUBLISHERS

SEVEN BRIDGES PRESS, LLC

NEW YORK • LONDON

MODERN POLITICS AND GOVERNMENT
6th edition

Seven Bridges Press, LLC
135 Fifth Avenue
New York, NY 10010-7101

Library of Congress Cataloging-in-Publication Data
Modern politics and government / Alan R. Ball and B. Guy Peters — 6th edition
p. cm.
Includes bibliographical references and index.
ISBN 1–889119–07–5
1. Political Science. I. Peters, B. Guy. II. Title

JA66 .B29   1999
320—dc21

99–51531

10 9 8 7 6 5 4 3 2 1

Printed in Great Britain

Contents

PART IV POLITICAL CHANGE

List of Tables

Preface to the Sixth Edition

Nearly 30 years have passed since the publication of the first edition of this book. They have seen dramatic changes both in the real world of politics and in the ways in which it is studied which have been reflected by the original author, Alan Ball, in successive revised editions. His retirement from active university teaching prompted the idea of adding Guy Peters as co-author for the sixth and subsequent editions.

Despite the change in authorship, the basic purpose of the book remains the same. As stated in the Preface to the First Edition, the intention is to provide a wide-ranging introduction to politics, and to the study of politics. Although no individual countries are discussed in great detail, the approach is inherently comparative, and attempts to demonstrate how politics plays out in a wide range of different settings. Also, as before, a variety of political phenomena are discussed, ranging from voting and public opinion to the formal actions of governments. There is an attempt to show how these institutions and political behaviour all influence the actions of government.

Although there is a great deal of continuity, this sixth edition has been very substantially revised, rewritten and updated to take account of the changing political world about which we are writing. Democratisation has brought about major changes in many countries of the world, as has the effect of reduced government involvement in the economy and the advent of a new – more market-influenced – form of public management. In Europe the continuing development of the European Union and the declining role of the nation state in some aspects of policy-making are transforming politics in the fifteen member countries, and potentially in an even larger number of potential members. These several changes in politics are posing new analytical and practical questions about politics. Finally, adding a new co-author with different interests and a different academic training has inevitably altered the focus of the book somewhat. In particular there has been an attempt to make the text reflect contemporary debates in political science and the intellectual questions that now drive the discipline.

We would like to thank our publishers, Steven Kennedy in Britain and Bob Gormley in the United States, for their patience, encouragement and numerous suggestions. The book is much better because of this editorial advice. We also want to thank our families for their support and understanding as we prepared this edition.

ALAN R. BALL
B. GUY PETERS

PART ONE

The Nature of Politics

1

The Study of Politics

Politics is one of the oldest activities of humanity. As soon as people began to live together in groups there was a need to devise ways to govern those societies. From modest beginnings the elaborate institutions and procedures of modern government have grown. Despite the increased formality and structure, many of the same issues exist in contemporary politics as existed when governing a band of hunter-gatherers. Who has the power, and do they exercise that power appropriately? Are the institutions of government stable, or are they subject to rapid changes of leadership? Are there processes for the average member of the society to influence government, or does it remain the domain of a few powerful individuals?

As well as being an important and sometimes amusing activity, politics is also a mechanism for achieving societal goals. In many modern societies more than one-third (and in some cases approaching – or even exceeding – a half) of what is earned in the economy is taken as taxes and then recycled through the public budget to achieve a variety of public purposes (Table 1.1). People in all countries depend upon government for protection against foreign enemies and domestic criminals, for some management of the economy, and public services such as roads. Citizens in most countries now depend upon government for their health care, for the education of their children, and for their own livelihoods during old age. Governing is about more than elections; it is also about providing for the collective welfare of the people. Further, a major political choice is what goods and services will be publicly provided and which will be left to the market or to other private organisations to provide.

Table 1.1   Government revenue as a percentage of Gross
Domestic Product (most recent year available)

Argentina	14.4
Australia	23.7
Canada	36.5
Czech Republic	41.3
France	40.7
India	34.3
Japan	22.6
Kenya	19.6
Sierra Leone	9.7
Sweden	46.8
United Kingdom	38.7
United States	33.6

Note: Government expenditures are often higher than their
revenues, given the tendency to use deficit finance.
Source: International Monetary Funds, *Government Finance Yearbook*
and *International Financial Statistics* (both Washington, DC,
annual).

The problem of boundaries

If there is agreement that politics is an important activity then
there is a marked lack of agreement on what constitutes the
best approach to the study of politics. The bewildering array of
titles of degree courses in the English-speaking world illustrates
some of the confusion: names such as Government, Politics,
Political Institutions, Political Science are umbrellas protecting
the various specialisations of Public Administration, Political
Theory, Political Philosophy, Comparative Government, National Politics, Public Policy and International Politics.[1] The
Oxford English Dictionary defines politics as: 'The science and art
of government: the science dealing with the form, organisation
and administration of a state, or part of one, and with the
regulation of its relations with other states.'

The restriction of the study of politics to a concern mainly
with public institutions and state activities is certainly disputed
by most contemporary students of the subject, who are more
likely to emphasise voting behaviour and the attitudes of the

public. When these students of political behaviour do look at government institutions, it is in order to examine how the individual members behave in office. For example, rather than being concerned so much with the content of Supreme Court decisions in the United States there is now a long tradition of studying the behaviour of individual judges, the consistency with which they vote along ideological lines, and attitudes that can be inferred from that behaviour.[2] This is very far from the traditional study of constitutional law, yet both studies can enrich the other.

The emphasis on the science of politics often has led to crude and confused analogies with the method of the natural sciences. Nevertheless, Professor W. J. M. Mackenzie pointed to some advantages of the term 'political science':

> So far as I can judge, 'political science' is still the name which carries meaning to the general public . . . The word science here indicates simply that there exists an academic tradition of the study of politics, a discipline communicated from teacher to pupil, by speech and writing, for some 2,500 years now. It does not mean that this discipline claims to be a 'natural science', or that it could be improved by copying the methods of physics and chemistry exactly.[3]

Although certainly not as formalised as the natural sciences, political science is now being studied much more scientifically than it was at the time that Mackenzie wrote, and there is a large body of quantitative, replicable analysis of political behaviour and political institutions.[4]

However, even with agreement on a title, or at least a recognition of where the disagreements lie, there still remains the problem of the content and orientation of the subject. This difficulty has been underlined by the dominance of American political scientists, especially since 1945, and their emphasis first on quantitative methods and later on formal models.[5] There has also been a more extensive borrowing of methods and concepts from other social science disciplines, such as economics, sociology and psychology, with varying degrees of success. These new developments which have been superimposed on traditional approaches to the subject have led to confusion of terminology as well as method, producing apparent confusion about what really constitutes the most appropriate ways of discussing political phenomena.

The apparent conceptual confusion in political science also results partly from the political changes in the twentieth century, in which the certainties of liberal democracy were assaulted by the rise of popularly supported totalitarian regimes. The fall of many of those regimes has, in turn, created a new wave of thinking about types of viable political regimes and the nature of governing. It is understandable that students fresh to the subject may feel rather uncertain as to what actually constitutes the study of politics. At the risk of promoting greater confusion, we will begin by briefly surveying the various approaches to the academic study of politics before examining, in Chapter 2, the nature of political activity itself.

Traditional approaches

Before 1900, the study of politics was largely dominated by philosophy, history and law. To use the label 'traditional' is neither a criticism nor a refutation of the obvious fact that they still play important roles in modern political studies although no longer monopolising the field. The modern student of politics is still faced with the works of great philosophers such as Plato or Hegel that require textual analysis and new interpretations, but the search for universal values concerning political activity tends to be avoided in most contemporary political analysis. At present 'ought' questions are not fashionable in political science, although not all critics of traditional political philosophy would travel as far as T. D. Weldon in his reduction to trivia and linguistic misunderstandings such ancient political concepts as freedom, justice, obedience, liberty and natural rights.[6]

It could not be thought that traditional political philosophy was concerned only with *a priori* deductions, that is, conclusions reached with little observation of political facts. Plato's search for his philosopher king, or Hobbes's 'leviathan', an all-powerful government that would end civil disorder, may be balanced by Aristotle's exhaustive collection of studies of the constitutions of Greek city-states, and Machiavelli's political advice resting on his observations and participation in the governments of Italian Renaissance states. But the seekers after the perfect state did base their answers on oversimplified assumptions over a wide variety of matters; thus Thomas Hobbes, with a generalised view of human nature, could speak of, 'a generall inclination of all mankind, a perpetuall and restlesse desire of Power after power, that ceaseth only in Death'.[7]

The classical political theorists are still important even in regard to the nature of the questions they posed, and certainly ignorance concerning them isolates any student of politics from some of the communication that passes among political scientists. Moreover, the descriptive work of these political philosophers, no matter how shaky their grand edifices may be, did supply the first explorations of the field of comparative government. Aristotle, for example, began to classify political systems in typologies in a manner not dissimilar to that used in contemporary political analysis, and the empirical evidence associated with normative problems provides a way to begin to understand the ways in which government functions.[8]

Also, there is significant interplay between the political theories and the nature of the society and its politics in which the theory originates. We can learn a great deal of the English revolution of 1688, its origins, the character and political aims of the men who controlled and guided it, by reading the political philosophy of John Locke. The nature of the American constitutional settlement of 1788–9 becomes clearer after examining the propaganda of the *Federalist Papers*. No student of the government and politics of the Soviet Union could avoid reference to Lenin's reformulation of Marxist philosophy, nor a student of those of China ignore the works of Chairman Mao. A student interested in feminist politics would do well to start with Simone de Beauvoir or Mary Wollstonecroft.

Given these particular approaches to political studies, it is easy to see why the historian played such a significant part in the discipline. The historical-descriptive technique examines past events through available evidence and draws tentative conclusions about some aspect of contemporary political activity. The sources vary from memoirs and biographies of important statesmen to journalistic accounts of particular events.

The historian becomes a synthesiser, using his own intellectual judgement and common sense to fit the various parts of the jigsaw into a coherent pattern. It is clear that many of the political institutions and political practices of the present day are explicable in terms of history, but past evidence leaves alarming gaps, and political history is often simply a record of great men and great events rather than comprehensive accounts of total political activity.

In British political studies, Sir Ivor Jennings, with his studies of parliament and cabinet government, favoured this approach, digging deep into nineteenth-century history to trace the growth of the office of prime minister or the rise of modern political parties. Robert McKenzie's pioneering work on British political parties lays great stress on their historical evolution. In American political science, Stephen Skowronek's study of the American executive and public administration enhanced understanding of contemporary institutions.[9] Likewise, Nelson Polsby has gone a long way in explaining the current state of the American Congress by looking at its pattern of development.

The study of constitutional law formed the third cornerstone of traditional political studies. There is now a closer relationship between the study of law and politics in the continental European tradition; in Anglo-Saxon countries the divorce has become more complete. Before 1900, a British student of politics would have devoted a major part of his energies to the study of legal institutions, and Dicey's *Law of the Constitution*, first published in 1885, loomed large on any politics reading list. Although arguments on such topics as the legal sovereignty of the British parliament, the rule of law and the separation of powers are no longer regarded as of first importance, the links between law and politics are not completely broken, the gap being bridged by bringing aspects of the judicial system firmly into the field of the political process. If anything, the role of the European Court of Justice has brought legal questions back to the centre of British politics. Of course, the importance of the Supreme Court and its judgements in American political life means that any student of American politics needs more than a nodding acquaintance with constitutional law.[10]

The strongest legacy that philosophy, history and law have bequeathed to the study of politics is in the field of descriptive and institutional approaches. Political scientists still, despite recent developments, concentrate chiefly on examining the major political institutions of the state such as the executive, legislature, the civil service, the judiciary and local government. These examinations yield valuable insights about the organisation and reform of political institutions. However, despite the point that all description involves some conceptualisation, no wide-reaching theories emerged from these studies. Bernard Crick's *Reform of Parliament* is representative of the British approach in this field, and Stephen Bailey's *Congress at Work* offers an early American example. They sought to explain how various political institutions work, and from that description come tentative proposals on how to remedy possible faults and inefficiencies.

There can, of course, be various different approaches within this descriptive–analytic field. If one were to study the contrasting examinations of the role of the president within the American system of government one could travel from the legal formalism of Edward Corwin's *The President – Office and Powers* to the invigorating emphasis on informal processes in Richard Neustadt's *Presidential Power*. Both, however, are concerned with the analysis of the president's role in American politics and seek to support their conclusions by citing case histories, personal observations and documentary evidence. They seek to show how that particular political institution works. It is interesting to note that some major contributions to this approach have been made not only by political scientists confined to their university desks, but by men actively engaged in public affairs. Walter Bagehot, for example, was a practising journalist when he wrote *The English Constitution* in 1867, but he produced a classic analysis of the working of the political process, an analysis that still has contemporary relevance; Woodrow Wilson's studies of politics – American and comparative – represented the work of someone who was both an academic and a major practitioner of governance.[11]

The study of institutional and policy processes continues to be a major component of political science. What has happened, however, is that the study has shifted from descriptive to more analytic studies of those processes. For example, Charles Jones has presented a 'stages' theory of the policy process that points to the steps through which a policy must go before it can be put into effect.[12] Following from that, there have been a number of theoretical and empirical studies of the various stages of the process, from agenda-setting through to evaluation.[13] All of these studies have pointed to the role that process has in determining the final solution of policy problems.

Comparative studies

Comparative government and politics was to provide the link between the traditional approaches to political science and the more recent developments in the discipline. We have already noted that the comparative method is a very old one; its origins and development can be traced from Herodotus and Aristotle through Bodin and Montesquieu. Yet despite the longevity of comparative political studies, many problems remain. It is not simply the difficulty of collecting enough relevant facts about different political systems but the organisation of the information gathered. Comparative politics has been mainly concerned with European and North American states, but the widening of horizons to countries referred to as 'developing' and 'transitional' states has led to greater scrutiny of what units should be compared.[14]

The geographical expansion of comparative politics led to the development of some theories that were so general as to be meaningless. For example, structural-functionalism argued that every government would have to perform certain requisite functions, and comparisons could be made according to how they were performed. Therefore, Joseph LaPalombara, among others, advocated the development of 'middle range theories' that would be applicable to a more limited range of countries or institutions.[15] A comparison of formal institutions such as legislatures and executives can be done across a range of countries, albeit still carefully. One cannot extract a particular political institution from its context and compare it with institutions in other countries without taking into account the whole political system in which that institution is set, but yet there may be some comparable features. Robert Dahl attempted a comparison of political oppositions in various liberal democracies, and reached the conclusion that it is a concept that has a particular meaning and relevance in the British system of government.[16] Still, all democratic countries do have opposition parties that function as alternative governments.[17]

The attempted transfer of European political institutions to former colonial territories, especially on the African continent, has illustrated the difficulty of comparative politics in a practical way. Parliamentary procedures, competitive party systems, neutral civil servants and soldiers grow out of integrated relationships and cannot be individually exported and expected to function in a manner similar to that found in the exporting country. That having been said, the more recent experience of building democracies in the former socialist systems in Eastern Europe reveals that institutional transfers can be made to work in some settings.[18]

Of course, the comparative method does not necessarily mean that the comparison must be cross-national to be rewarding. The existence of fifty American states with some degree of independence of the federal government provides a fertile field for comparison.[19] Even the apparent uniformity of English local government allows some scope for comparison.[20] Nor does the comparative method imply a disinterest in the political processes of one's own country; on the contrary it may be the most rewarding means of discovering information about the politics of one particular state. However, the recent advances in the theory and methodology of the political sciences have resulted partly from the fact that the basic questions of the comparative approach, such as 'Why do certain types of political institutions and political activity exist in certain states?', are still largely unanswered.

To some extent it has been in response to these problems that political science has attempted to formulate general or partial theories and advance certain models in some way comparable to those used in the other social sciences. Indeed, we could argue that comparative politics is the crucial component of political science.[21] Unlike the natural sciences, political science does not have the possibility of doing experiments. There are some natural experiments, e.g. New Zealand changing its voting system while retaining the other formal aspects of the political system, but these are rare. Therefore, comparison becomes the fundamental method by which political scientists test theory and develop the science in political science.

Transitional approaches

The publication of Graham Wallas's *Human Nature in Politics* and Arthur Bentley's *The Process of Government,* both in 1908, symbolised the beginning of a change in political studies. With these changes there would be a greater emphasis on the informal processes of politics and less on state political institutions in isolation.[22] There also would be freer borrowing from other social science disciplines of sociology and psychology, and the new empirical orientation of political studies was ultimately to lead to an examination of such political concepts as power, authority and political élites. It should be remembered that these new approaches have been neither uniformly accepted nor universally applied, nor should we ignore the nineteenth-century predecessors such as de Tocqueville or even Bagehot, who foreshadowed much of what is contained in this empirical aim of examining politics in action to discover what makes the machine tick.

Graham Wallas, an Englishman with practical political experience, was to emphasise a demand for a new realism in political studies. His central theme, borrowed from psychology, was that humans were not rational creatures whose political actions were totally guided by reason and self-interest. Human nature was far too complex for simple explanations. Wallas was, therefore, attacking not only the deductive reasoning of the political philosophers, but also the approach of the classical economists that explanations could be found in man's eagerness to follow rationally his own economic self-interest. Wallas demanded facts and evidence, claiming that advances in the discipline should be attempted quantitatively not qualitatively. It is true that many of Wallas's methods and conclusions were extensively criticised and that political science's enthusiasm for psychology was not to bear the fruit that these early hopes had raised, but Wallas did carry the important message that to understand the political process one must examine how people actually behave in political situations, not merely speculate on how they should or would behave. The other pioneer who symbolised new stirrings in political studies was Arthur Bentley. He too has been widely criticised, but nevertheless his pragmatic realism and his demand for measurement and facts succeeded in weaning the discipline away from political philosophy and descriptive formalism. His aim was not to describe political activity but to provide new tools of investigation, and he believed that he had found these in the study of groups in politics: 'When groups are adequately stated, everything is stated'.[23] He was therefore prepared to ignore almost completely formal political institutions. His behaviouralism owed much to sociology, and he pointed the way to the study of the roles of pressure groups, parties, elections and public opinion in the political process.

These new orientations have produced several dangers for political science. First, politics has been seen as a subsidiary, a satellite of sociology, in that political activity and institutions reflect the nature of society and are determined and patterned to a large extent by divisions within society. Politics in this sense can be seen as dependent on forces outside the political system, and as such ceases to have a major role as an independent social science. Thus the way people vote is seen to depend particularly on class, ethnic and religious divisions in society, and the activities and programmes of political parties and of governments are considered less important. Giovanni Sartori has strongly argued for a re-emphasis on the mutual contributions of politics and sociology and recognition that political factors – as manifested in governments and political parties – independently affect political behavior.[24]

A second danger is that political sociology tends to emphasise only the 'inputs' of the political system, by which we mean emphasis on the role of political parties, pressure groups, voting behaviour, political communication and public opinion, to the detriment of other political factors such as governments, legislatures, administration and judiciaries. Linked to this is a third danger, which is that of examining only those aspects of the political system that are amenable to measurement or quantification. It has been part of the search for a pure science of politics in which the findings and conclusions would depend not on subjective judgements but on measurable factors. Quantitative methods would allow description and values in political studies to be banished at least from the research laboratories.

The quantitative approach to politics has been of immense advantage in some fields of political science, especially voting behaviour and elections, in which mass behaviour could be more readily analysed by these tools. Sample surveys used by opinion pollsters have illuminated many aspects of political behaviour undiscoverable by other means, and used correctly in skilled hands have enriched the discipline. However, they are tools of analysis that can only be usefully employed in certain fields, and their findings have to be treated with care. The polling failures in the 1992 election pointed out the problems that even well-managed and well-funded sample surveys can encounter.[25] The problem is that for some scholars quantification becomes an end in itself; meticulous care is often taken to discover the class readership of newspapers and the political views of the editors before the more important question of whether newspapers actually influence political opinion is discussed.

The search for a science of politics and the fashioning of new tools of analysis and more sophisticated concepts was dominated after the First World War by American scholars. Their lines of inquiry took them into the fields of psychology and the empiricism of quantitative methods. Political power became one of the key concepts of political scientists. The two giants of this approach were Charles Merriam[26] and Harold Lasswell,[27] who spoke of the 'science of power' and widened the discussion of such concepts as political élites. It is interesting to note that the development of the discipline from Merriam to his pupil Lasswell is also an indication of the relative failure of liberal democratic systems of government, especially in Europe, and the rise of totalitarian regimes of the fascist and communist varieties. Of course, a study of political power was not previously foreign to political science, and intellectual forerunners may be found in Machiavelli and Hobbes, just to mention two, but the new approach was far more rigorous and systematic, and was ultimately to blossom into the studies of communities and power in the 1950s with the arguments over methodology that they entailed.[28]

Further developments

Following the Second World War, there were other major shifts in the direction of political science. One of these was the extension of behavioral and quantitative analysis to a degree probably unanticipated by the early pioneers in this form of analysis. This was clearly seen in areas such as voting behaviour, with a number of major studies in the United States and others coming somewhat later in Britain.[29] There was also an extension of behavioural analysis to the members of major institutions, including legislatures and the courts.[30] In addition, there were a number of new theoretical departures reflecting in part the felt need to make political science more capable of coping with the development of newer governments in the former colonies.

Systems analysis

David Easton published *The Political System* in 1953, claiming that he was attempting to construct a theory to embrace all the social sciences.[31] He was emphasising the need to theorise about the whole political process, not simply about related aspects of it. Since then, Easton has become one of the prominent supporters of the application of 'general systems' theories to political science,[32] and one of the few to come from within the discipline rather than from the other social sciences. Briefly, Easton focuses on the system – that is, a pattern of related structural and behavioral elements that are interdependent. He defines the political system as 'that system of interactions in any society through which binding or authoritative allocations are made'.[33] Authoritative allocations may be roughly translated as policy-making, although the term may have somewhat broader, symbolic implications.[34]

There are in this political system inputs from the various environments and these are converted into outputs, i.e. authoritative decisions. Feedback mechanisms put outputs back into the system as inputs, thus completing a complex, cyclical operation. Many demands will be made, or 'articulated', but some are lost in the conversion process and do not reach the output stage. If there are too many demands, or particular types of demand, stress arises, and the channels are then overloaded. There are various regulatory mechanisms to control demands and minimise overloading: firstly, the structural mechanisms, 'the gatekeepers', e.g. pressure groups, political parties; secondly, cultural mechanisms, the various norms which consider the appropriateness of the demands; thirdly, communications channels, which can be increased. Fourthly, demands may be controlled in the conversion process itself by the legislators, executives and administrative bodies. Authoritative decisions that displease too many members of the system will lose support for the system.

The model is far more complex than described here, but the outline is sufficient to indicate the systemic approach. It is an attempt to provide a framework for organising and conceptualising information. The approach has been variously criticised for failing to accommodate adequately major concepts such as political power, or for being unable to handle mass political behavioural aspects such as voting.[35] Further, it says virtually nothing about the 'withinputs' of the system, or the institutions of conversion that had been central to most previous comparative politics. Still, it may be said to be one of the more ambitious attempts to construct a theoretical framework from within political science.

Structural-functionalism is an important off-shoot from general systems theories.[36] It is a means of explaining what political structures perform which basic functions in the political system, and it provides a set of general questions for investigation. A political party is a structure within the political system that performs many functions, including those of communicating the desires of the mass electorate to their government, informing the electorate on important political issues, and allowing for wider participation by more people in the political system. The party helps to maintain the system because it performs these tasks, but other structures such as pressure groups or formal government institutions may also carry out these same functions, and in other political systems other structures may carry out the functions in the absence of institutionalised political parties. A particular function may not be recognised or intended by the participants, and this is called a *latent* as opposed to a *manifest function*. The structural-functional approach was more widely adopted in the field of comparative government because it provides standard categories usable for analysing markedly different political systems.[37] The approach has been criticised, in part because it was concerned centrally with systems maintenance, and, as such, tended, it was argued, to justify the status quo. Even if not completely conservative, the structural-functional approach did appear to have an implicit bias in favour of Western-style democratic systems. One of the criteria advanced for development in this approach, for example, was the differentiation of subsystems, something akin to developing autonomous political institutions.[38] Some of the criticisms could be met if the claims of the structural-functionalists had not been exaggerated, and it has become recognised that this approach, while rewarding, cannot provide a general theory for all aspects of political science.

Other theoretical developments

New approaches in the theories of political science have been borrowed from the technical advances of electronic communications and large-scale computers. Karl Deutsch is one of the foremost advocates of communication theory, and his approach is clearly set out in his book *The Nerves of Government: Models of Political Communication and Control*. 'This book,' says Deutsch, 'concerns itself less with the bones or muscles of the body politic than with its nerves – its channels of communication and decision. This book suggests that it might be profitable to look upon government somewhat less as a problem of power and somewhat more as a problem of steering; and it tries to show that steering is decisively a matter of communication.'[39] He then proceeds to talk of channels, loads, load capacity, flows, lag, etc., as these concepts have relevance for the study of political phenomena. The main point made was that communications limits the capacity of any organisation, including political organisations, to make good decisions and implement them, and therefore this process should be analysed intensely.

Emphasising the necessity of steering foreshadowed later development of ideas concerning 'governance', a concept also closely related to the idea of government steering its society. Governance is a vague term and it can be construed to mean a number of different things, including self-management of societies through networks and other social actors.[40] However governance is conceptualised, this approach to politics emphasises that the basic function of government is to make policy and to influence the situation in the surrounding economy and society.

In the search for new theoretical approaches, it may be said that the wheel has turned full circle, and the latest enthusiasm is for application of economic theory to politics. This approach is titled variously 'new political economy'[41] to distinguish it from the political economy of the classical nineteenth-century liberal economists, or 'rational choice'.[42] The attempts to apply economic models to the study of politics are particularly associated with the names of Anthony Downs,[43] J. M. Buchanan and G. Tullock,[44] and more recently with scholars such as Kenneth Shepsle[45] and George Tsebelis.[46] The essence of the approach is the view of the political process as a process of exchange; the vote, for example, is a type of money that can be exchanged for something else. Politics is a market place. The political economist sees the behaviour of individuals and organisations as rational, and as the pursuit of self-interest. He or she is inclined to stress the co-operative elements in the political process as opposed to the conflict approach. Politics is concerned with the allocation of resources, and the optimising of social welfare, and thus choices within the political process are concerned with government finance, budgets, types of taxes, and the effect of these choices on political structures. The application of economic models in competition with political sociology has resulted in an ironic state of affairs for the study of politics. In the words of W. J. M. Mackenzie: 'Hence a curious situation. Sociology and economics have both occupied the traditional territory of political science: but what is left to arbitrate their dispute – except political science.[47]

Political science in the 1990s is left in a rather confused situation. Any enthusiasm for functionalism and systems analysis in comparative politics has long since passed, and the limits of behaviouralism have become very evident. Likewise, rational choice approaches are demonstrating more appeal to technicians than to people genuinely interested in political phenomena. Policy analysis continues to attract some attention, and political scientists are directing more of their energy toward understanding what governments do, and the consequences of government policies. This direction may involve a return to organisational theory, as well as a wider investigation of the constraints on policy-making and policy alternatives.[48] Changes in Latin America and above all in Eastern Europe and the former USSR have also led to renewed interest in the factors affecting the development of democratic government,[49] and the work of Robert Putnam and others has revived some interest in political sociology and the importance of civil society in promoting effective democracy.[50]

A major set of challenges to the existing canon of political science comes from changes in the international environment, generally discussed in terms of 'globalisation' and 'regionalisation'. The international economy and the creation of regional political and economic blocs such as the European Union are tending to erode the power of national governments and to make governance more difficult. These movements may be exaggerated by some advocates of the ideas, but it is also clear that national governments are not the only actors involved in making public policies, and that political science needs to find ways of including these emerging patterns in our analyses of both developing and more-developed political systems.[51]

The new institutionalism is one of the more important reactions to the perceived excesses of rational choice analysis and behaviouralism.[52] Unlike the older version of institutionalism described above, the new institutionalism is less concerned with describing organisations than with developing theoretical means for understanding political outcomes and processes. Although discussed in the singular, the 'new institutionalism' is actually a variety of different approaches, some focusing on the role of norms,[53] while others are more concerned with the effects of structure on the choices made by individuals.[54] Still other institutionalist approaches study the effects of initial policy choices and the 'path dependency' of institutions.[55]

All of these various institutionalist approaches, however, move political science away from an emphasis on individuals and back – at least in part – to its roots in the study of structure. These approaches also promote the necessity of thinking about the interaction of individual behaviour and the formal structures within which they function. For example, where do the preferences of the members of the institution come from? Are they the result of their own previous socialisation, or the result of values being inculcated from within the institution? Also, are individual leaders capable of transforming institutions or are the transformations only the product of longer-term, and impersonal, processes of change?

Political studies and practical politics

Aristotle once said that 'the end of politics is not knowledge but action', and certainly an overview of political studies must acknowledge the links between the academic approach and practical activity. There is, of course, a danger of being accused of political and social engineering in that the labours of the political scientist may be applied to normative ends. This is especially dangerous when university departments come to rely more and more on direct grants and particular private funds to conduct research, a danger more acute in the United States. But the history of political studies has illustrated the benefits received from practising politicians and the returns that political science has been able to repay. Machiavelli may not have secured the post in the Florentine government which he hoped would follow the dedication of *The Prince* to the Medici, but the realism of that treatise owes much to his former public service. The founding fathers of the American constitution are a foremost example of a mixture of political theory and practical realism; they wanted their system of government to embody certain political principles, but they also wanted it to work and endure. Herbert Morrison utilised his political and ministerial experience to provide valuable insights into the working of British governments. Lenin's *What Is to Be Done?*, a pamphlet of

1902, and Hitler's *Mein Kampf*, written in 1923, are superb examples of mixtures of political theory, political strategy and political propaganda.

American political scientists appear to be more willing to involve themselves in practical politics than are their European counterparts. Zbigniew Brzezinski was an influential foreign policy adviser to President Carter in the late 1970s; Jeane Kirkpatrick taught political science in Washington before being chosen by President Reagan in 1980 to be American ambassador to the United Nations. Donna Shalala, formerly president of the University of Wisconsin, became Secretary of Health and Human Services in the Clinton Administration. Prominent British political scientists, such as Anthony King and Ivor Crewe, were actively engaged in advising the British Social Democratic Party, founded in 1981. However, this level of involvement appears pallid when compared to that of the American political scientists of the Progressive era, the first two decades of the twentieth century, with their confidence in the future of liberal democracy, and their determination to set the world to rights. Woodrow Wilson not only wrote two important books on the nature of the American system of government, but was president between 1913 and 1920. Charles Merriam was a passionate and eloquent advocate of personal political involvement by political scientists amongst others, and was heavily involved himself in the politics of Chicago until 1920 as a political reformer, a passion reflected in his academic work.

Some professional political scientists argue that personal involvement in practical politics can only harm the work of the political scientist. In this view, he or she will not achieve objective understandings of the nature of the political process without dispassionately standing aside. However, this raises the more important question of how neutral can the study of politics be? The question of the political scientist's involvement in practical politics has become a central question of the so-called 'post-behavioural revolution'. This movement is mainly a reaction to the post-1945 American behaviouralist school; as one political scientist has remarked: 'It is rumoured that the positivist-behavioural political science is moribund if not dead. It is said that we now live in the post-behavioural period of political science.'[56]

The post-behavioural approach accepts the need to make political science relevant to real political problems; it is suspicious of the traditional defences of American pluralism, and emphasises that political scientists should perhaps seek some of their inspiration in traditional political philosophy.[57] The reaction against behavioralism has also included a concern about the role of government in making public policies. If we go back to early scientific studies of politics, scholars such as Lasswell were concerned about policy, but that was lost in the concerns about explaining individual political behaviour. As political science returned to think more about 'relevance', policy concerns came back on to the agenda.

The 'new institutionalism' discussed above has been another reaction to the dominance of behaviouralism and rational choice theories in political science. This approach seeks to remove the focus in the discipline from individuals and to return it to structures. The several versions of institutionalism all attempt to point to the ways in which individuals have their political values and their political actions shaped by the institutions to which they belong. This approach argues that individual preferences are not the result of their social backgrounds, or of their calculations of self-interest, but rather are a result of social interactions.

Summary

Defining the nature and scope of contemporary political science is a difficult undertaking. If we focus excessively on recent theoretical and methodological issues we run the risk of devaluing the roots of the discipline and the need of contemporary students to understand those roots. On the other hand, excessive emphasis on the formal institutions of government, and on the ideas of the traditional canon of political theory, may lead us to ignore important contemporary developments. A self-conscious blend of these various approaches to politics and political science is likely to achieve a richer and more powerful understanding of the political than would the simpler course of a commitment to one path or the other.

The eclecticism of our approach may appear to reflect an unwillingness to make a difficult choice, but in fact it reflects a willingness to utilise all the tools available to us to understand and interpret a crucial aspect of human life. Unlike the natural sciences, where new theories often dismiss and supplant the old, any study of human behaviour must have strong roots in traditional concerns such as political philosophy. We need to understand the moral basis of politics, not just the technical aspects of procedure and behaviour, if we are to understand what actually drives many of the participants in the process, and if we are to be able to make our own judgements about politics.

As well as being somewhat eclectic, we will stress the importance of comparison in political analysis. Although much of the writing in political science tends to focus on individual countries, the only real source of generalisation is comparison. As important as comparison is, it also introduces a number of difficult interpretative and methodological issues. As we discuss institutional and behavioural factors in politics we will point to some of those issues and possible means of resolving them. Even if the methodological issues, such as the cultural element inherent in most comparisons, are not totally resolvable we still believe that the study of politics can only make progress by being explicitly comparative in its focus.

Notes and references

1. See B. Crick, 'The Tendency of Political Studies', *New Society*, 3 November 1966, for a brief survey of the position in Britain.
2. Harold Spaeth, *The Supreme Court and the Attitudinal Model*, 2nd edn (Cambridge: Cambridge University Press, 1993)
3. W. J. M. Mackenzie, *Politics and Social Science* (London: Penguin, 1967) p. 17.
4. For a review of the current state of the discipline, see R. E. Goodin and H.-D. Klingemann (eds), *A New Handbook of Political Science* (Oxford: Oxford University Press, 1996). For a more American view, see Ada Finifter (ed.), *Political Science: The State of the Discipline, II* (Washington, DC: American Political Science Association, 1993).
5. See G. A. Almond, 'The History of the Discipline', in Goodin and Klingemann, *A New Handbook*.

6. T. D. Weldon, *The Vocabulary of Politics* (London, 1953).
7. Thomas Hobbes, *Leviathan* (Everyman's Library edn, London, 1914) p. 49.
8. See B. Guy Peters, *Comparative Politics: Theory and Method* (London: Macmillan, 1998).
9. S. Skowronek, *Building a New American State: The Expansion of National Administrative Capacities, 1877–1920* (Cambridge: Cambridge University Press, 1982).
10. L. Epstein and T. G. Walker, *Constitutional Law for a Changing America: Institutional Powers and Constraints* (Washington, DC: CQ Press, 1998).
11. Wilson's works include *Congressional Government* (1882), a plea for reform of American government, and *The State* (1887), a comparative institutional analysis of major governments at his time.
12. Charles O. Jones, *Introduction to the Study of Public Policy*, 3rd edn (Monterey, CA: Brooks/Cole, 1984). See also B. Guy Peters, *American Public Policy*, 5th edn (Chatham, NJ: Chatham House, 1999).
13. John S. Kingdon, *Agendas, Alternatives and Public Policies*, 2nd edn (Boston: Little, Brown, 1993).
14. The end of colonialism and the creation of numerous new countries during the 1950s and 1960s was associated with this expansion in the domain of comparison. See G. A. Almond and J. S. Coleman, *Politics in Developing Areas* (Princeton: Princeton University Press, 1958).
15. Joseph LaPalombara, 'Macro-Theories and Micro-Applications: A Widening Chasm', *Comparative Politics*, 1 (1968), pp. 52–78.
16. Robert A. Dahl, *Political Oppositions in Western Democracies* (New Haven: Yale University Press, 1966).
17. M. Laver, and K. Shepsle, *Making and Breaking Governments: Cabinets and Legislatures in Parliamentary Democracies* (Cambridge: Cambridge University Press, 1996).
18. L. Diamond, 'Promoting Democracy in the 1990s: Actors, Instruments and Issues', in A. Hadenius (ed.), *Democracy's Victory and Crisis* (Cambridge: Cambridge University Press, 1998).
19. See V. Gray, H. Jacob and R. Albritton (eds), *Politics in the American States: A Comparative Analysis*, 5th edn (Glenview, IL: Scott, Foresman, 1990).
20. See James Alt and Alec Crystal Political Economies (Berkeley: University of California Press, 1970).
21. See B. Guy Peters, *Comparative Politics*.
22. See Arthur F. Bentley, *The Process of Government: A Study of Social Pressures* (Chicago: University of Chicago Press, 1908). For a good summary of the theory developed since that time, see F. R. Baumgartner and B. L. Leach, *Basic Interests: The Importance of Groups in Politics and in Political Science* (Princeton: Princeton University Press, 1998).
23. Bentley, *The Process of Government*, p. 77
24. Giovanni Sartori, *Comparative Constitutional Engineering* (New York: New York University Press, 1994).
25. David Sanders, 'Why the Conservatives Won – Again', in A. King *et al.*, *Britain at the Polls 1992* (Chatham, NJ: Chatham House, 1993).

26. Charles Merriam, *New Aspects of Politics* (Chicago: University of Chicago Press, 1925) and *Political Power* (New York: Collier, 1934).
27. Harold Lasswell, *Politics: Who Gets What, When, How?* (1936, reprinted Glencoe, IL: Free Press, 1951) and with A. Kaplan, *Power and Society: A Framework for Political Enquiry* (London, 1952). Bernard Crick, *The American Science of Politics*, (London: Routledge & Kegan Paul, 1959) chs 8 and 10, provides a discussion of the work of both Merriam and Lasswell.
28. On the community power literature, see Nelson W. Polsby, *Community Power and Political Theory* (New Haven: Yale University Press, 1963).
29. One of the earliest studies was P. F. Lazarsfeld, B. Berelson and H. Gaudet, *The People's Choice* (New York: Columbia University Press, 1948). For perhaps the defining study, see A. Campbell *et al.*, *The American Voter* (Ann Arbor: University of Michigan Survey Research Center, 1960). In Britain the Nuffield Studies of every general election since 1955, conducted by David Butler with various colleagues, have been the standard studies of voting behavior.
30. K. Karl Deutsch, *The Nerves of Government* (New York: Free Press, 1966) p. xxvii.
31. D. Easton, *The Political System* (New York: Knopf, 1953).
32. For a brief discussion of general systems theory, see Oran Young, *Systems of Political Science* (Englewood Cliffs, NJ: Prentice Hall, 1969) ch. 2.
33. David Easton, *A Framework for Political Analysis* (Englewood Cliffs, NJ: Prentice Hall, 1965) p. 50. Also D. Easton, 'Systems Analysis in Political Science Today', *Political Science Review*, 19, 1 (1980) pp. 1–25.
34. See *The Political System* (New York: Knopf, 1953) for Easton's famous definition of politics as 'the study of the authoritative allocation of values in a society'.
35. See Young, *Systems of Political Science*, pp. 37–48, and Mackenzie, *Politics and Social Science*, pp. 102–10, for a brief appreciation of Easton's work.
36. For a description see G. W. Stocking, *Functionalism Historicized* (Madison: University of Wisconsin Press, 1980). Although largely discredited there are still some reasons to consider functional analysis. See R. Lane, 'Structural Functionalism Reconsidered: A Proposed Research Model', *Comparative Politics*, 26 (1994), pp. 461–77.
37. See particularly G. A. Almond and G. Bingham Powell Jr., *Comparative Politics, System, Process and Policy*, 2nd edn (Boston, MA: Little, Brown, 1978) and G. A. Almond and J. Coleman (eds), *The Politics of Developing Areas* (Princeton, NJ: Princeton University Press, 1960).
38. At the extreme this could even be seen as resembling the American separation of powers doctrine. Most of the developers of the approach did happen to be American.
39. Deutsch, *The Nerves of Government*.
40. J. Kooiman, *Modern Governance* (London: Sage, 1993).
41. See W. C. Mitchell, 'The Shape of Political Theory to Come: From Political Sociology to Political Economy', in *Politics and the Social Sciences*, ed. S. M. Lipset (New York: Oxford University Press, 1969).

42. See R. Czada, A. Hertier and H. Keman, *Institutions and Political Choice: The Limits of Rationality* (Amsterdam: VU University Press, 1996).
43. A. Downs, *An Economic Theory of Democracy* (Chicago: Rand-McNally, 1957).
44. J. M. Buchanan and G. Tullock, *The Calculus of Consent* (Ann Arbor: University of Michigan Press, 1962).
45. Laver and Shepsle, *Making and Breaking Governments*; K. Shepsle, 'Studying Institutions: Some Lessons from the Rational Choice Approach', *Journal of Theoretical Politics*, 1 (1989), pp. 131–47.
46. George Tsebelis, *Nested Games* (Berkeley: University of California Press, 1993).
47. Mackenzie, *Politics and Social Science*, p. 152.
48. Charles O. Jones, *An Introduction to the Study of Public Policy*, 3rd edn (Monterey, CA: Brooks/Cole, 1984); Wayne Parsons, *Public Policy* (Aldershot: Edward Elgar, 1996).
49. See Chapter 13.
50. R. D. Putnam, *Making Democracy Work* (Princeton: Princeton University Press, 1993); V. Perez-Diaz, *The Return of Civil Society* (Cambridge: Harvard University Press, 1994).
51. See Janet Weiss, *The Myth of the Powerless State* (Oxford: Polity, 1997).
52. James G. March and Johan P. Olsen, 'The New Institutionalism: Organizational Factors in Political Life', *American Political Science Review*, 78 (1984), pp. 734–49.
53. March and Olsen, *ibid.*; *Rediscovering Institutions* (New York: The Free Press, 1989).
54. A. Hertier, 'Institutions, Interests and Political Choice', in R. Czada, A. Hertier and H. Keman (eds), *Institutions and Political Choice: The Limits of Rationality* (Amsterdam: VU University Press, 1996).
55. K. Thelen, T. Longstreth and S. Steinmo, *Structuring Politics: Historical Institutionalism in Comparative Perspective* (Cambridge: Cambridge University Press, 1992).
56. Ellis Sandoz, 'The Philosophical Science of Politics: Beyond Behavioralism', in *The Post-Behavioral Era: Perspectives on Political Science*, ed. G. J. Graham and G. W. Carey (New York: David McKay, 1972).
57. See H. S. Kariel, *Saving Appearances: The Re-establishment of Political Science* (Amertherst: University of Massachusetts Press, 1972).

2

Politics, Power and Authority

Politics is certainly an important human activity, but except for politicians, some members of the media, and of course political scientists it is rarely a primary concern. Thus Quintin Hogg, defining the attitude of British Conservatives towards politics, said: 'Conservatives do not believe that political struggle is the most important thing in life . . . The man who puts politics first is not fit to be called a civilised being, let alone a Christian.'[1] American responses to survey questions reveal a rather minor, and generally declining, interest in politics[2]. Even efforts to 'rock the vote' by music television channels appear unable to excite much interest in politics among younger Americans. The evidence on political interest in Europe shows a lesser, but still significant, decline[3].

However, this casual approach to political activity does tend to raise some problems for the analyst, and for society. First, it is often assumed that politics is only concerned with the public sector, with parliaments, elections, cabinets, and has little relevance to other spheres of human activity. Second, there is the danger of confusing politics solely with party politics, that it is somehow concerned with having a political opinion, or that it at least implies a distaste with the intrigues and tricks of party politicians seeking power. Political activity is, on the contrary, a far more universal phenomenon. It involves disagreements and the reconciliation of those disagreements, and therefore can occur at any level. Two children in a nursery with one toy which they both want at the same time presents a political situation. There is conflict and there is the need to resolve that conflict. The two children could resort to violence, with the stronger claiming the toy, or the mother could appear and use her stronger position to arbitrate between the quarrelling children.

Although the possibilities for resolution are numerous, the essence of a political situation remains: that of conflict and the resolution of that conflict. A Hapsburg emperor, Charles V, once said of his relations with the French King: 'Francis I and I are in complete agreement. We both want Milan.' The attempts to resolve this particular 'agreement' alternated between military clashes and summit conferences. It does raise the interesting point of whether physical force is the end of politics, or the continuation by other means.[4] It also points to the alternative strategies available to actors in international, domestic and more localised political situations.

The failure to recognise these basic elements of politics gives rise to various confusions and misconceptions even if we concentrate our attention on the arena of public affairs. British civil servants are said to be politically impartial, but this does not mean that they do not make political decisions, i.e. decisions that resolve conflicts. Nor does it mean that they will not sometimes apply their own standards and values in reaching a decision. Political neutrality, in the context, merely implies that they will not openly support or favour one or other of the political parties by means other than voting. Judges are in a similar position. Their political neutrality, in one sense, is a vital source of the confidence people show in their competence, but this does not mean that conflict-resolving decisions are not made by judges within the discretion allowed to them by written laws. This role is especially apparent in societies such as the United States and Germany where the courts play major roles in resolving social conflicts.

The constant demands for an all-party government in some countries or the desire to turn government functions over to individuals who have displayed competence in other fields, such as business men, is again evidence of these misconceptions about political activity. Competing parties or factions are evidence of policy disagreements, not causes of those disagreements, and coalitions and all-party governments are attempts to cure an illness, if political conflict could be regarded as unnatural, by treating the symptoms not the cause. George Washington, the first American president, at the end of his second term of office criticised what he called 'the baneful effects of the spirit of party', but the factionalism of the young conservative United States stemmed partly from disagreement on how wide the powers of the national federal government should be over the individual states. The parties were expressing this disagreement. The new political institutions and growing political parties were successful means of reconciling those differences while preserving the unity of the country. The disagreement was the cause of party growth. When the parties and other political institutions failed to continue to reconcile that particular disagreement in the middle of the nineteenth century, the result was civil war.

Single-party states do not signify an end to disagreement among political leaders. Khrushchev was overthrown by his own Communist Party colleagues in 1964 because, amongst other things, they disagreed with his foreign policy and his economic policy.[5] Internal conflicts within the Communist Party in China were in part the cause of the cultural revolution and the political turmoil following the death of Chairman Mao Tse-Tung. Even the military-dominated regime of Saddam Hussein has encountered internal opposition based on both political ambition and religious differences, although the regime has managed to suppress most of the discontent.

Even in multi-party democracies crises tend to suppress disagreements. British political parties buried most of their disagreements between 1940 and 1945 because of the demands of total war, but some conflicts persisted even at parliamentary level, on such issues as personal liberties, social welfare and the nature of the governments to be supported in former enemy-occupied territories.[6] Politicians have long known that one way to divert attention from domestic problems, and to create at least short-lived unity, is to create an external political crisis.[7]

The belief that a general interest exists is held by those who hold that the promotion of certain interests and opinions is for the good of all, not recognising the sectional nature of those interests. It may result from a deliberate attempt to confuse people as to the selfish aims of a particular group by disguising those claims. Usually, this concept of the general interest is a criticism of the political process, and a failure to understand that political activity is concerned with conflict and conciliation. Thus the Duke of Norfolk, criticising the party electioneering before the 1970 British general election, said: 'This is not a time for politicians to get at one another's throats. It must be clear that in the interests of the nation they must come together with reasoned consideration and sane appreciation of all problems . . . We must not be divided and embattled, but think of the nation and what we can do together to help the nation.'[8] This seemed to be a plea not merely to take politics out of general elections, but really to substitute one form of political activity for another, simply to change the arena of the political conflict.

Sources of political conflict

Politics arises from disagreements and conflicting interests, and those differences arise from a number of sources. Economics are a common source of these disagreements, but in this age there is no country that is not afflicted by other social cleavages.[9] Even for countries that have not been divided by language, race or religion, continuing immigration and the development of cleavages along lines of gender and 'lifestyle' produce conflict. The problem that these social cleavages present is that they are not as bargainable as readily as are cleavages based on money.

Political activity may result from the scarcity of resources. An expensive space research programme may only be possible at the cost of ignoring social problems such as housing, education and the relief of poverty. An increased road-building programme may necessitate increased taxation. Political activity results from the necessity of choosing and reaching a decision about alternative policies when only one is economically possible. Differences between individuals and groups provide reasons for disagreements. The poor may be jealous of the rich and form groups and political parties to work for a more equal distribution of wealth. Men may wish to perpetuate the inferior position of women in society, and struggle may ensue for the political emancipation of women. This is not to say that all differences are a source of potential conflict at public level; the differences between tall men and short men do not give rise to political conflict. Some differences are more important than others, and there will be variations between different countries. However, economic differences appear to provide a universal source of political disagreement.

The diversity that gives rise to conflict need not have an objective base such as economic or racial differences. Opinions not directly linked to objective social differences may form the source of political activity. Non-smokers have been engaged in campaigns to eliminate smoking in all public places, and to eliminate tobacco sales entirely. Religious diversity substitutes for race and social class as the chief basis for political conflict in some societies, and in the form of debates over moral issues such as abortion has become more central in a number of other countries.[10] The personality of leaders may be a factor in the political mobilisation, such as Hitler's desire to impose his will on others, irrespective of his views on German nationalism, Jews or class differences; at a less extreme level the personalities of leaders such as Margaret Thatcher, Charles de Gaulle and Bill Clinton have been major political issues. The degree of diversity in a society may vary, but diversity of some form is an inherent feature of every society. It is a permanent feature, and therefore political activity is not an abnormal aspect of human behaviour. It is the process of accommodating the conflict that stems from that diversity.

Means of reconciling political conflict

At public levels there are various means of reconciling political conflict. An election decides which of the competing parties or individuals may translate their programme into public policy. A debate in the legislature or in a legislative committee allows opponents to express their views and provides an opportunity to try to defeat unwelcome legislation. A revolt in a political party or a cabinet crisis may force the resignation of a particular leader and reversal of his policies. A constitutional court may have the authority to declare certain government actions or legislative enactments unconstitutional. Pressure groups, such as business organisations or trade unions, may effect a change in government policy, or seek to balance and defeat the counter-claims of opposing groups by aiming for closer relations with political leaders.

The above political institutions and political processes provide a framework within which political conflict may be channelled and reconciled and decisions reached. However, there must be agreement that these are acceptable means of accommodating disagreements. If some groups are barred from participating, or feel that a particular political institution is a means of frustrating their political demands, they may seek change by acting outside the recognised political channels, illegally or unconstitutionally, and attempt to provoke violence, or seize power by a *coup d'état*.

A comparison of national and international politics provides an interesting contrast in this respect. There is more stability in national politics because of a greater willingness to work through the existing institutions, and to recognise the legitimacy of existing political processes. Relations between states are more anarchic, and the efforts to reconcile conflicts by institutional means such as the United Nations are less successful. This difference, of course, partly stems from reasons of historical development, and from the inability to impose sanctions, short of war, at international level. Some aspects of international politics, e.g. international trade regulated through the World Trade Organisation or finances controlled through the International Monetary Fund, are however acquiring substantial control over national policies.[11]

It is important not to overemphasise the formal and institutionalised aspects of the political process, such as elections, cabinet meetings and parliamentary debates. The reconciliation of conflict may be achieved at various levels, which are accepted but not formalised. *Ad hoc* arrangements may equally be a necessary part of the political process. Professor T. H. Williams has provided an interesting and informative example of the settlement of political conflict in Louisiana in the 1920s. Governor Parker had promised in his election campaign that he would impose a tax on private companies such as Standard Oil which were exploiting the natural resources of the state. He asked the companies, informally, to agree to a small tax, but they refused. Parker then threatened a smaller tax which would be pushed through the state legislature whether the companies agreed or not. The combined opposition of the companies collapsed, and in return for their agreement Parker not only promised not to raise the level of the tax in the future, but even allowed representatives of the larger companies to draft the proposed legislation imposing the tax. Unfortunately for Parker, the state legislature was not committed to the governor's 'gentleman's agreement' with the companies, and wanted a higher tax imposed. Whereupon Parker called the legislative leaders and company representatives to a meeting which actually took place on the steps of the governor's home, and various concessions and compromises were proposed and accepted. The tax was limited: it was not to be increased for a set period, and part of the proceeds of the tax were directed to help the constituencies the legislators represented. As Professor Williams observes: 'Every party to the controversy got something, and everyone seemed satisfied.'[12]

Political activity is simply a means of reconciling differences. In itself it is neither good nor bad. Particular politicians or political methods of achieving certain goals may be disliked, but politics itself is neutral. However, this should not lead to the acceptance of the liberal view of political activity, which holds that governments are neutral and merely referee between competing interests in society. Governments are composed of different opposed interests, and may be dominated by one particular interest. Certainly governments generate interests of their own, even if it is simply that of preserving the status quo. Organisations in government tend to embody those interests and often compete among themselves for resources and for control over policy areas.[13]

If political activity is based on diversity, and is the attempt to reconcile conflicts flowing from that diversity, through, at public level, a political framework of accepted political institutions and processes, political activity is then universally applicable to all types of governments. No political regime has succeeded in suppressing differences, none has established a uniformity of behaviour, nor have any ended disagreement; the Franco regime in Spain was able to suppress disagreements for some time but the differences certainly did not disappear.

Therefore politics cannot be confused with liberal freedoms such as the rights of individuals in society, or denied to socialist or fascist states. Politics is an activity, not a moral prescription; it is a universal activity. The propaganda myths that propose the end of conflict with the realisation of certain social and economic changes should not be accepted as the actual creation of a conflict-free society.[14]

Political power

So far in the discussion we have avoided any direct reference to the concept of political power. It is a key concept in the study of politics: for if politics is the resolution of conflict, the distribution of power within a political community determines how the conflict is to be resolved and whether the resolution is to be effectively observed by all parties. However, there are numerous terminological difficulties, for political scientists disagree on the definitions of such terms as 'power', 'authority' and 'influence'.[15]

Political power may be broadly defined as the capacity to affect another's behaviour by some form of sanction. Sanctions may take the form of coercion or inducement: power may be backed by the carrot or the stick and it may be exercised in a positive or negative fashion.[16] Thus, political leaders may acquire compliance with their wishes by promising wealth or honours to their supporters; or they may threaten to deny such rewards to their opponents. Most exercises in political power include both elements. The negative penalties for opposing the holder of power may be extreme, such as imprisonment or death. These penalties are usually in the hands of those who control the institutions of the state, and those who control the state usually wield the greatest political power. However, it is the fear of these coercive sanctions which promotes obedience, not the coercion itself. Indeed, too frequent use of these penalties may be an indication of the weakening of political power.

Political power must also be seen as a relationship: the holder of political power has the capacity to make another behave in a manner that he, she or it was unwilling to do before the threat or application of sanctions.[17] Thus Robinson Crusoe had no power until the arrival of Man Friday on the island. The actors in a power relationship may be individuals, groups, or institutions. If political power implies a relationship, it is important to discover who or what has power in relation to whom or what. The claim that a Secretary of Education in the central government is more powerful than the chairman of a local authority education committee is a different type of statement from that which concludes that the British Prime Minister is more powerful than the American President. The first statement is clearly concerned with decision-making in the field of education. The second could refer either to the ability of the Prime Minister and the President to change the behaviour of a third party, say the Prime Minister of Canada, or to their respective power relationships with their own cabinets, assemblies, or civil servants.

It is also important to compare like with like. The claim that modern British cabinets do not control the decision-making processes of modern government as effectively as nineteenth-century cabinets, where all major decisions were considered, ignores the limited scope of cabinet decision-making a hundred years ago. Then government responsibility was confined chiefly to matters of foreign policy, defence and internal order, not to economic regulation or the wide field of social welfare. These later additions to government responsibilities involve many more actors and complex patterns of implementation that may limit the apparent power of political leaders. Indeed, as governments shift to third-party delivery systems of various sorts they have increased that complexity and reduced their control over outcomes of their policy choices.[18]

There are further problems in deciding who or what has power. The individual, group or institution may be initially unwilling to act in the manner desired by the wielder of power, and obviously there can be no agreement between the actors in the relationship. Thus, if a prime minister asks for the resignation of a member of the cabinet and the resignation takes place with little or no political damage to the prime minister, we can say that in relation to the resigning member of the cabinet, the prime minister has political power. However, if the cabinet member resigned for other reasons and it was a coincidence that his resignation occurred at the same time as the prime minister's request, we have no evidence either way about the power of the prime minister in this relationship. Similarly, if a trade union threatens industrial action in order to compel a government to agree to policy changes, and the government successfully resists the union's demands, we cannot claim the union is powerful if, as a result of the consequent industrial action, there is economic dislocation. The union is not powerful as a result of consequences it did not primarily intend.

Political power cannot be measured satisfactorily. Any attempt to measure the amount of political power that individuals or groups hold must be a very careful exercise. The relevant questions involved in this exercise include the following: How many times has A effected a change in the behaviour of B in the manner intended? Did B's behaviour change dramatically, or was B almost at the position that A desired? Was the change in B's behaviour relatively permanent or did B quickly return to the position previously occupied before A's exercise of power? Was A trying to change only the behaviour of B at the time or were there attempts to change the behaviour of C, D and E? What were the political costs to the actors involved? If A induced a change in B's behaviour at enormous political costs to A and few costs to B, then A's power is less than if the reverse was the case. As Pyrrhus, the ancient king of Epirus, remarked: 'One more such victory over the Romans and we are utterly undone.'

Measurement of political power is not the only difficulty facing the political scientist. There is also the problem of non-decisions.[19] An actor may be powerful enough to keep certain issues off the political agenda. A political élite may have sufficient political power to keep out of the political debate any issue which would provide a threat to its own power and the élite may attempt to restrict political conflict to 'safe' issues.[20] Most analytic approaches to power and decision-making are ill-suited to situations in which one or more actors are seeking to prevent those decisions from being made.

The complex issue of potential power presents yet more analytic difficulties. Those with power may act in such a way to avoid creating political opposition; they anticipate the possible or potential power of groups, individuals or institutions that as yet have not emerged as opponents of the power-holders. Yet although the power relationship is not overt, it is difficult to claim that a power relationship does not exist.[21] Further, some political cultures place greater emphasis on achieving consensus than in exercising power than do those of the United Kingdom or the United States, so that power often remains potential.[22]

Political authority and influence

Obedience secured solely by the threat of sanctions is unstable. Political power is usually accompanied by authority. Political authority is the recognition of the right to rule irrespective of the sanctions the ruler may possess. Another way of saying this is that power is the ability to get things done in spite of opposition; authority is the ability to get things done without opposition. Governing is rarely so easy that there will no disagreement, but possessing authority may prevent overt opposition to the policy. David Easton's famous definition of politics as the 'authoritative allocation of values for a society' emphasises the importance of authority in governing.[23]

Thus a ruler may be obeyed because of the belief that he was chosen by divine authority, and obedience to the ruler is obedience to God's laws. Supporters of the theory of the Divine Right of Kings could seek verification in the New Testament: 'Let every soul be subject unto the higher powers. For there is no power but of God: the powers that be are ordained of God. Whosoever therefore resisteth the Power, resisteth the ordinance of God. . .'[24] Shakespeare's distorted view of King Richard III was that of a man who monopolised the coercive powers of the state, but whose right to rule was disputed because he had usurped power. The challenge to his authority, because of that usurpation, was the reason for his ultimate downfall. Thomas Hobbes's prescription of strong government to end the civil wars was a concentration on the coercive powers of governments, but Rousseau was nearer the truth underlying political stability when he observed: 'The strongest

is never strong enough to be always master, unless he trans-
forms strength into right, and obedience into duty.[25]

The German sociologist Max Weber suggested a threefold
classification of the sources of political authority in the modern
state. First, traditional authority is the right to rule resulting
from the continuous exercise of political power. Hereditary
ruling families fit into this classification. Second, charismatic
authority results from exceptional personal characteristics of
the political leader, e.g. Hitler or perhaps Charles de Gaulle.
Third, there is legal-bureaucratic or legal-rational, in which
authority emanates from the political office the individual
holds, not from the individual who holds the office. The
American president is obeyed because he is the American
president, not because of the particular individual holding
that office; the emphasis is on the acceptance of constitutional
rules. Weber recognised that none of these categories existed in
pure form. The British political system provides an example of
a mixture of traditional and legal-bureaucratic sources of
authority. American presidents often combine charismatic
authority with the legal-bureaucratic.[26]

We have noted that political power may be divorced from
political authority in that the right to exercise political power
may not be recognised. Some political leaders may possess
political authority but be unable or reluctant to translate it
into political power. General de Gaulle's authority was recognised in German-occupied France, but the coercive powers of
the German and pro-German French governments prevented
the conversion of that authority into political power. Political
authority is buttressed and perpetuated by the use of symbols
such as the use of the national flag or a coronation ceremony,
but an important basis of political authority can be found in
the pattern of political ideas.

Political influence, like power and authority, implies the
ability to change the behaviour of other actors. However, here
the cause of the behavioural change is not the application of
sanctions or the acceptance of the authority of those seeking a
change in the behaviour of others. The change in behaviour
resulting from influence is the result of rational persuasion or of
mutual recognition of the advantages of co-operation. Influence differs from power in the sense that with the former the

behavioural change is not reluctant. Naturally, it is often difficult to ascertain clearly the degree of unwillingness on the part of those whose behaviour is changed.

Distribution of power

Political power is not distributed evenly in any political system. The rich possess more political resources than the poor in that they can finance election campaigns, bribe supporters and opponents, and purchase other political advantages such as a good education. The rich may be individuals or they may be corporate bodies. Some individuals have more political skills than others in that, like Hitler or Lloyd George or John Kennedy, they may be able to influence audiences by their oratory or political intelligence. Prestige gained in non-political activities such as the army and the church may be translated into political power. Even those in possession of certain political skills and resources may be reluctant to turn them into political assets. However, all theories concerned with the distribution of political power agree on one main point: political power in all political systems is unequally distributed. Nevertheless, there are key differences between the various models of how political power is distributed.

Pluralism

An influential approach to the distribution of political power in modern political systems is that adopted by the pluralists. The pluralists hold that political power in liberal democracies is widely distributed, that there is continual competition between groups and that new groups constantly emerge. Decisions are seen as the outcome of bargaining between influential groups, and although political power is not equally distributed, no one group has a monopoly, especially when different policy areas are considered.[27] The membership of the groups overlaps and the leadership interacts to produce an overall consensus on the aims of the political system and the methods for maintaining political stability; there is élite consensus. The resolution of conflict tends to be non-violent, taking the form of bargaining and procedural devices such as elections.

Modern pluralism is partly the result of the behavioural revolution in political science that emerged in America after the Second World War. However, there are many varieties of pluralism. Some early pluralists adopted what came to be known as the 'balance of power' theory, implying a dynamic equilibrium between competing groups.[28] Dahl, the most influential of the American pluralists, however, has never held such views and he is far more explicit on the relationship between political and economic inequality: some are more equal than others.[29] Another area of disagreement among pluralists is concerned with the degree of neutrality of the modern state; whether the state is a passive mediator between competing interests or whether the state has interests of its own.[30] The return to concern with the state in American political theory has tended to emphasise the existence of interests of the state in policy and politics.[31] Further, there is an understanding that pluralism has become more organised and better structured as government organisations attempt to ensure greater control over their political environments.[32]

A variety of the pluralist model was also implemented in certain socialist states during the 1970s and 1980s. This approach, sometimes known as bureaucratic or institutional pluralism, recognised that in a modern, differentiated society even a dominant Communist Party had to reach some accommodation with increasingly diverse social and economic interests.[33] In the late 1980s Mikhail Gorbachev himself began to use the term 'socialist pluralism', and as his reform programme unfolded, it came to include greater freedom of association and expression and finally, in 1990, the acceptance of multiparty politics. Thus, it appears that as societies modernise there is less capacity to maintain political uniformity and homogenity.

The pluralist approach to the distribution of political power, particularly in liberal democracies, has been widely criticised. It ignores non-decisions, it ignores social class as a basis for élite rule: 'The flaw in the pluralist heaven is that the heavenly chorus sings with a strong upper-class accent.[34] Pluralists, it is alleged, have tended to isolate important decisions, but this methodological approach tends to create a criterion of 'importance' which underpins the pluralist conclusions. Critics argue that the alleged balance of groups, countervailing power, does not exist. Pluralists unfairly distinguish between legitimate rule and illegitimate protest, and term 'extremist' those of whom they disapprove. Above all, pluralists are criticised for faults in their methodology that their approach intended to avoid: namely the adoption of an approach that favours their own political preferences.[35]

Elitism

Elitist models of the distribution of political power share many of the characteristics of pluralist approaches. However, all élite theorists accept one key element which separates them from the pluralists and brings them close to Marxist views: all societies are divided into two groups, the rulers and the ruled. The smaller group, the political élite, controls the majority. Mosca, an early twentieth-century originator of modern élite theories, said: 'In all societies . . . two classes of people appear – a class that rules and a class that is ruled. The first class, always the less numerous, performs all the political functions, monopolises power and enjoys the advantages that power brings, whereas the second, the more numerous class, is directed and controlled by the first in a manner that is more or less legal.[36] The wishes of the smaller group generally prevail over the wishes of the majority,[37] and the élite is cohesive and united on most important issues. This closed nature of the political élite and its common social background is common to all political systems, although there are certainly marked degrees of openness in recruitment, as well as in the degree of social mobility within societies.[38]

There are several important differences between the élite theorists; élite models do not agree on the sources of power of the élite, whether it is economic, social, the possession of certain psychological characteristics such as the will to power, and/or the ability of the élite to organise. The major division among élite theories is whether the power of the élite stems from the occupation of certain political offices, such as party or military leadership, or whether élite power stems primarily from economic and social bases.[39] However, whatever these differences, élitists differ from the pluralists on the crucial point of the concentration of power; they differ essentially from the Marxists over the sources of that élite power.

Elite models, like those of the pluralists, are criticised for a flawed methodological approach; a concentration on those assumed to have political power will result in the conclusion that they do indeed have political power. Pluralists will not accept that power is cumulative; as Robert Dahl has observed: 'Neither logically nor empirically does it follow that a group with a high degree of influence over one scope will necessarily have a high degree of influence over another scope within the same system.'[40] Also, élitists have been criticised for inadequately dealing with the problem of political change in society and, importantly, the problem of identifying the élite itself.

Marxism

As with pluralism and élitism, there are numerous, varied Marxist models of the distribution of political power. However, the essential basis of all Marxist approaches is that the economic order of society determines how political power is distributed; political power is concentrated in the hands of a ruling class as a consequence of the concentration of economic power in the hands of the few. The state is a coercive mechanism designed to keep the ruling class in power. Marxism recognises divisions within the ruling class, and as a result of these divisions the state has a degree of autonomy and regulates political and economic conflicts. Moreover, to maintain the stability of the ruling class domination, the state will attempt to mitigate the worst consequences of the division of political power, and to appease those who may seek to disturb the status quo.

Marxism in all its varieties offers a rich and complex explanation of the distribution of power. Unlike elitism it offers a more persuasive explanation of change in political societies. However, there are serious divergences between Marxists themselves and many trenchant criticisms of the Marxist approaches.[41] The concentration on the importance of social class, the conflicts over the nature of the state, a monocausal approach to the nature of political change and the inability to test certain Marxist assumptions empirically are some of the criticisms levelled at this explanation of the distribution of political power. The Eastern European 'revolutions' of 1989 and the collapse of the USSR in 1991 fuelled the view that Marxism was discredited, not only as a model of development but also as a tool of political analysis. It is important to remember that no approach to the study of power is value free; the analysis of political power is generally not a neutral occupation.

Corporatism

Corporatist approaches emerged (or re-emerged) in the 1970s to analyse the distribution of power in liberal democracies. Germany and Austria were seen as examples where corporatist mechanisms had proved highly successful, and though this view appeared more questionable from the mid-1980s, the new post-communist government in Czechoslovakia self-consciously prepared to adopt a form of corporatism. Corporatism stresses the incorporation of certain (largely economic) groups in society into the decision-making process. The state benefits from the co-operation and expertise of the groups, such as industrialists and trade unions, in the implementation of political decisions, while the groups gain a share in political power and the recognition of their monopoly as representatives of certain societal sectors.[42] As a result of this incorporation of key groups, large areas of the decision-making process are depoliticised; that is, the formal bodies such as cabinets and assemblies appear to make the decisions, but they are in effect only endorsing decisions reached by other means. Corporatism implies that the state is not, as the Marxist claims, a repressive means of coercion but a mechanism for engineering consent.

There are many different emphases among corporatism theorists, and none claim that it is a complete theory of the distribution of power, nor that it can be applied to all political systems. The empirical foundations of corporatism are disputed,[43] and there are serious divergences on the role of the state. To some, corporatism is merely 'a variety of pluralism'.[44] Further, with the continuing fiscal crises of government in many countries, interest groups found that all they were able to do was to participate in distributing cuts, rather than distributing benefits to their members. We will explore the various dimensions of corporatist theory later when we discuss the role of interest groups in the political process.

Power distribution in modern societies

The student of politics is faced with competing and complex models seeking to explain how political power is distributed. They all agree that power is not distributed equally but disagree on whether it is concentrated in the hands of an élite or ruling class, or whether it is more widely distributed between competing élites. The debate is of crucial importance, since the whole approach of the political scientist will be coloured, unconsciously or not, by the ideological assumptions implicit in the competing models. Politics is concerned with conflict and the resolution of that conflict, but how the resolution takes place and the consequences of that resolution will be coloured by the investigator's 'bias'. The different institutions of the state, executives, bureaucracies, assemblies and judiciaries, plus parties, pressure groups and the procedural devices such as elections, are analysed within each political investigator's ideological preferences, raising the question of whether political study cannot be completely value free?

Notes and references

1. Quintin Hogg, *The Case for Conservatism*, 2nd edn (London: Collins, 1959) pp. 12–13.
2. For example, Gary Orren, 'Fall from Grace: The Public's Loss of Trust in Government', in J. S. Nye, P. D. Zelikow and D. C. King (eds), *Why People Don't Trust Government* (Cambridge, MA: Harvard University Press).
3. Max Kaase and K. Newton, *Beliefs in Government* (Oxford: Oxford University Press, 1995).
4. This echoes von Clausewitz's maxim that 'War is the continuation of politics by other means.'
5. See W. Tompson, 'The Fall of Khrushchev', *Soviet Studies*, 43, 6 (1991), especially pp. 1109–13.
6. For an interesting account of the opposition to the policies of the National government during the Second World War, see A. Calder, *The People's War* (London: Heinmann, 1969).

7. In the United States this has come to be known as the 'Wag the Dog' scenario, after the movie of that name portraying a president using a faked war to divert attention from a domestic scandal.
8. *The Times*, 3 June 1970.
9. On the concept of cleavage, see E. H. Bax, *Modernization and Cleavage in Dutch Society* (Aldershot: Avebury, 1998).
10. E. Lee, *Abortion Law and Politics Today* (London: Macmillan, 1998); M. Dillon, *Debating Divorce: Moral Conflict in Ireland Today* (Lexington, KY: University of Kentucky Press, 1994).
11. Anne O. Krueger, *The World Trade Organization as an International Organization* (Chicago: University of Chicago Press, 1998).
12. T. H. Williams, *Huey Long* (London, 1970) p. 144.
13. See Junko Kato, *The Problem of Bureaucratic Rationality* (Princeton, NJ: Princeton University Press, 1994).
14. See B. Crick, *In Defence of Politics*, 3rd edn (London, 1982), for the argument that 'Politics is the way in which free societies are governed' (p. 5).
15. The classic statement is Robert A. Dahl, 'The Concept of Power', *American Behavioral Scientist*, 2 (1957), pp. 201–15. Also R. Heinemann, *Authority and the Liberal Tradition* (New Brunswick, NJ: Transaction, 1993).
16. See Ray C. Rist, Ernst Vedung. *Carrots, Sticks and Prayers* (New Brunswick, NJ: Transaction Books, 1998).
17. The classic statement of this position is Robert A. Dahl, 'The Concept of Power' (see note 15).
18. D. F. Kettl, *Government by Proxy: (Mis)Managing Federal Programs* (Washington, DC: CQ Press).
19. See P. Bachrach and M. S. Baratz, 'Two Faces of Power', *American Political Science Review*, 56 (1962) pp. 947–52.
20. Ibid; Also see a case study in the area of non-decisions, M. A. Crenson, *The Un-Politics of Air Pollution* (Baltimore: Johns Hopkins University Press, 1971).
21. See D. Truman, *The Governmental Process* (New York: Knopf, 1951).
22. Japan and the Scandinavian countries are obvious examples. See N. Elder, A. H. Thomas and D. Arter, *The Consensual Democracies?*, rev. edn (Oxford: Basil Blackwell, 1988).
23. D. Easton, *The Political System* (New York: Knopf, 1953) p. 2.
24. Romans: 1 and 2.
25. *The Social Contract* (Everyman's Library edn, 1913) p. 6.
26. See Max Weber, *The Theory of Social and Economic Organisations*, trans. A. M. Henderson and T. Parsons (Glencoe, IL: Free Press, 1947).
27. That is, doctors may be extremely powerful in health policy but virtually impotent in agricultural policy.
28. For a discussion of pluralist theory see Nicholas Rescher, *Pluralism* (Oxford: Clarendon Press, 1995).
29. See R. A. Dahl, *Dilemmas of Pluralist Democracy* (New Haven: Yale University Press, 1982).

30. See Earl Latham, *The Group Basis of Politics* (Ithaca: Corwell University Press, 1952) p. 390. He depicted the state as a body which 'referees the group struggle'.

31. See Gabriel Almond, 'The Return to the State', *American Political Science Review*, 82, pp. 853–74.

32. Edward P. Weber, *Pluralism by the Rules* (Washington, DC: Georgetown University Press, 1998).

33. See S. Soloman (ed.), *Pluralism in the Soviet Union* (London: Macmillan, 1983). See also D. Hammer, *USSR. The Politics of Oligarchy*, 2nd edn (Boulder, CO: Westview, 1987).

34. E. E. Schattschneider, *The Semi-Sovereign People* (Homewood, IL: Dryden, 1960) p. 35.

35. For criticisms of the pluralist approaches, see W. Connolly (ed.), *The Bias of Pluralism* (New York: Atherton, 1969); R. Miliband, *The State in Capitalist Society* (London: Weidenfeld & Nicolson, 1973); P. Dunleavy and B. O'Leary, *Theories of the State: The Politics of Liberal Democracy* (London: Macmillan, 1987) pp. 59–70.

36. Gaetano Mosca, *The Ruling Class* (New York: McGraw-Hill, 1939) p. 50. For a general view of élite theories, see G. Parry, *Political Elites* (London, 1969).

37. See R. Michels, *Political Parties* (Glencoe, IL, 1958 reprint) p. 418 for his famous depiction of élite rule in his 'Iron Law of Oligarchy'.

38. Although the evidence is somewhat dated the basic conclusions of H. Eulau and M. M. Czudnowski remain valid. See their *Elite Recruitment in Democratic Politics* (Beverly Hills: Sage, 1976).

39. For examples of the 'positional élite' argument, see Mills, *The Power Elite* (New York: Oxford University Press, 1956) and E. Nordlinger, *The Autonomy of the Democratic State* (London, 1981).

40. R. A. Dahl, 'Critique of the Ruling Elite Model', in F. G. Castles *et al.* (eds), *Decisions, Organisations and Society* (London, 1971).

41. There is not the space to identify the wide literature, but see Karl Marx and Friedrich Engels, *The Communist Manifesto* (London edn, 1967); B. Jessop, *The Capitalist State* (London, 1982); R. Miliband, *Marxism and Politics* Merlin (London, 1977).

42. For corporatist theories, see P. Schmitter and G. Lehmbruch (eds), *Trends Towards Corporatist Intermediation* (London: Sage, 1979); O. Newman, *The Challenge of Corporatism* (London, 1981); H. Wiarda, *Corporatism and Comparative Politics: The Other Great 'Ism'* (Armonk, NY: M. E. Sharpe, 1997).

43. See M. Heisler, 'Corporate Pluralism Revisited: Where is the Theory?', *Scandinavian Political Studies*, 2 (new series), 3, 1979, pp. 285ff.

44. G. Almond, 'Corporatism, Pluralism and Professional Memory', *World Politics*, 35, 2 (January 1983) p. 251.

...

of

...ding comparative political
...ign political systems, and types of behaviour,
to usable categories. Categories are a way of placing the rather confusing range of political activity into more usable groupings. Those groupings then can be used to develop further theories about politics, or at a minimum simply to understand the nature of several different political systems. Until we can classify them, however, all political systems and all political behaviour is really the same.

Aims of classification

Attempts to produce a classification of political institutions can be dated back to the beginnings of the study of political science. Aristotle made one of the earliest attempts to classify government structures. He distinguished between states ruled by one person, by the few and the many – monarchy, aristocracy and mixed government. His intention was not only to describe but to evaluate governments, and thus he extended his classification scheme to their 'perverted' forms, which he labelled tyranny, oligarchy and democracy. He realised, however, that these types did not exist in their pure forms, thus noting that classification in political science is a search for 'ideal' types.[1]

Jean Bodin, writing his *Six Books on the Commonwealth* in the sixteenth century, pushed Aristotle's classification further.

Although he was still primarily concerned with the question 'Which type of constitution is best?', his immense arsenal of facts on contemporary constitutions and his insistence that the type of government depended on economic and geographical factors as well as political factors, allowed him to make significant advances in the study of politics. There was still the emphasis on legal sovereignty that was to be the hallmark of political science until the twentieth century.[2]

Montesquieu, a French philosopher of the eighteenth century, produced one of the most famous schemes of classifying governments: 'There are three species of government: republican, monarchical and despotic.[3] Montesquieu's classification differed from Aristotle's in that aristocracy and democracy were part of his republican type of government, but his categorisation was firmly in the classical mould since the type of government depended on the number of people holding power. Republican government divides power between the many or the few; 'the more an aristocracy borders on democracy the nearer it approaches perfection: and in proportion as it draws towards monarchy, the more it is imperfect'.[4] Monarchy is a system of government in which power, although in the hands of a single person, is regulated by fundamental laws and by the power of other groups in the society. Despotism is the worst form of government since power is in the hands of one man. There is in Montesquieu the important recognition of the relationship between the type of government and the type of society. Education, morals, patriotism and the level of economic equality all help to determine the type of government, and a most important variable is the extent of the state's territory: 'A large empire supposes a despotic authority in the person who governs',[5] a monarchical state possesses moderate territory, but 'It is natural for a republic to have only a small territory otherwise it cannot long subsist.[6]

These brief glimpses at early attempts to produce schemes of classification help to illustrate some of the difficulties in their construction. Classification is essentially an attempt to isolate the most important characteristics of the political system from the less important. Classification presupposes a comparative approach, and is fundamental to comparison.[7] Further, classification in political science is no different in terms of its aims from classification in the natural sciences; it is to simplify, to ensure the grouping of like with like, to allow for significant comparison and thereby extend our understanding of the phenomenon in question.

It is important to remember, however, that all classification in the social sciences is somewhat arbitrary; the classification scheme depends on what aspect of the political system one wishes to isolate and emphasise. Because of the numerous criteria that could be applied, no one scheme of classification can be suitable for all purposes. It is important to ask the question: 'What is the purpose of a particular scheme of classification?' Although the conclusions arising from a system of classification can only be tentative, the mark of good categorisation is its simplicity. A categorisation scheme should be sufficiently transparent for it to be replicated, and the logic of a country being located in one group or another made clear.

Several examples will illustrate the importance of the question being asked. We noted Weber's classification of different types of political authority in Chapter 2, but like other simple taxonomies it has its limitations; it only provides answers to the question that it asks and it is concerned solely with the sources of political authority. Robert Dahl has emphasised this point: 'Even as a scientific classification, however, Weber's typology seems deficient, since it makes no place for a number of distinctions that most students of politics would regard as interesting and significant.'[8] If one were concerned to emphasise civil liberties, one might distinguish liberal democracies from non-liberal democracies and discuss the emphasis that certain civil freedoms appear to receive in political systems of the former type. However, if one wanted to examine the degree of executive independence of the legislature, it would be rewarding at some stage to compare presidential systems of the type found in the United States and the parliamentary systems prevalent in most of Western Europe.[9] Even that seemingly clear distinction, however, does not account for the hybrids such as 'semi-presidential systems' (France and Israel[10]) not for marked differences in types of parliamentary regimes.

If we asked questions concerning the degree of public participation in the decision-making process, we would find a distinction between presidential and parliamentary systems most unrewarding; even a distinction between democratic regimes and non-democratic regimes would produce difficulties. There is a distinction between participatory systems such as the United States and non-participatory systems such as Saudi Arabia. The former communist systems of the USSR and Eastern Europe placed great stress on popular participation, and many authoritarian systems utilise mass participation as a means of attempting to demonstrate their legitimacy to the rest of the world. Further, different types of participation – voting as compared with more direct interventions in policy-making – may vary significantly across democratic systems.[11]

The classification scheme may point to interrelations between different variables. The connection between the type of political system and the socio-economic structure is an important one in this respect. The French writer Alexis de Tocqueville emphasised this relationship when examining the basis of American democracy in the early nineteenth century:

> Among the lucky circumstances that favored the establishment and assured the maintenance of a democratic republic in the United States, the most important was the choice of the land itself in which the Americans live. Their fathers gave them a love of equality and liberty, but it was God who, by handing a limitless continent over to them gave them the means of long remaining equal and free. General prosperity favors stability in all governments, but particularly in a democratic one.[12]

This relationship between socio-economic development and the type of political system has been echoed by S. M. Lipset. He has argued that a liberal democratic system is only possible where relative social and economic equality produces political stability, and where economic and industrial development has produced a high level of material prosperity.[13] Basically, there is a relationship, in his view, between the capitalist mode of production and liberal democracy, and there is the presumption that liberal democracy is not consistent with a peasant, non-industrial economic base. Non-liberal democracies, or authoritarian regimes, may therefore be a product of economic underdevelopment. This also argues that advocates of liberal democracy would do well to promote economic development along with democracy.

Barrington Moore developed this link between the type of political system and other socio-economic factors.[14] He isolated three types of political system: the democratic or parliamentary, such as Britain, France and the United States; the fascist, such as pre-1945 Germany and Japan; the communist regimes, such as the Soviet Union and China. He allowed for types of political system that do not follow this threefold pattern of development, giving India as the main example of this hybrid type. Moore argued that the interaction of lords, peasants, the middle class and government bureaucracies will tend to produce in certain circumstances a particular type of political system. Theda Skocpol has built on this work, examining the effects of socio-economic factors on the revolutions in France, Russia and China.[15]

The number of typologies and taxonomies of political systems is very large, and the choice of an appropriate scheme will depend on the type of variables that are being considered. More importantly, the choice of schemes depends heavily on the nature of the comparative questions being asked. Before any particular scheme is adopted the aim of the classification must be clear, as well as the range of cases to which it will be applied. Even with this qualification in mind, however, there are still innumerable problems of methodology that must be identified before moving to the adoption and use of any particular schemes for classification.

Problems of classification

One aim of all schemes of classification is simplicity, although the choice of what aspects of political systems to highlight may be arbitrary, depending on the nature of the question being asked. Yet even given these qualifications to the utilisation of particular typologies, there are certain fundamental problems that are common to all schemes of classification. There is the problem of defining the concepts being used: civil liberties meant different things in the United States and the former

Soviet Union, while countries with a predominantly Islamic culture also have a different conceptual understanding of rights and freedoms. Giovanni Sartori talks about this problem in terms of concepts that do not 'travel' well beyond the political context within which they were developed.[16] To make classifications useful we will need to be clear about our concepts and also have concepts that are usable in a variety of political and cultural settings.

The use of quantification may complicate the already difficult question of conceptualisation. Weber's concept of 'charisma' provides an illustrative example here; how does one measure charisma? If one claims that the source of a leader's authority is charismatic rather than legal-bureaucratic, how much charisma is necessary before this claim is made and how is it measured? Hitler was certainly obeyed because he had outstanding powers of leadership, but he was also appointed chancellor in a legal manner by the German president; how are we accurately to estimate the different contributions to his authority over the German people? Again, Sartori is concerned with this problem as he discusses the dangers of 'degreeism' and the arbitrary use of a cut-off point to define the presence or absence of an attribute.[17]

The problem over labels is another difficulty in the classification of political systems. Political institutions with the same label may perform similar functions in different political systems.[18] Take for example the familiar term 'executive'. The British monarchy has similar political functions and political influence to those of the German president. The French president of the Fifth Republic has more political power than either. The president of the United States combines, in some respects, the political features of the British prime minister and the British monarchy. We will see in Chapter 5 that the labels of multi- or two-party systems may be most confusing in terms of how the party system actually works. Thus it is very important and often very difficult in the construction of typologies to make sure that like is being compared with like.

Another difficulty concerns value judgements. Classification is sometimes used to praise or condemn a particular regime. Regimes are labelled 'democratic' or 'autocratic' not simply to describe, categorise and analyse the political institutions, but to indicate preferences. To a certain extent all political scientists are culture-bound: they use the political institutions and the political processes with which they are familiar as a yardstick with which to measure others. They seem to state preferences almost unconsciously; they see types of governments they dislike as resting on force or fraud. Political descriptions then become full of words of abuse. Bernard Crick has pointed out the difficulties of using the word 'democratic', given the desire on the part of practising politicians and political scientists to consecrate different regimes with this holy description:

> Democracy is perhaps the most promiscuous word in the world of public affairs. She is everybody's mistress and yet somehow retains her magic even when her lover sees that her favors are being, in his light, illicitly shared by many another. Indeed, even amid our pain at being denied her exclusive fidelity, we are proud of her adaptability to all sorts of circumstances, to all sorts of company. How often has one heard: 'Well, at least the Communists claim to be democratic'? But the real trouble is, of course, that they do not pretend to be democratic. They are democratic in the sound historical sense of a majority actively willing to be ruled in some other way.[19]

The dangers are, in some cases, unavoidable, but awareness that value judgements often may interfere with a more objective analysis helps in weighing the utility of the process of classifying political systems.

A further difficulty in the development of typologies is the failure to recognise that regimes change; any system of classification must allow for the processes of change, avoiding excessive rigidity. The collapse of the communist systems of the USSR and Eastern Europe in the late 1980s produced enormous political, social and economic changes in these countries. The changes were rapid and dramatic, as have been those of other democratising regimes.[20] The political scientist must now adjust the classification schemes to take these changes into account. Yet the present political fluidity in these former communist political systems and the uncertainty as to future political developments in these countries make new classification to encompass the changes hazardous.[21] These developments provide a clear warning against rigid systems of classification.

Systems of classification

Many of the methodological problems of classifying political systems can be appreciated by examining particular examples of classifying political systems and political institutions. We have already seen in Chapter 1 that the political system includes all types of political activity within a society, not only the formal political institutions. We also saw that the concept of a political system implies the interdependence of the various parts of the system and that changes in one aspect of the system will affect other parts. There are many different ways in which political systems have been classified,[22] but for the purpose of underlining the difficulties associated with typologies as well as indicating some of the advantages, the following broad typology would be sufficiently representative:

1. Liberal democratic systems.
2. Communist systems.
3. Post-communist systems.
4. Authoritarian systems.

Each of these categories may also have sub-categories that help to clarify the meanings of the category and to enhance understanding of the term.

As we begin to use these categories, we can use the 'liberal democratic system' as an example. This system could be characterised as follows:

1. There is more than one political party competing for political power.
2. The competition for power is open, not secretive, and is based on established and accepted procedures, including elections.
3. Entry and recruitment to positions of political power are relatively open.

4. There are periodic elections based on universal franchise.
5. Pressure groups are able to operate to influence government decisions. Associations such as trade unions and other voluntary organisations are not subject to close government control.
6. Civil liberties, such as freedom of speech, freedom of religion, and freedom from arbitrary arrest, are recognised and protected within the political system. This assumes that there is a substantial amount of independence and freedom from government control of the mass media, i.e. radio, television, newspapers (even though government may own and operate some components of the media).
7. There is some form of separation of powers – i.e. a representative assembly has some form of control over the executive, and the judiciary is independent of both executive and legislature.

This broad description of commonly accepted attributes of liberal democracy bristles with conceptual and methodological dangers. The difference of degree becomes very important and the measurement of this degree difficult, as we saw earlier with civil liberties. A major problem is the relative importance of the different variables. For example, South Africa always had a competitive party system, but given the police powers used to control the majority of the population who were excluded from legitimate political competition, civil liberties for the majority were non-existent. Yet one-party states to the north in Africa, such as Zambia, were transformed in the late 1980s to relatively competitive systems in a peaceful manner by the exercise of rights within the existing political structures.

On another continent, critics of the government of Indira Gandhi after the declaration of the state of emergency in 1975 argued that the government's control of the press and imprisonment without trial of political opponents no longer entitled India to be categorised as a liberal democracy. But here we meet the problems of change and the fact that few political systems are static; India has since returned to being a highly competitive party system. The British government possessed the most far-reaching powers during the Second World War, including powers of imprisonment without trial, to ban newspapers, to direct labour, to seize property by new procedures; there was, moreover, a postponement of elections and an electoral truce between the political parties. Did all this imply that Britain ceased to be a liberal democracy? Of course, the nature of the emergency, the agreement of all the main political parties and the apparent consent of the British people to these draconian powers were very important considerations, yet the example does underline some of the difficulties in classification.

There is no doubt that the problems are formidable. Jean Blondel has observed: 'Liberal democracy is . . . difficult to define, as the major components of the combined index (free elections, existence of an opposition, etc.) seem to defy rigorous operationalisation.'[15] However, in spite of all the problems, the concept of liberal democracy is flexible enough to be able to group together various systems by emphasising certain essential characteristics and usefully to contrast these systems with other broad categories of political system. The political systems of Britain, France, Sweden, the United States, Germany, etc. can be grouped together under the label 'liberal democratic', thereby stressing certain important characteristics these political systems possess in contrast to other political systems.

This general category of 'liberal democracy' is useful, but may be more useful if it is differentiated further. Arend Lijphart, for example, differentiates between majoritarian and consensual democracies. In the former category – e.g. the United Kingdom and many other Westminster democracies – the institutions are designed to produce government through a dominant party. The other type of democracy, typified by the Low Countries and the Scandinavian countries,[23] focuses on the creation of broad political consensus and the involvement of as many actors as possible in the process of governing. Also, although they are certainly liberal democracies, several countries such as Sweden and Japan have been dominated by a single political party.[24] Another group of countries such as the Netherlands and Belgium can be characterised as 'consociational' involving élite consensus to overcome social divisions in the mass public.[25]

The second category, that of communist systems, presents greater operational problems than that of liberal democracy.

Many scholars traditionally saw the communist regimes as a sub-category of totalitarian systems, which aimed to exercise total control of the lives of their citizens. The most widely accepted characterisation of totalitarian systems was that of Friedrich and Brzezinski, who stressed the features of a dominant official ideology, a single mass party, a monopoly of control of communications and the use of force, widespread use of terror, and central direction of the economy.[26] However, difficulties abound with the concept of totalitarianism, and criticisms proliferated with the post-war evolution of the communist states.[27] The term has some historical relevance, particularly to the regimes of Stalin and Hitler in the 1930s, while some would also add Cambodia under the leadership of Pol Pot. Moreover, its strong normative overtones and its inability to explain change were major disadvantages, and other labels such as socialist or communist became widespread.

The term 'communist political system' also has certain disadvantages, not least that it reflects an aspiration to communism rather than its achievement. Yet it is widely understood and can be characterised in the following manner:

1. There is an official ideology linked in some fashion to the writings of Karl Marx.
2. The political system is dominated by one political party.
3. There is central planning of the economy and a relative absence of private ownership.
4. Freedom of association and expression are limited by control of organisations and the censorship of a state-owned press.
5. There is no concept of the separation of powers and, consequently, limited judicial independence.

Historically this category has been quite large. It persists in 1998 with only China, Cuba, North Korea, and Laos providing clear examples.[28] However, countries formerly in this category have been subject to recent major upheavals. Before 1989 the category included not only the USSR and the countries of Eastern Europe, but also Afghanistan, Angola, and Ethiopia. The revolutions in Eastern Europe, the disintegration of the USSR, civil war in Afghanistan and foreign pressures on Angola and to a lesser extent Ethiopia brought in their wake a rejection of communism. In Cambodia direct foreign intervention and a continuing civil war have resulted in a somewhat shaky democratic regime.

It should be remembered that even before the upheavals of 1989–90 the category of communist systems embraced considerable diversity. There was a great deal of private ownership in Poland, for example, while East Germany and Poland continued to permit some non-communist parties to function. The autonomy of organisations like churches or trade unions was very varied within different communist systems. Changes were under way in a number of states such as Hungary before the 'revolutions' occurred. Poland led the way with the establishment of the independent trade union, Solidarity, in 1980. In particular, the level of economic development differed enormously before 1989–90. Since the more industrialised states have now renounced their communist character, the most important characteristic of the current communist states is their economic underdevelopment.

The third category, that of post-communist systems, is a new one resulting from changes in the communist world. The accession of Gorbachev as party leader in the USSR was an important milestone in this process. By the end of 1989 communist regimes in Poland, Hungary, Czechoslovakia, East Germany and Romania had collapsed. Bulgaria and even the hard-line communist bastion of Albania followed. Old states have disappeared. The collapse of the Soviet Union in 1991 resulted in fifteen successor states, while the break-up of Czechoslovakia and civil war in Yugoslavia also produced a number of new states. All of these states have had to develop their own ways of governing, often with a strong emphasis on meeting rather severe demands of democratisation and the creation of modern welfare states in a short period of time.

Of course, given the rapidity and the contemporary nature of these changes, categorisation of the new regimes is fraught with difficulties. Many observers feel that given the economic and social problems facing the new regimes, a form of authoritarian populism is likely to emerge, as it already has in several countries.[29] Yet the post-communist states appeared to share particular characteristics dividing them from other types of political system. These characteristics could include:

1. The state is weak and viewed with suspicion.
2. Party systems are weak, with numerous parties competing for power with thinly articulated programmes and a reluctance to compromise.
3. Civil liberties generally enjoy little regard, especially concerning the protection of minorities.
4. There is extensive state ownership, but the aim is to move toward a capitalist economic system.
5. There is a 'low civic culture', and a relatively small number of the civic organisations that would support liberal democracy.[30]

The fourth category, autocracy, probably gives rise to more difficulties of conceptualisation than either liberal democracy or communist systems. It becomes a heterogeneous collection of all the political systems that cannot be fitted into the other three categories. Furthermore, the political systems that can be classified as autocratic are often unstable and likely to change more rapidly than others, and therefore the examples are often soon dated. Descriptions such as 'modernising regimes' or 'third world states' are useful in some exercises, but tend to emphasise only certain aspects of the political system. The level of socio-economic development, the nature of the party system, and the role of the military are all important variables; but the classification cannot rest on these alone. Certainly, characteristics such as limitations on open political competition, the role of ideology, the overt deployment of coercion, weakly supported civil liberties, lack of judicial independence and the role of traditional or military élites are important and perhaps would allow a way forward. Thus, oligarchic or authoritarian regimes as opposed to liberal democratic or socialist regimes may be classified as follows:

1. Conservative regimes:
   (a) Traditional monarchies, with traditional ruling groups and little political institutional infrastructure, e.g. Saudi Arabia, Morocco and Nepal.

(b) Conservative dictatorships where the personality of the leader is important and there are few institutional forms of legitimacy, e.g. Malawi before recent attempts to create an effective democracy.

(c) Theocracies, revolutionary regimes that attempt to mobilise mass support. The few examples can be drawn from the Islamic states such as Iran and Afghanistan.

2. Façade liberal democracies where there are competitive elections but restrictions on the opposition and limited civil liberties. Examples in this category could include Malaysia, Peru and (decreasingly so) Mexico.

3. Military regimes:

(a) Direct military rule. The military has usually seized power in a *coup*, and there are no elections (or only sham elections), and there is a poor level of economic development and often a marked degree of political instability. Examples are to be found in contemporary Pakistan, Myanmar, and the Democratic Republic of the Congo.

(b) Civilian–military regimes. These portray far more political stability than those regimes with direct military rule, but the power relationship between the civilian and military within the government is difficult to assess, and subject to constant change. The best example of this type of regime is Peru under President Fujimori, and Egypt and Syria also would fit into this category.

(c) Radical military regimes. This provides a most controversial category since there is considerable overlap between this and categories (a) and (b) above and even with the socialist systems. Tentatively, one could put Algeria into this category.[31]

Certainly, it would not be difficult to quarrel with any of these categories, nor with the examples chosen to illustrate them. This exercise illustrates the advantages of attempting some form of explicit classification, and also underlines the pitfalls. All systems of classification should be tentative and flexible and possess a clear idea of the purpose of the classification exercise.

Classification of political structures

Attempts to classify particular elements of the political system are fraught with the same difficulties outlined above. We shall see this more clearly when we examine different types of party systems in Chapter 5. However, if we recognise such limitations, the comparison of different structures or processes assists students of politics in understanding the working of various aspects of the system, especially in terms of the relationship of the separate parts to the whole. The division between a federal and a unitary system, or that between parliamentary and presidential systems, can serve to illustrate the advantages of such an approach.

Federal and unitary division cuts across the fourfold typology outlined for political systems. A federal form of government is one in which political power is divided between the central federal government and the constituent states or provinces that compose the federal union. Further, in a federal system the constituent units have some right to existence, and to perform certain functions, that are guaranteed by a constitution or other basic law. Indeed, the constituent units often predated the central government, e.g. in the United States or Australia, and that central government resulted from a compact among those units. The European Union appears to be becoming a particular form of federal or confederal system in which the constituent units retain an even larger share of power than usual, although the creation of the Economic and Monetary Union moves the system more towards a federal entity.

The federal structure can lead to significant differences in the way in which the political process works. We shall see in later chapters that federalism affects the working of the party system, the operation of pressure groups, the relationships between assemblies and executives, the status of the judiciary and the organisation of the bureaucracy. Therefore, for certain patterns of interrelationships, the division between the federal systems of the United States, Canada, Australia and Germany on the one hand and the unitary systems of Great Britain, Sweden and France on the other is an advantage in the examinations of individual systems and the comparison of these systems.[32] The former Soviet Union was characterised by such a high degree of centralisation that many observers regarded its federal character as a sham. This is an exaggeration; but the erosion of the centralising forces of the Communist Party and the system of central economic planning led the constituent Soviet republics first to demand a profound renegotiation of the federal arrangements and then, increasingly, to reject the federal structure for full national independence.

Another useful division is that between presidential systems and parliamentary systems.[33] A comparison of the two patterns of relating the executive and the legislative powers in a government throws up certain important distinctions between the two, emphasises the essential characteristics of each form, and, moreover, further underlines the limitations of any form of classification.

The major characteristics of the parliamentary type of government could be listed as follows:

1. There is a nominal head of state whose functions are chiefly formal and ceremonial and whose political influence is limited. This head of state may be a president, as in Germany, India and Italy, or a monarch, as in Japan, Sweden and the United Kingdom.
2. The political executive (prime minister, chancellor, etc.), together with the cabinet, is part of the legislature, selected by the legislature, and can be removed by the legislature if the legislature withdraws its support.
3. The legislature is elected for varying periods by the electorate, the election date being chosen by the formal head of state on the advice of the prime minister or chancellor.

There are significant differences within parliamentary types of government. The legislature may consist of one chamber or two, and there are variations in the methods of selecting the second chamber if it exists; there are variations in the power of the executive to dissolve the assembly and call an election, and even in the capacity of the parliament to dismiss the executive; there may be a supreme court to interpret the constitution, or the position may be that of Britain, where the legislature is legally supreme. The number and type of political parties will have important consequences for the operation of these systems.

The chief characteristics of the presidential type of government are as follows:

1. The president is both nominal and political head of state.
2. The president is not elected by the legislature, but is directly elected by the total electorate. (There is an electoral college in the United States, but it is of political significance only in that each states votes as a unit and hence the system tends to disadvantage small parties.)
3. The president is not part of the legislature, and he cannot be removed from office by the legislature except through the legal process of impeachment.[34]
4. The president cannot dissolve the legislature and call a general election. Usually the president and the legislature are elected for mixed terms.

The outstanding example of the presidential form of government is that of the United States. Most other examples are imitations of the American presidential system, found chiefly in Central and South America.

The division between presidential and parliamentary regimes can be most useful for comparison. There are numerous examples of political scientists using a comparison of, say, the United States and Britain, in terms of this division in order to emphasise significant aspects of both systems. Other scholars have argued that presidentialism is a danger for developing countries, given that it may be more subject to instability.[35] The assumption is that presidentialism focuses too much on the personality and capacity of a single individual, so when that individual is undermined the system as a whole is also undermined.

But there are serious limitations to this approach. We have already hinted at one difficulty: the small size, and somewhat skewed nature, of the sample of presidential systems. Also, all our examples come from liberal democratic systems. Although there are a number of new examples, they are not yet fully institutionalised. Gorbachev attempted to introduce a presidential system into the USSR, and Boris Yeltsin also accrued considerable executive powers in his role as president of Russia. In Poland, the example of France proved an attractive one to President Lech Walesa, whose efforts to increase his own powers referred frequently to the French presidency as a model to be emulated.

France of the Fifth Republic is a good example of the limitations of this approach. France adopted a new constitution in 1958 after the accession of de Gaulle to power. Formerly under the Fourth Republic (1946–58), French political institutions could be firmly classed as 'parliamentary'. The constitution of the Fifth Republic strengthened the political power of the president and he ceased to be merely the ceremonial head of state. Basically, the new constitution demoted the National Assembly, as the president is not dependent on its support but is elected for a fixed term by the whole electorate. French political institutions are no longer parliamentary, but the political structure cannot be clearly classified as a presidential type of system on the American model. The system can now be classified as 'semi-presidential', having some aspects of the presidential regime but retaining some of those of a parliamentary system.[36]

These examples serve to highlight some of the empirical difficulties we encountered in attempts to compare political systems or their constituent elements. Few political systems fit neatly into any one pigeon-hole. Categories are elaborated in terms of general, abstract characteristics, while each political system is in some respect a unique combination of particular features. Thus, the more clearly defined a category, the more difficult is the problem of empirical fit. This factor has led many political scientists to succumb to the temptation to proliferate their categories by adding further divisions and sub-divisions.[37] To carry this process to its logical conclusion would be to obviate the purpose of classification, for it would result in a separate category for each political system.

It appears more useful, therefore, to accept the utility of various types of classification, recognising the fluid nature of political systems, and accepting that for some purposes it will be useful to treat certain countries as having crucial similarities, while for others the systems concerned will appear diametrically opposed to one another. Thus, classification remains a very useful means of approaching understanding of political systems, but care must always be exercised, and the degree of variance that exists within each category must also be recognised.

Further, classification may be the beginning rather than the end of the process of comparison. Once a country or an institutional arrangement has been classified, that provides a beginning for comparing it with others, but only a beginning. Even if two political systems are explicitly parliamentary, for example, they may still have different conventions about how parliamentary government is to function. For example, both Italy and Norway are parliamentary but have very different histories of dissolutions of government and instability, and somewhat different conceptions about the role of government in society.

Summary

Classification and categorisation are essential parts of the scientific process, whether in the natural sciences or the social sciences. Although basic, classification is not easy and frequently involves the use of judgement as much as hard, 'scientific' evidence. We may say, for example, that we want to distinguish democratic from non-democratic systems, but how much democracy is needed to fit into the more virtuous category? Decisions about what to include and what to exclude in a measure of democracy will determine what countries are democratic, and may in turn influence any analysis of democratic politics.

Further, in political science there is no single scheme of classification that conveys all the information that is needed about a political system. In biology, for example, the hierarchy of class, phylum, genus and species places all living things in an accepted position *vis-à-vis* all other cases. In political science there is little or no agreement on how to classify and therefore there are almost as many classification schemes as there are scholars interested in classifying systems.

Notes and references

1. *The Politics of Aristotle,* trans. with an introduction by Ernest Barker (Oxford: Oxford University Press, 1946) particularly Book IV.
2. See J. W. Allen, *A History of Political Thought in the Sixteenth Century* (London: Methuen, 1957) ch. 8.
3. Baron de Montesquieu, *The Spirit of the Laws,* trans. T. Nugent (London, 1966) bk II, ch. 1, p. 8.
4. Ibid, bk II, ch. III, p. 15.
5. Ibid, bk VIII, ch. XIX, p. 122.
6. Ibid, bk VIII, ch. XVI, p. 120.
7. See Giovanni Sartori, 'Comparing and Miscomparing', *Journal of Theoretical Politics,* 3 (1991), pp. 243–57.
8. R. A. Dahl, *Modern Political Analysis,* 4th edn (Englewood Cliffs, NJ: Prentice-Hall, 1964) p. 30.
9. See, for example, Kurt Von Mettenheim, *Presidential Institutions and Democratic Politics* (Baltimore: Johns Hopkins University Press, 1997).
10. M. Duverger, 'A New Political System Model: Semi-Presidential Government', *European Journal of Political Research,* 8 (1980), pp. 165–87.
11. See R. D. Putnam, 'Democracy in America at Century's End', in A. Hadenius (ed.), *Democracy's Victory and Crisis* (Cambridge: Cambridge University Press, 1998).
12. Alexis de Tocqueville, *Democracy in America* (London, 1968) p. 345.
13. See especially S. M. Lipset, *The First New Nation* (London: Faber, 1963).
14. Barrington Moore, *Social Origins of Dictatorship and Democracy* (London: Methuen, 1967).
15. Theda Skocpol, *States and Social Revolutions: A Comparative Analysis of France, Russia and China* (Cambridge: Cambridge University Press, 1979).
16. Giovanni Sartori, 'Concept Misinformation in Political Science', *American Political Science Review,* 64 (1970), pp. 1033–41,
17. Sartori, 'Comparing and Miscomparing'.
18. See G. A. Almond and G. B. Powell, *Comparative Politics: System, Process and Policy,* 2nd edn (Boston: Little, Brown, 1978).
19. B. Crick, *In Defence of Politics* (London, 1964) p. 56.
20. A. Stepan and J. J. Linz, *Problems of Democratic Transition and Consolidation: Southern Europe, South America and Post-Communist Europe* (Baltimore: Johns Hopkins University Press, 1996).
21. But see P. C. Schmitter and T. L. Karl, 'The Conceptual Travels of Transitionologists: How Far East Should They Attempt to Go?', *Slavic Review,* 53 (1994), pp. 3–28.
22. See A. Bebler and J. Seroka (eds), *Contemporary Political Systems: Classifications and Typologies* (Boulder, CO: Lynn Reinner, 1990).
23. E. S. Einhorn and J. Logue, *Modern Welfare States: Politics and Policies in Social Democratic Scandinavia* (New York: Praeger, 1989).
24. T. J. Pempel (ed.), *Uncommon Democracies: The One-Party Dominant Regimes* (Ithaca: Cornell University Press, 1990).

25. Arend Lijphart, *The Politics of Accommodation* (Berkeley: University of California Press, 1968).
26. C. Friedrich and Z. Brzezinski, *Totalitarian Dictatorship and Autocracy*, 2nd edn (Cambridge, MA: Harvard University Press, 1965) p. 22.
27. For wide-ranging discussion of the usefulness of the concept of 'totalitarianism', see, *inter alia*, C. J. Friedrich, B. R. Barber and M. Curtis, *Totalitarianism in Perspective: Three Views* (London, 1969); L. Schapiro, *Totalitarianism* (London, 1972); R. Burrowes, 'Totalitarianism: The Revised Standard Edition', *World Politics*, vol. 21, no 2 (Jan. 1969) pp. 272–89; R. Cornell (ed.), *The Soviet Political System* (Englewood Cliffs, NJ: Prentice Hall, 1970).
28. See S. White *et al.*, *Communist and Post-Communist Political Systems* (London: Macmillan, 1990) pp. 1–35.
29. D. Nelson, 'The Comparative Politics of Eastern Europe', in S. White, J. Batt and P. Lewis (eds), *Developments in Eastern European Politics* (Durham, NC: Duke University Press, 1993).
30. Robert D. Putnam, *Making Democracy Work* (Princeton, NJ: Princeton University Press, 1993).
31. For a discussion of the problem of classifying radical military regimes, see J. Markakis and M. Waller (eds), 'Military Marxist Regimes in Africa', *Journal of Communist Studies*, vol. 1, nos 3 and 4 (Sept./Dec. 1985).
32. On federalism, and the variety of ways in which it functions, see E. Ahmad, *Financing Decentralized Expenditures: An Institutional Comparison of Grants* (Cheltenham: Edward Elgar, 1997); C. Bolick, *European Federalism: Lessons from America* (London: IEA, 1994).
33. See R. Kent Weaver and Bert A. Rockman (eds), *Do Institutions Matter?: Government Capabilities in the United States and Abroad* (Washington, DC: The Brookings Institution, 1995).
34. The celebrated attempt to impeach President Clinton brought this possibility to the attention of the world in 1998. See also R. Berger, *Impeachment: The Constitutional Problems* (Cambridge, MA: Harvard University Press).
35. Riggs, 'The Survival of Presidentialism in the United States: Para-Constitutional Practice', *International Political Science Review* 9(1988), 247–78.
36. Maurice Duverger, 'A New Political Systems Model: Semi-Presidential Government', *European Journal of Political Research* 8(1980), 165–87; see also, J. Nonsianen, 'Bureaucratic Tradition: Semi-Presdential Rule and Parliamentary Government: The Case of Finland', *European Journal of Political Research*, 16, pp. 221–49, 1988.
37. See, for example, the work of COCTA – the Committee on Conceptual and Terminological Analysis of the International Political Science Association.

4
Political Culture

As well as being a function of structures and constitutions, the behaviour of political systems, and of the people within them, is a function of *ideas* about politics. People have pictures in their heads about what constitutes appropriate political behaviour, and will evaluate the performance of their governments accordingly. Likewise, members of the political élite learn their roles from observing their predecessors, and as they actually participate in institutions. As well as cultural differences between the mass public and élites, there may be differences among different groups in society, whether defined by region, ethnicity, or social class. No matter how differentiated or how uniform political culture may be, to understand politics in a country it is necessary to understand something about the ideas that influence the political behaviour of individuals.

The nature of the political culture

A political culture is composed of the attitudes, beliefs, emotions and values of society that relate to the political system and to political issues.[1] These attitudes may not be consciously held, but may be implicit in an individual or group relationship with the political system. Nor are they necessarily amenable to rigid definition, but, nevertheless, an awareness of the basis of a political culture allows a more detailed picture of the political system to emerge. Building this picture would be difficult if reference were made only to the political institutions and the policy issues of the political process. In Britain during the early 1990s there was dissatisfaction with the way the country was governed and weaker attachment to the institutions and processes of government. There was substantial discussion of reforming political institutions and more support for political innovations such as membership of the EU, changes in the electoral system, and for a strengthening of civil liberties. However, there was at that time still a fundamental consensus on the major aspects of the political system and lack of support for revolutionary changes, so that we can say that a degree of consensus exists. Where this consensus is weak, there is greater likelihood of the political system being challenged by public disorder or even revolution. The consensus may exist on the goals of the political system as well as the means of reaching those goals.

That is not to claim that even in politically stable societies the political culture is homogeneous; where differences between one group and others are marked, a political sub-culture is said to exist. This is not a completely distinct set of attitudes, beliefs and values, but rather a set of attitudes some of which are in common with other sub-cultures and some of which are distinctive. Thus many Spanish Basques, as well as Catalans and Galicians, feel that loyalty to their group is more important than loyalty to Spain as a whole, and because of the strength of these attitudes there is a strong separatist movement in the Basque provinces (see Table 4.1). Likewise, different linguistic components of Belgium have different degrees of attachment to the federation (see Table 4.2). African-Americans in the United States constitute a distinct political sub-culture, sharing some values of the larger society but also having their own orientations to politics.[2] The growth of the

Table 4.1 National identification in Spanish regions

	Nation	*Region*
Asturias	93	5
Aragon	61	31
Galicia	38	53

Source: J. E. Lane and S. Ersson, *Politics and Society in Western Europe* (London: Sage, 1996).

Table 4.2   Major political identification in Belgian regions

Region	Belgian	Other
Flems	33	67
Brussels	57	43
Walloons	50	50

Source: J. E. Lane and S. Ersson, *Politics and Society in Western Europe* (London: Sage, 1996).

Scottish National Party, especially in terms of electoral support, has illustrated the strength of separatist feelings within the United Kingdom. Most political cultures are in fact heterogeneous, whether that heterogeneity is a function of regionalist or more strictly political considerations.[3]

Political cultures differ according to the degree to which they stress participation in the political process by the citizens of the political system. In some systems, individuals take a more active role in the political process, possess a great deal of political information, and expect to influence decisions made by governments. In the United States, despite an increasing political cynicism and mistrust of political leaders, political participation generally remains high, although electoral turn-out is low.[4] Soviet political culture placed great stress on public participation, with citizen involvement encouraged by drawing people into a variety of agencies to assist the implementation of central policies. At the same time, the ruling élite expected obedience from the governed and conformity to the directives of party and government organs.[5] Some observers of the post-communist states have expressed anxiety at the continuing influence of the deeply ingrained attitudes of *homo sovieticus* and the difficulties that these attitudes may present for making democracy work.

The German political culture presents interesting contrasts. Germans profess to be very interested in politics, possess impressive political knowledge and consume a great deal of political media, but while electoral turn-out is high, other types of political activity are less common, and even after decades of democracy Germans remain less likely than Americans to believe that they have the ability to influence the government.[6] In Germany, however, there seem to be marked generational differences in political culture, with younger people being more participatory and also perhaps less accepting of the authority of the state than are their elders.[7]

Foundations of the political culture

A political culture, whether diverse or homogeneous, is a product of many interrelated factors. *Political continuity* is important in Britain, and the older values have been allowed to merge with modern attitudes, undisturbed by violent internal strife or domination by a foreign power; what Rose called the 'modernity of tradition'.[8] Structurally, as well as in attitudes of the public, the British political system has evolved gradually. That having been said, first the radical programme of the Thatcher years,[9] and then the equally radical constitutional programmes of the 'New Labour' government elected in 1997,[10] have challenged the conventional interpretation of continuity and stability. Still, compared with many political systems the process has been gradual and conducted without fundamental, systemic challenges.

France offers a sharp contrast in historical development. The revolution of 1789 violently overthrew the existing political structures, and the political conflicts and antagonisms of the nineteenth and twentieth centuries may have been largely determined by the attitudes, values and beliefs formed by that revolutionary upheaval. French political culture is often described as two subcultures derivative of factions within the Revolution. One, the Jacobin, stresses the power of the centralised state, while the Girondist strand of thinking is more manifestly participatory and democratic.[11] Further, despite the strength of the French state, some components of the political culture stress individual resistance to that power.

Violent historical changes may, however, result in a conservative consensus. The American War of Independence, although accompanied by certain social changes, was primarily a break of the political links with Britain. It established agreement on certain liberal democratic procedures which were affirmed by the American constitution. Thus, although there was no complete rejection of the past, the Revolution did establish a stable political system based on new egalitarian and competitive values which were not fundamentally changed by the later industrialisation and mass immigration.[12] The political culture emerging from this revolution is also deeply sceptical about the role of government, especially the central government, and also extremely optimistic about the possibilities of human improvement.

The *impact of European colonial domination* on many new states in Africa and Asia is an important factor explaining some aspects of the political culture of these states. The extent of this colonial influence is disputed, but one may recognise the different effects of, for example, British and French control, or even, in Nigeria's case, a more flexible policy of the colonial power toward different areas of the same colony. The northern area of Nigeria was subject to indirect rule and the coastal areas were controlled more directly by British administrators, a policy which was to re-emphasise the different political cultures of the north and south, and was to have profound consequences on the post-independence politics of the country. India provides an illustrative example of colonial domination extended over a long period of time, and the gradual introduction of the Westminster model of government. There was indirect rule in the case of the princely states, but the British system of conciliar local government was established in other areas, with apparently some enduring consequences.

Besides historical development, *geography* is another important factor in fashioning a political culture. Britain's being an island protected the country from foreign invasion and permitted the development of its pragmatic and evolutionary approach to government. The seemingly limitless frontier of the developing United States is said to have forged the political values of independent egalitarianism in spite of ethnic differences,[13] a theme that also appears in Australian and Canadian politics. The interrelationships in culture also are apparent here; the United States possessed an abundance of natural resources and was protected by two oceans from hostile neighbours.[14]

The impact of *ethnic differences* on a particular political culture varies. Ethnic differences have only recently begun to affect attitudes in Great Britain, largely because of the expansion of immigrant populations. Yet the United States, with a more polyglot population, has succeeded in assimilating the vast numbers of immigrants, at least the voluntary ones, so that different groups think of themselves primarily as Americans, owing allegiance to the government of the United States. In contrast, European immigration into Canada has not removed the consciousness of being members of different ethnic groups, and the contemporary politics reflect this consciousness very clearly. The very existence of Canada as we now know it is threatened by the deep differences between the Anglophone and Francophone communities.[15] This is true even though Canada has successfully assimilated numerous immigrants from other European and many Asian societies, and has made progress in addressing the grievances of its indigenous peoples. It is significant that in Canada, unlike America, the two dominant ethnic groups retained their own languages, and reinforced their separate identities by retaining the link between ethnicity and religion.

Religion, not language, was utilised by the Irish to emphasise their separateness from the British in the long struggle for independence before 1922.[16] Religion has also divided societies in European countries such as the Netherlands and to some extent Germany, as well as a number of countries such as Sri Lanka, Nigeria, and the Sudan in the Third World. Again, the United States has been able to cope successfully with a huge variety of religious affiliations. In a few countries such as Switzerland the society is divided by both language and religion, but yet the country manages to survive with little or no overt strife among the groups (Table 4.3).

The instability in the political system caused by ethnic groups, with loyalties being directed to themselves and not to the national government, is increased if allegiances are also focused on another state. European history is littered with such historical accidents, and the inclusion of Serbians in the Hapsburg Empire, and of numerous Germans in the Czechoslovakian state, were important factors in the events leading up

Table 4.3 Principal identifications in Swiss cantons

	Nation	*Language group*	*Canton*
German-speaking	53	16	31
Romance-speaking	40	40	20

Source: J. E. Lane and S. Ersson, *Politics and Society in Western Europe* (London: Sage, 1996).

to the 1914 and 1939 European wars. The multiple allegiances in Bosnia-Herzogovina are the major source of the conflicts there. The arbitrary boundaries of former European colonies in Africa were drawn with little reference to the divisions of tribal groups, so that an ethnic group in one country may have close ties with groups, perhaps dominant groups, in neighbouring countries.[17]

The *socio-economic structure* is another determinant of the political culture. A predominantly urban, industrialised society is a more complex society, putting a premium on rapid communications. Educational standards are higher, interest groups proliferate, and public participation in the decision-making process is, of necessity, wider. Rural societies are not geared to change and innovation, and states with a predominantly peasant population tend to be more conservative. We observed in Chapter 3 that there is not always a direct link between the level of socio-economic development and participatory liberal democracies, but none the less there are repercussions on certain political attitudes and values. Loyalty to national, as opposed to regional, groups is more a characteristic of an industrialised society, but the examples of states such as Belgium warn us that this is not a rigid correlation; Belgium is highly industrial but the terminal loyalties of most citizens appear to be to either the Flemish or Walloon community.

A simple division between urban-industrialised states and agrarian ones is too crude a categorisation. American farming, even when it employed the majority of the working population, was always a more capitalist and commercial activity than farming is, or was, in predominantly peasant societies, and therefore the values were those more associated with modern industrialised states. Modern New Zealand and Denmark are illustrations of farming economies with this commercial foundation. In societies in which peasants form the major part of the population, conservative attitudes and a resentment of government activity and an ignorance of its scope may dominate. What the central administration does may be known, but there is little awareness of how these policies can be changed and influenced.[18]

An industrialised society will have a complex class structure, but the distinctness of class as a sub-group will vary. In the United States it is claimed that the working class have been more *bourgeois* and lack the consciousness of European working classes. But even in Britain, where social class is more closely aligned to voting behaviour for the different political parties, consciousness of class membership does not mean that the working class identify their values and interests as being in conflict with those of other social classes. A greater conflict between class sub-cultures may be seen in certain European liberal democracies, such as France and Italy, where hostile attitudes to the values of the dominant political élites is seen through electoral support for communist, fascist and other anti-system parties.

Some scholars have argued that in the industrialised democracies there has been a shift away from viewing politics in bread-and-butter, materialist ways toward a 'post-materialist' ethic. In post-materialist politics, values such as equality, participation and environmental protection become paramount.[19] These values appeared especially relevant for the generation that came of age politically during the 1960s, but these ideas continue to be manifested through a variety of new political parties and social movements, as well as in the attitudes that the public express in surveys. These attitudes are not, however, constant but appear to vary with changes in the economy, and also vary with other social and political changes.

One increasingly important aspect of post-materialism in Europe is the increasing self-identification of citizens as European and a declining commitment to individual nation states. Especially for many young people the nation state is a symbol of the past and the war and division that characterised much of

European history. The European Union, on the other hand, is seen as a way to move away from that conflictual history. It should be noted, however, that at the same time as there is growing European identity, there is also an increasing awareness of sub-national loyalties.[20]

Aspects of the political culture

There are two important components of a political culture: attitudes to the political institutions of the state, and the degree to which citizens feel they can influence and participate in the decision-making process. However, there are problems of measuring both how much pride people have in the political system and their perceptions of political efficacy.[21] A distrust of the political office-holders may not affect positive feelings about the political institutions themselves. Americans express great support for the American political structure as a whole, admire the Constitution and will not support any anti-system parties. Yet Americans are also critical of particular political institutions, have become more electorally volatile and independent in terms of party support, and are disillusioned with politicians – especially Congress – as well as other major social institutions (see Table 4.4).

Table 4.4   Citizens' confidence in American institutions (% saying 'a great deal' or 'quite a lot')

	Military	Church	Presidency	Supreme Court	Congress	Organised labour
1975	58	68	n/a	49	40	38
1981	60	54	n/a	46	29	28
1985	61	66	n/a	56	39	28
1989	63	52	46	43	32	26
1991	69	56	50	39	18	26
1993	68	53	43	44	22	26
1996	66	57	39	45	20	25
1997	63	53	36	44	18	22

Source: Gallup Monthly Poll.

That having been said, however, there are some differential views about politicians among the public. Americans express very little – and declining – confidence in Congress, but yet also tend to express support for their own Congressman. Further, they tend to re-elect incumbent Congressmen in large numbers – 96 per cent of incumbents who ran were elected in 1996. It seems that the public recognise the benefits brought to the district by the incumbent but also see the institution as a whole as deeply flawed by its partisanship and difficulties in decision-making.[22]

Italians, on the other hand, show far less support for the total political system, and are more inclined to vote for anti-system parties, but have expressed an increasing pride in the economic system.[23] One could therefore presume that political stability in Italy rests more on the satisfactory performance of the economic system than on the structure of representative parliamentary democracy. In Britain, surveys consistently show that there is often admiration for political leaders and a desire for strong government, even if particular political leaders are not greatly liked. Margaret Thatcher was regarded as a strong, decisive leader and this image was strengthened by the Falklands conflict of 1982. Yet, she was also regarded as an opinionated and unsympathetic individual whose policies were politically divisive.[24] She led the Conservative Party to three successive general election victories, although her autocratic style in pushing the 'poll tax' through parliament (along with several other unpopular programmes) ultimately produced her downfall.[25]

Change can also pose problems for an evaluation of political cultures. Almond and Verba's pioneering work of 1963 comparing political cultures in several political systems was extensively re-evaluated in 1980. Besides the methodological problems involved in cross-national comparisons, the contributors to the new study found evidence of important changes in the political cultures of the countries investigated.[26] In stable liberal democracies, the boundaries of the political system are fairly firmly drawn. There is a belief in the limitation of government activity. Thus the freedom of the individual is emphasised, and at the same time there is an expectation of benefits for the individual ensuing from government activity.

This again stems from the basis of trust in political leadership, and a belief that the unwritten rules of the political game will be respected by all the participants.

The degree of political stability is linked to the level of socio-economic development. We have noted the effects of relative economic prosperity on Italian attitudes, and the level of education will affect the sense of competence on the part of the citizens. In Britain, the relative economic decline and the accompanying rise in educational levels have reduced the importance of deference in the political system, deference being the belief that socially superior individuals are best suited to political decision-making. Deference in Britain is now largely confined to the older generation,[27] and deference in almost all countries appears to be declining.

In the former West Germany, the 'economic miracle' of the post-war years may have assisted the emergence of more positive attitudes to political institutions in the 1980s than were found in the 1950s, and there developed a greater willingness to participate politically, especially among the young. Of course, there are other variables involved, such as the longevity and the political successes (including reunification) of the Republic itself. Yet there is a link between political consensus and political stability, and a comparison between the West German system and the Weimar Republic is indicative of that link.

Economic growth also appears to be affecting political attitudes and the practice of democracy in Southern European countries.[28] Economic development during the 1960s and 1970s helped to weaken the legitimacy of the former dictatorial regimes and to create more positive attitudes toward representative democratic institutions. The successful democratisation of Spain, Greece and Portugal was aided by economic growth and sustained by membership in the European Union.

There is little doubt that the rapid deterioration of the economies eroded the legitimacy of the communist regimes. In Poland, a new wave of strikes in 1988 proved the final straw for the government of General Jaruzelski, which then embarked on a process of dialogue with Solidarity (then still an illegal organisation), specifically aimed at transforming the system into a genuine parliamentary democracy. The upshot was the so-called Round Table election of 1989, repudiating the communists and leading to the installation of the first non-communist prime minister in Eastern Europe since the 1940s.[29] In the Soviet Union, economic chaos was a major reason for the decline in the popularity of Mikhail Gorbachev; significant elements of the population transferred their allegiance to their own republican capitals, with an upsurge of anti-Moscow nationalism gradually spreading from the Baltic throughout the European territories of the Soviet state. Unfortunately, economic chaos continues to threaten the fragile democratic system in place in Russia and the Ukraine, and has led to reassertion of more authoritarian rule in several other former Soviet Republics.

Symbols and political culture

Political attitudes and values in a society are symbolised by such things as the flag and the national anthem. The monarchy may be a symbol of national pride for some political systems – King Juan Carlos is widely credited with being a key to the success of Spanish democratisation. These symbols express the idealised elements of the political institutions and are not necessarily related to the level of political knowledge and competence of the people whose emotions are channelled through such symbols. Bagehot, writing in the middle of the nineteenth century, recognised the importance of such symbols, arguing that 'we have whole classes unable to comprehend the idea of a constitution – unable to feel the least attachment to impersonal laws. Most do indeed vaguely know that there are some institutions besides the Queen, and some rules by which she governs. But a vast number like their minds to dwell more upon her than upon anything else, and therefore she is inestimable.'[30] Although the relationship between political symbols and stability is difficult to analyse, even after the damaging publicity surrounding the death of Diana, Princess of Wales, there are still problems of initiating a rational public debate about the place of the monarchy in the British system, as its role does not seem open to utilitarian analysis, and the treatment given to critics is a measurement of the strength of the emotional attachment.[31]

The American president attracts a similar emotional adherence, in spite of the more overt political role he performs. President Kennedy was more popular after his death than before, perhaps because he was no longer a politician, and because of the ability of his successors to construct an image of Camelot in which the best and brightest could govern. The negative image of a president being tried while in office was in some ways one of President Clinton's strongest assets during the time leading up to his eventual impeachment. This affair has exposed the presidency to substantial negative attention and that may reduce the symbolic capacity of the presidency in the future.

All political systems place great emphasis on the use of symbols. They give reality to abstractions and embody some aspects of the dominant political values, such as the hammer and sickle emphasising the unity of workers and peasants. The uniforms and the flags of the Nazi mass rallies presented an image of strength, unity and authority. Lenin's memory was used as a symbol of the continuity and ideological purity of the Soviet leadership. Religious symbols may take the place of secular symbols in some political cultures. Profound significance is attached to coronation ceremonies in the national church, national holidays are chosen from the church calendar, and particular saints are used to symbolise national unity. The symbolism of religion was crucial for the transformation of Poland from communism, and remains central in defining the nature of Israel.[32]

Myths play an important role in the political culture. They may be very important as a foundation of national identity. Myths about certain historical periods are used to evoke a sense of national greatness. The 'Elizabethan age' is important in the British context – the image of small ships defying the overwhelming might of Spain, basing their victories on superior courage and seamanship. A former prime minister, Harold Wilson, constantly evoked the 'spirit of Dunkirk' in his political speeches. Myths emphasise certain half-truths and therefore are distortions, although politically important distortions.

They were especially important in totalitarian systems; thus the Bolsheviks are portrayed as playing the major role in the 1917 revolution, and the parts played by other groups are largely ignored. Hitler emphasised the 'stab in the back': the German armies were not defeated by the western allies in the 1914–18 war, but were betrayed by traitors at home.

It is interesting to note that the more artificially created state of West Germany was unable to evoke a sense of national unity or national pride by the use of the various symbols of flag and national anthem. West Germans were less patriotic after 1945 and, in spite of official efforts, the new flag did not inspire the reverence paid to former national symbols. This problem was repeated when the former East German *Länder* were added after the fall of the Berlin Wall (November 1989). For other 'new countries', such as those emerging from colonialism, national symbols became extremely important. Having never had nationhood those symbols were important, while where symbols had proved extremely destructive they were greeted with greater caution.

The symbols need not be directly relevant to the existing political system, and may be regarded with incredulous amazement by outsiders. Thus the Protestants of Northern Ireland symbolise the religious unity of their allegiance to the British crown by yearly celebrations of the victories of William III in the late seventeenth century, and the anniversary of his defeat of the Catholics at the Battle of the Boyne is treated as a sectarian holiday. In some cases, even in Europe, national myths are relatively recent inventions, for example the epic poem the *Kalevala* in Finland.

The emotional intensity that embraces these symbols is a means of identifying the political values and attitudes in the political system, but these symbols are also used by governments to ensure their own legitimacy and to foster national unity. This creation of unity is particularly important in new nations or in states that have experienced a profound political upheaval. Efforts are made to eliminate memories of previous regimes by new anthems and flags, and by rewriting history – in some cases inventing it – establishing new national heroes or resurrecting forgotten ones, changing street names and even those of towns, and a constant ritual bombardment of the population to provoke manifestations of national unity. This sense of unity can often be intensified by whipping up feeling against foreign symbols such as foreign embassies or the economic role of foreign companies.

Development of a political culture

A political culture is not static but will respond to new ideas generated from within the political system or imported or imposed from outside. Japan furnishes an interesting example of a state subject to these internal and external pressures, resulting in bewildering and rapid changes within the last hundred years. In 1868 the Meiji Restoration ended a long period of centralised feudalism; it also coincided with the intrusion of the western industrialising societies after long international seclusion. Japan then embarked on a period of rapid industrialisation that was to make the country the equal of the western nations in economic and military strength, and also adopted some of the forms of European autocratic government, especially those of the German Empire.

The complete defeat of the Russians in their 1904–5 war represented the emergence of Japan on the world scene, a victory that was to become in some ways a blueprint for strategy in the Second World War. Then total military defeat in 1945, the occupation until 1952, and the imposition of the liberal democratic constitution by the Americans in 1946, all superimposed great changes on an already changing society. The result has been the coexistence of traditional norms and modernising western characteristics, which, while not completely conducive to political stability, has, nevertheless, produced a viable political system. As in Germany, this system was supported by a rapidly growing economy. Fortunately, the major recession in the Japanese economy in the 1990s did not occur until democracy had been well institutionalised.

Industrialisation is an important factor in changing values and attitudes. Rapid influxes of immigrants, war, and especially defeat in a major war or a revolution, all may provoke changes in political values and beliefs, with subsequent strains on the political system. The relationship of change and continuity is illustrated by the course of twentieth-century American foreign policy. The end of isolationism, or rather increased intervention in world affairs since 1900 made possible (and perhaps necessary) by American industrial and economic developments, was made more acceptable to the American public by projecting American values on to a world stage. Thus American foreign policy was designed to encourage liberal democracies and national self-determination. These were factors in American political development believed to have led to American prosperity and power. This sense of mission to extend American values to less fortunate nations was readily amenable to an anti-communist crusade, a crusade to which American liberals more eagerly subscribed than the conservative isolationists, at least until the Vietnam War reduced commitment to this style of foreign policy.

The stability of a political system is underlined by the relative success or failure of the assimilation of new attitudes into the existing value structure, and we must now examine the means of effectively transmitting the political culture from generation to generation.

Political socialisation

Political socialisation is the institutionalisation and development of attitudes to, and beliefs about, the political system. The process may encourage loyalty to the nation and the fostering of particular values, and it may increase either support for, or alienation from, the system. It is particularly important in influencing the degree of participation in political life that is expected of groups and individuals. Political socialisation is not a process confined to the impressionable years of childhood, but one that often continues throughout adult life. It happens through formal attempts to inculcate political values, as well as more informally as people participate in families, schools, clubs and the workplace.

Before examining the agencies of the socialisation process, some words of qualification are needed. First, there are as yet various conclusions about socialisation, and most of these are disputed.[33] It is easier to examine the deliberate attempts of

governments to influence the socialisation process than to come
to some firm views about the effects of those attempts, especially as it is easier, for example, to conduct a survey of mass
opinions in Great Britain than in China. Second, the values
and attitudes developed by political socialising agencies are
often mistakenly confused with voting intentions and party
allegiances, partly, one suspects, because it is easier to measure
the latter. While there may be considerable overlap between
voting and party partisanship and broader political values and
attitudes, they are not the same. Thirdly, one needs to
distinguish clearly between intentional efforts to influence the
establishment of political values and socialisation processes
over which the government has no influence. With the former,
manifest, as opposed to latent, political socialisation, we are
usually referring to political indoctrination. Non-political experiences, such as participation in school societies and sporting
clubs, may be as important in later adult political life as a
weekly civics course on the structures of the country's political
institutions. Finally, one needs to be aware when examining
the agencies of the political socialisation process of the interrelationships between them, and this in turn can lead to
general conclusions as to whether they can complement each
other or whether there is conflict between them. In stable
political systems there are fewer antagonisms between such
socialising institutions as the family, school and the various
voluntary groups in society.

Agencies of socialisation

The principal determinants of the development and establishment of various attitudes and values about the political system
may be listed as: (1) the family; (2) the schools and other
institutions of education; (3) voluntary groups, work and
informal relationships; (4) the mass media;[34] (5) government
and party agencies. We have noted the necessity of remember-
ing the overlap between them; they cannot be examined in
complete isolation. Moreover, all these factors are affected, in
varying degrees, by other factors, such as social and geographical mobility. For example, people moving upwards on the

social class ladder tend to acquire new values and attitudes, whereas those whose social class is lower than their parents' are more likely to retain former political attitudes. Geographical mobility has several consequences, such as the reluctance to discuss political questions or participate in political activities after moving into a new district.

The influence of the family in the process of political socialisation seems obvious. The family is the child's first window on the world outside; it is the child's first contact with authority; it is here that the first differences in the role expectations between the sexes are implanted, and surveys have shown the strong link between the voting behaviour of parents and their children.[35] Of course there are other agencies exerting influences on the child from an early age, and it may be that the family is divided in its political attitudes, and the political values of the child may be formed in opposition to one of the parents. Also, the longer the period of formal education and the higher the intelligence of the child, the smaller will be the extent of parental influence.

Yet a great deal will depend on the relationship with other socialising agencies. In Britain and the United States family life tends to encourage many of the values that will find support in later political life, whereas it is claimed that in the Soviet Union the constant propaganda efforts of the government and the emphasis on political education in the schools were evidence of the regime's relative failure to eradicate 'deviant' influences of the family. The conflict of values in families and those of other agents becomes more complicated when there are major regime changes and families have to explain their support for the previous regimes. Political attitudes are not formed in terms of opposition to parents, however much they may differ, but parents are only one agency, and not always as influential as one would suspect, at least in terms of political values if not in terms of party allegiance.

The educational system has important effects on the process of socialisation, the more so if it is extended to cover higher and university education. The values imparted by schools and universities may not be the result of direct political indoctrination, but are none the less important. A decentralised educational system may prevent direct government interference and may encourage and support sub-cultures. In France there is a high degree of centralisation, but state and local control of schools in the United States allows for regional variations, variations in which family attitudes are reinforced by the schools. American education, however, does tend to support the major values apparent in the political system; it encourages the notion of equal and democratic participation, and there are strong links with the parents which temper authoritarian tendencies on the part of the schools.

The structure of British education, on the other hand, is more likely to encourage inequality and deference, especially with the existence of a strong private sector of education for middle-class children, with its emphasis on character-building and other individual and social virtues.[36] The arguments over comprehensive schools in the state sector of British education are more concerned with social inequalities than academic or administrative arguments. The implicit inculcation of political attitudes in any educational system can be in the role that religious education plays, and in the continuation of somewhat different expectations of boys and girls in education.

Yet manifest socialisation is important in many political systems. The educational programme of Soviet schoolchildren traditionally included an overt element of 'moral education' with stress on discipline, Soviet patriotism and proletarian internationalism, and dedication to the goals of the community, the state and the Communist Party.[37] Civics and 'Americanism' courses have been a necessary part of American education to allow for the assimilation of vast numbers of immigrants from diverse backgrounds. The teaching of history is an important part of any education course; accounts of past national heroes, coupled with a timely neglect of other aspects of history, are an effective means of encouraging patriotism and a general pride in the achievements of the state. It is noticeable that for understandable reasons recent history is a neglected aspect in many German schools, and what history is to be taught remains a contentious issue in Japanese education.[38] African-Americans have become more vocal in their criticisms of the neglect of Black contributions to American history as outlined in American schools and textbooks, and have successfully demanded the inclusion of 'Black studies' programmes in many colleges.

The effect of education on political values can be partly illustrated by the upsurge of student radicalism in the late 1960s, especially in more industrialised countries. Even though it may represent only a minority of the young people at the time, the students' role in the French crisis of May 1968, and the American student opposition to the Vietnam War are illustrative examples of the impact of education.[39] However, the impact of university education on political values is complex, and it may be that a university environment merely heightens political awareness without affecting basic political attitudes.[40]

The other agencies of political socialisation are regarded as less direct (or measurable) and are closely interrelated to the influence of family and school. Political parties have more diffuse impacts because of their need to win wider support among the public. Direct government intervention may be a sign of failure to receive the type of support from either the family or school in socialisation that government might desire. The German and Austrian governments provide financial support to voluntary youth groups and organisations and to the political parties to encourage political education. Youth movements do play an important part in the process of national integration in developing countries, e.g. the youth wing of the United National Independence Party (UNIP) in Zambia. Nearly all Soviet schoolchildren were members of the Party-controlled Octobrists and Pioneers, and the majority of university students were members of the Komsomol, the youth wing of the CPSU.

The mass media, whether directly controlled by the government or not, tend to reinforce existing political values, and this aspect also highlights a negative weapon of the government, that of political censorship. Further, media laws in most democratic countries attempt to impose limits on the degree of concentration of ownership of media, both electronic and print. Even when the press is free of political control, it may not be free of economic control, and these laws promote some variety in the sources of political ideas available to the public.

Perhaps the most important socialising agency in this voluntary category for most countries is the church. Its effect on political attitudes is less apparent when it reinforces other socialising agencies, but the role of Roman Catholicism in many European countries offers illustrations of its conflict with both state and education, and is possibly a vital factor in the political behaviour of women in some countries. Outside of Europe, Islam is an increasingly powerful force shaping behaviour, and its influence now extends into Europe as larger number of immigrants bring with them the political and social values of their homelands.

It is also worth noting the socialisation role of compulsory military service in some states; especially in multi-ethnic societies this may be one common experience, at least for males.

Socialisation and the political system

We have seen that manifest socialisation may be the result of several socialising agencies, and that interrelationships are important. One cannot simply seek links between, for example, an authoritarian family structure and the establishment of values that expect a subject role in the political system. There are too many variables, such as generational differences, the greater adult socialising influences on political leaders and the question of individual personality, which are more defiant of analysis. Yet the values established need neither be coherent nor consciously held to contribute to the stabilisation of the political system. Some processes of socialisation are more homogeneous, and the various agencies will complement each other rather than conflict; yet this does not preclude change, nor does it stifle variety. Political socialisation is a continuous process, and as such is not completely static. The test for a stable political system is whether the socialising agencies are sufficiently flexible and sufficiently interdependent to permit political change without violent disruption.

We have been discussing political socialisation in the context of the nation state, but with globlisation and the increased importance of regional entities such as the European Union the values being inculcated are not necessarily those of the nation state within which citizens live. Especially in Europe these values may vie strongly with national values, as citizens begin to think of themselves as members of a political unit that transcends conventional national boundaries. It is not only identification with transnational political forces that is changing, it is also that more substantive values about politics are also being spread globally.

Summary

Political culture is one of the many possible explanations for political behaviour and the decisions made by political actors – whether individual voters or political élites. Some of the ideas contained in a political culture are very general notions about democracy or what constitutes good government, while others may be more specific assessments of policies or particular forms of political participation. In some countries the political culture is homogenous while in others it may be divided along ethnic, class or even gender lines. However it is structured, the political culture does influence behavior.

The difficulty from an analytic point of view is that identifying exactly how political culture exerts its influence in political life is difficult. Too often the cultural elements of politics become a residual explanation – when more objectively demonstrable variables are unsuccessful in explanation then the outcomes *must* be the consequences of political culture. Several of the approaches to political culture discussed above do provide some objective measures of culture, but even with those it is difficult to establish a clear link between the indicators of individual political values and the behaviour of whole political systems. Making this linkage remains one of the major challenges for the advocates of political culture.

Notes and references

1. See D. Kavanagh, *Political Culture* (London: Macmillan, 1972) pp. 9–19.
2. H. L. Perry and W. Parent, *Blacks and the American Political System* (Gainesville: University Press of Florida, 1995).

3. Greens and other ecologists may, for example, constitute a distinct political subculture.

4. See J. S., Nye, P. D. Zelikow and D. C. King, *Why People Don't Trust Government* (Cambridge, MA: Harvard University Press, 1997).

5. See S. White, *Political Culture and Soviet Politics* (London, 1979). See also A. Brown (ed.), *Political Culture and Communist Studies* (London, 1984).

6. See L. J. Edinger, *West German Politics* (New York: HarperCollins, 1986) pp. 95–100.

7. See J. Thomassen, 'Support for Democratic Values', in H.-D. Klingemann and D. Fuchs, *Citizens and the State* (Oxford: Oxford University Press, 1995; J. M. Mushaben, *From Post-War to Post-Wall Generations* (Boulder, CO: Westview, 1998).

8. Richard Rose, 'England: The Traditionally Modern Political Culture', in L. Pye and S. Verba (eds), *Political Culture and Political Development* (Princeton: Princeton University Press, 1967).

9. See D. Marsh and R. A. W. Rhodes, *Implementing Thatcherite Policies: Audit of an Era* (Buckingham: Open University Press, 1992);

10. Michael Foley *The Politics of the British Constitution* (Manchester: Manchester University Press, 1999).

11. On contemporary French political culture, see S. Hazareesingh,*Political Traditions in Modern France* (Oxford: Oxford University Press, 1994).

12. See F. Thistlethwaite, *The Great Experiment*, 3rd edn (Cambridge, 1967) for a broader view of the development of the American political culture. See also M. Schudson, *The Good Citizen: A History of American Civic Life* (New York: Martin Kessler, 1998).

13. This is in part the famous thesis of Frederick Jackson Turner about the frontier. See *The Frontier in American History* (New York: H. Holt, 1920).

14. See S. M. Lipset, *The First New Nation* (London: Faber, 1963). Hugh Seton-Watson, remarking on the effect of these interrelationships, has observed: 'one reason for the prevalence of autocracy in Russian history is military. Russia has no natural boundaries except the Arctic ice and the mountain ranges of Caucasus and Central Asia. It was subject for centuries to invasion from both west and cast. Imagine the United States without either the Atlantic or the Pacific, and with several first-rate military powers instead of the Indians, and there would be some form of parallel. . . . In America the open frontier meant opportunity, and so freedom: in Russia it meant insecurity, and so subjection' (*The Russian Empire 1801–1917* (Oxford: Oxford University Press, 1967) pp. 12–13).

15. See A. A. Barreto, *Language, Elites and the State: Nationalism in Puerto Rico and Quebec* (Westport, CT: Praeger, 1998); K. McRoberts, *Misconceiving Canada: The Struggle for National Unity* (Toronto: Oxford University Press, 1997).

16. See E. Norman, *A History of Modern Ireland* (London, 1972) pp. 237–41, for an account of Irish cultural nationalism in the early twentieth century, especially the attempts of the Gaelic League to revive the Irish language.

17. G. Hyden and M. Bratton, *Governance in Africa* (Boulder, CO: Westview, 1992).
18. This is similar to the idea of 'subject culture' in Gabriel Almond and Sidney Verba *Civic Culture.* (Princeton: Princeton University Press, 1963).
19. R. Inglehart, *The Silent Revolution* (Princeton: Princeton University Press, 1979); Inglehart, *Culture Shift* (Princeton, NJ: Princeton University Press, 1990);
20. See Michael Keating, *Nations Aginst the State* (New York: St Martin's, 1996).
21. See A. C. MacIntyre, 'Is a Science of Comparative Politics Possible?', in *The Practice of Comparative Politics,* ed. P. G. Lewis *et al.* (London, 1978) pp. 266–84, for a discussion of the problems of comparing political cultures. MacIntyre is a rather strict anti-empiricist so these critiques should be considered with some caution.
22. See Morris P. Fiorina, *Congress: The Keystone of the Washington Establishment,* rev. edn (New Haven: Yale University Press, 1992).
23. For an overview of the Italian political culture, see G. Sani, 'The Political Culture of Italy: Continuity and Change', in Gabriel Almond and Sidney Verba, *The Civic Culture Revisited* (Newbury Park, CA: Sage, 1989). pp. 273–324.
24. See D. Kavanagh, *Thatcherism and British Politics: The End of Consensus?* (Oxford, 1987) pp. 270–4. See also H. Young, *One of Us: A Biography of Margaret Thatcher,* rev. edn (London: Macmillan, 1991) pp. 601–3.
25. D. Butler, A. Adonis and T. Travers, *Failure in British Government: The Politics of the Poll Tax* (Oxford: Oxford University Press, 1995).
26. See G. A. Almond and S. Verba, *The Civic Culture* (Princeton, NJ: Princeton University Press, 1963) and *The Civic Culture Revisited* (Newbury Park, CA: Sage, 1989).
27. See R. Rose, *Politics in England,* 4th edn (London: Faber, 1985) pp. 141–2.
28. V. Perez-Diaz, *The Return of Civil Society: The Emergence of Democratic Spain* (Cambridge, MA: Harvard University Press, 1994).
29. See P. Winczorek, 'The Internal Evolution and Changing Policies of the Democratic Party', in *Democratization in Poland, 1988–90,* ed. G. Sandford (Basingstoke: Macmillan, 1992) pp. 177–94.
30. W. Bagehot, *The English Constitution* (Fontana Library edn, London, 1963) p. 85.
31. See R. Rose and D. Kavanagh, 'The Monarchy in Contemporary Political Culture', *Comparative Politics,* 8, 4 (1976) pp. 548–76.
32. There are manifest conflicts between secular and orthodox Jews, but there is little doubt that religion helps define the State.
33. One particularly interesting discussion is provided in J. P. Euben, *Corrupting Youth: Political Education, Democratic Culture and Political Theory* (Princeton: Princeton University Press, 1997). See also R. F. Fahren (ed.), *Democracy, Socialization and Conflicting Loyalties in East and West* (New York: St Martin's, 1996).

34. The influence of the mass media will be examined in Chapter 7.
35. For a discussion of the family and the socialisation process, see B. Stacey, *Political Socialisation in Western Society* (London: Macmillan, 1978) pp. 1–18. See also J. Gibbins (ed.), *Contemporary Political Culture: Politics in a Postmodern Age* (London: Sage, 1989).
36. See Rose, *Politics in England*, pp. 170–7.
37. See D. Lane, *Soviet Society under Perestroika*, 2nd edn (London: Unwin Hyman, 1992) pp. 289–314.
38. And to some extent in America. See E. T. Linenthal and T. Engelhardt, *History Wars: The Enola Gay and Other Battles for the American Past* (New York: Metropolitan Books, 1996).
39. A. Schnapp, *The French Student Uprising, November 1967–June 1968* (Boston: Beacon Press, 1971).
40. See Stacey, *Political Stabilisation in Western Society*, pp. 92–9, for a discussion of American student opposition to the Vietnam war.

PART TWO

Parties, Pressure Groups and Representation

5

Political Parties and Electoral Systems

The opinions or actions of individuals may count for little in the political process unless expressed through some form of organisation. Organisations can bring together the voices of thousands or even millions of people and provide the political power needed to produce action. We will now begin to discuss the groups in society that collect, process and articulate the wants and demands of the public – political parties and then (Chapter 6) interest groups. These groups are crucial for the performance of modern democracy. Although direct democracy has some appeal as an ideal,[1] in practice it is often unwieldy and subject to demagoguery.[2] Interest groups, and especially political parties, are important for mediating between the demands of the public and the formal institutions of decision-making by government. These organisations are mechanisms of channelling and aggregating demands, and providing an institutional basis for relating the people to their government. They further provide a means of organising within government, and give the public some continuity in politics. Even for citizens who may not be adherents of one party or the other the parties are in most systems points of stability.

Political parties

Political parties are also often crucial for the success of non-democratic political systems. Certainly the Communist Party was a central player in the regimes of the former Soviet Union and Eastern Europe, and remains so in China and Cuba.[3] Similarly extreme right-wing parties have been crucial sources of governance in countries such as Nazi Germany, Franco's Spain, and Pinochet's Chile. The Ba'athist party has played a major role in the governance of Syria. Dominant political parties such as Congress in India and the Partido Revolucionario Institutional (PRI) in Mexico have been central to developmental efforts in those countries, and in the management of the polity, particularly linking local and national politics.[4] This list could be extended, but the basic point is that even in less than fully democratic systems political parties are important elements in supplying governance.

Definition

Political parties may be principally defined by their common aim. They seek political power either singly or in co-operation with other political parties. As Joseph Schumpeter has observed: 'The first and foremost aim of each political party is to prevail over the others in order to get into power or to stay in it.'[5] It is this goal of attaining political power that distinguishes political parties from other groups in the political system, although the distinction is rather blurred at times, especially in regard to pressure groups (see Chapter 6). This flexible definition presupposes organisation, and to distinguish political parties from legislative cliques there must be the assumption that the organisation has some extra-parliamentary bases of support. Otherwise one would have to include within the definition of parties the pre-nineteenth-century West European parliamentary organisations that differed markedly in structure and in functions from modern political parties.[6] Parties may retain a strong parliamentary basis for their decision-making, but there must be some relationship with the public.

Given this definition we can avoid evaluative approaches to the study of parties – whether parties are 'conspiracies' against the rest of the nation, whether they are inimicable to the 'national good', etc. Political parties exist in differing forms in various political systems, and while not essential to the political process, it is difficult to imagine the political consequences of their absence in the vast majority of states. Also the definition avoids examining the ideological and programmatic aspects of political parties. Parties are important for the functioning of the political system, whether a party is ideologically united or simply exists as an electoral machine, but the presence or absence of ideology does not determine the right to the title of political party. Again it is important whether particular parties compete against each other for political power, but this does not mean that we can only meaningfully discuss political parties in liberal democracies and deny their existence in state socialist or authoritarian systems.

The capture of political power, or indeed its retention, can be achieved within existing political structures or by over-throwing them. Working within the political system, parties present candidates and leaders to the electorate and seek to mobilise the support of the electorate by propaganda, orga-nised activities and by emphasising programmatic differences with other parties in competitive party systems. Even parties such as the National Socialists in Germany in the early 1930s and Communists in some Eastern Europe countries after the Second World War first may achieve power through elections and then use that electoral base to legitimise their transforming the political system more fundamentally. The word 'Party' often is used by groups seeking political power, whether they seek it though elections or through less democratic means, e.g. the 'Black Panther *Party*' active during the 1960s and 1970s.

Functions of political parties

One of the most important functions of political parties is that of unifying, simplifying, and stabilising the political process. Parties do not divide, in spite of the claims of advocates of non-party or coalition-national governments, they tend to unite. In most political systems, parties can bring together sectional interests, overcome geographical distances, and provide coher-ence to sometimes divisive government structures. The Amer-ican Democratic Party long provided a bridge to bring together, albeit uneasily, southern conservatives and northern liberals.[7] It was a sectional split among Democrats that encouraged the outbreak of the American Civil War over a century ago. The French UDF gives a parliamentary coherence to a loose group of locally based notables whose only elements in common have consisted of an anti-clerical and anti-Marxist platform. The German Christian Democratic Party (CDU) has likewise bridged the gulf between Protestants and Catholics in Germany, although most Catholic adherents actually are organised through the partner party, the Christian Social Union (CSU) in Bavaria and in parts of Baden-Wurtemberg.

All political parties in federal systems emphasise the uniting of different government structures, the extreme example being the one-party system of the Soviet Union which almost completely undermines the federal constitutional division of decision-making. Even in such politically homogeneous systems as Great Britain's, there is some bridging between local and national government through parties. This function of political parties also may be seen in the unity of Cabinet and House of Commons. Some of that capacity for bridging depends upon the integration of the parties themselves; if parties mean one thing in local communities and another at the national level then there will be more conflict than linkage occurring.

This bridging function of political parties is an important factor in political stability.[8] There are many other variables, but nevertheless political parties in their search for political power do form order out of chaos. They seek to broaden the range of interests they represent and harmonise these interests with each other. This 'aggregation' of interests is carried out by other groups in the political system as well as by political parties, but in the main the function is performed by the parties.[9] The representation of interests is a safety valve; it brings diverse interests into the political process, and appears at least to be attempting to satisfy their demands. We have already noted this co-ordination and compromise aspect of the American Democratic Party. The British Conservative Party, one of the most successful parties in competitive party systems, has, in spite of the nature of its internal organisation and distribution of power, won at times the support of diverse economic, social and geographical sections in British politics.

Political parties often seek to widen their support, whether they are parties fighting competitive elections or single parties dominating the political process, and in doing so they not only reflect divisions in society, but tend to mitigate their divisiveness. The major exception to this generalisation is the behaviour of sectional or ethnic parties that might lose support from their main base if they were to attempt to be more inclusive. For example, the Hindu Nationalist Party in India might well lose its appeal if it attempted to be a 'catch-all' party in the mould of the Congress Party. The same could be said of regionalist parties in Spain or Belgium.[10]

Political parties provide a link between government and people. They seek to educate, instruct and activate the electorate. They use the mass media and local organisations to maintain contacts with relatively politically inactive citizens and lead them to the awareness and acceptance of various policies. They also seek to mobilise and involve the population in politics. These activities may be restricted to election periods, with various methods of increasing the party's votes, but they may extend far beyond electoral propaganda, and the party may seek to mobilise support by channelling its supporters' non-political activities. Thus political parties may create and control trade unions and cultural and leisure organisations. The French Communist Party provides an excellent example of this 'occupational and social implantation' by a political party.[11]

The mobilisation of support by activating the population may be carried further by mass rallies, uniforms, mascots, flags and other displays of unity, to emphasise the identification between the individual and the political party. This aspect of political mobilisation is usually associated with parties in totalitarian systems, and the German Nazi Party provides some spectacular illustrations:

There were posters, always in red, the revolutionary colour, chosen to provoke the Left; the swastika and the flag, with its black swastika in a white circle on a red background, a design to which Hitler devoted the utmost care; the salute, the uniform and the hierarchy of ranks. Mass meetings and demonstrations were another device which Hitler borrowed from the Austrian Social Democrats. The essential purpose of such meetings was to create a sense of power, of belonging to a movement whose success was irresistible.[12]

While increasing the scope of political activity and widening popular participation, political parties perform the important function of recruiting political leaders. Recruitment is a very important party function in socialist regimes (China, Cuba) where the party provides the only avenue to political power, but it is as significant in competitive party systems in which the main source of political recruitment is through the political parties.[13] In political systems where political parties are absent or very weak, the political élites are recruited from traditional élites, such as hereditary ruling families, or through religious or military organisations. The recruitment of political élites without the existence of a popular base of party leaders may have significant negative effects on the stability of the regime, given that the leaders have less of an anchor in society. Parties thus create 'political opportunity structures' for present and future leaders, and help the political system by training future leaders and weeding out the less capable.[14]

Parties present ideas and issues; they articulate alternative value goals for the society in ways that may enhance the opportunities for choosing those values. All political parties have philosophical bases, no matter how blurred and no matter how divorced from the actual political behaviour of the party these foundations may be. The more coherent this philosophical base is, the more inclined we are to talk of ideological parties. The ideology may be important for party workers and voters to justify their commitment to the party, but it also serves to distinguish the party from others and allows the party to attempt to organise public opinion in a given ideological or policy direction. The ideology of the party may be a challenge to the prevailing ideologies, as when socialist parties appeared in Western Europe at the end of the nineteenth century to oppose the existing conservative and liberal consensus among the political élites. The ideology may, on the other hand, express an agreement among the parties on existing political structures and political goals.

The different levels of ideological commitment could be illustrated by distinguishing between American political parties, European social democratic parties, and parties in socialist states. American political parties remain largely pragmatic, despite increasing levels of commitment to particular policies and ideals; Robert Dahl speaks of 'ideological similarity and issue conflict'.[15] This does not mean that American parties are not ideological, but that they agree fundamentally on the goals of American society: there is no challenge to existing orthodoxies, and most parties, socialist or radical right-wing, that have challenged the consensus have failed even at state level. Indeed, part of the failure of the Republican Party in the 1998 Congressional elections is that it came to be seen as excessively committed to a 'right-wing' ideology. One recent exception to the generalisation of the failure of third parties is the success of the populist Reform Party in electing the governor of Minnesota. The major Irish parties, Fianna Fail and Fine Gael, are the nearest European equivalents of the American parties in respect to lack of clear ideological differences.[16]

Some degree of pragmatism is evident even in West European communist and social democratic parties, for although they have wished, at least theoretically, to challenge the existing social and economic system, they do not aim to overthrow the prevailing political structures. Rather, these parties are content to work through the existing structures, attempting to realise their goals gradually, as 'Eurocommunist' parties.[17] Party members who do not subscribe to the ideological goals of the party may be disciplined, and more passion is often spent on internal doctrinal feuding than on the mechanics of winning elections. There are wide differences between social democratic parties that have dominated government for long periods, as in Sweden, and communist parties that formed opposition groups for long periods, as in Italy, for example. It is easier to remain ideologically pure without the responsibility for pragmatic adjustments of government. Yet the ideological base of these parties is sufficiently flexible to allow accommodation to parliamentary forms of government, and the parties tend to be dominated by their legislative wings, and an increasing number of communist parties have entered into coalition governments with social democratic parties.

The single parties in socialist or fascist systems set more rigid ideological goals for society. The German Nazi Party emphasised racial purity; communist parties proclaim the dictatorship of the working class, and economic and social equality. The aims of the party become the total aims for the society, and the party goals assume the form of a secular religion. They are more than statements of party programmes; they are also general guides to social action and appropriate behaviour on the part of citizens. Thus, disagreement with the ideology of the party is both treason and heresy, and usually was punished accordingly. The same style of ideological preoccupation is found in some developmental parties that attempt to use the party and its ideology as a means of transforming the society; examples are found across Africa and the Middle East.

It is difficult to imagine modern political systems without political parties; certainly liberal democratic institutions imply

Table 5.1 Examples of types of political parties

Communist	Communist Party of Cuba
	Communist Refoundation (Italy)
Social Democratic	Labour Party (UK)
	Social Democratic Party (Germany)
Centre	Center Party (Sweden)
Liberal	Free Democrats (Germany)
Conservative	People's Party (Spain)
	Progressive Conservative Party (Canada)
Extreme Right	Progress Party (Norway)
	Freedom Party (Austria)
Ecological	Greens (Germany, and elsewhere)
Regional	Northern League (Italy)
	Christian Social Union (Bavaria)
Religious	Hindu National Party (India)
	Christian People's Party (Sweden)
Linguistic	Russian People's Party (Estonia)
	Swedish People's Party (Finland)
Catch-All	Fianna Fail (Ireland)
	Democratic Party (United States)

political parties, and the reliance on parties is greatest in socialist regimes. This is not to overlook the distorting features of political parties. The German Weimar Republic collapsed as a result of the polarisation of the electorate between the Nazi and Communist Parties. The Portuguese military rulers feared that the election results of the 1976 general election would polarise opinion between the left and the conservative parties. The military had, in fact, banned the more conservative parties in previous elections that followed the 1974 coup.[18] More recently, fractious political parties have presented real governance problems for post-socialist regimes.

In general, the better political parties are at fulfilling their representative functions the less capable they may be of fulfilling the governing functions that are at least as important. Moreover, the various functions of the political parties may clash within the political system; thus Fred Greenstein observed that the supporters of the decentralised, consensual party system in the United States emphasise the success and consequent stability of that system, whereas its critics argue that it has been achieved at the expense of democratic control of government, and at the expense of efficient and effective government. The experiences of Americans with more centralised and 'responsible' parties during the Clinton impeachment debates, and indeed their behaviour in Congress during the post-1994 period, has led many scholars, and citizens, to recognise the virtues of less responsible parties.

Party structure

The structures of political parties relate very closely to the functions and the methods that political parties employ to realise their aim of capturing or retaining political power. Thus, parties that desire to widen their electoral support and be effective participants at a parliamentary level will need a different structure from a party forced underground by restrictive legislation, or from a party conducting guerrilla operations from a rural base against urban-centred political élites. Parties that attempt to attain wider democratic participation, such as the extension of the franchise, may have, in theory, a more democratic structure than parties which seek to perpetuate the power of existing political élites.

An important analysis of party structure has been offered by the French political scientist Maurice Duverger. Duverger advanced a fourfold classification of party structure.[19] The alternatives were: (1) the caucus; (2) the branch; (3) the cell; (4) the militia. The caucus or committee is characterised by its small membership and its resistance to seeking wider mass membership; it emphasises quality in its membership and its leadership potential. It concentrates mainly on electoral activities, remaining dormant between elections. Its members consist either of local notables elected for their individual qualities and local influence ('direct caucus'), or of delegates of local organisations which have combined to form the party ('indirect caucus'). Duverger cites the French Radical Party and the British Labour Party before 1918 as two examples of this type of party, and he argues that the caucus-type party declines with the extension of the franchise. American political parties retain some of these features, with the voting strengths of the parties being as much as [20] times their formal membership;[20] the British Conservative Party also continues to behave much as if it were a legislative caucus, with the party still dominated by the 1922 Committee in the House of Commons, and by its leader.[21]

Many of the parties emerging in the new democracies in Eastern Europe have the characteristics of caucus parties, having few members and being essentially small groups of elites. Given this pattern, and electoral laws that tend to reward small parties, there may be dozens of parties standing in elections. The many small parties that get elected then make forming governing coalitions more difficult, and rather than enhancing respect for democracy by being representative may actually bring democracy into some disrepute for being apparently ineffective.

The branch party is the product of the extension of the franchise in Western Europe. Unlike the caucus, the branch party is a mass party seeking to enrol the maximum membership. It usually has a centralised party structure, the basic units being distributed geographically according to the constituency arrangements. Moreover, its political activities are permanent, not merely confined to election periods. The branch structure was invented by the European socialist parties after the extension of the franchise to the working class, and has been imitated by a number of Catholic and conservative parties with varying degrees of success. Indeed, the branch is the typical form of organisation for political parties in the industrialised democracies.

The German Social Democratic Party (SPD) provides a good example of the branch from of organisational structure. Delegates are elected via the branches and the regions to the biennial party congress, which in theory is the highest policy-making body in the party. The congress elects the party executive, which controls the party organisation outside the German parliament. (Although a new competing organisation, the party presidium, was established in 1958, and is more tightly controlled by the SPD parliamentary group.) The real centre of power in the party is, in fact, in the hands of the parliamentary group, which consists of all SPD members of the Bundestag, the German lower chamber. The organisation of the SPD is similar, in many ways, to that of the British Labour Party, especially in regard to the distribution of power inside the party. The principal difference is the greater power of trade unions within the British Labour Party.

Duverger's third type of structure, the cell, is an invention of the revolutionary socialist parties. Its organisational structure is based on the place of work, not, as with the branch parties, on geographical areas, although some area cells do exist and in some parties are quite important. The cell is smaller than the branch and is geared to continual political activity. The cell structure was essentially conspiratorial; it was designed to ensure that the whole party structure was not imperilled by the infiltration or destruction of one cell, as there was no contact between individual units at the same level. The secretive activities of the cell were more widely political and more demanding on the individual than in branch parties. Cell-structured parties tended to regard the winning of elections as of secondary importance. Elements of the former cell structure still remain in European parties, but there is hostility among French Communist Party members to this form of structure. The French Communist Party, like other Western European 'Euro-Communist' parties, has long attached far more importance to winning parliamentary elections, and the structure of the party now resembles more closely parties with a branch form of structure.

Duverger's fourth form of party structure is the militia type of organisation in which the structure takes on the hierarchical character of an army. Like the communist party cell structure, the militia form of organisation is adopted by revolutionary parties, and the two principal European examples have been Hitler's Storm Troopers and Mussolini's fascist militia. As the name implies this form of organisation mimics a military system, with the same hierarchical control over party members. But Duverger does point out that 'no political party has ever been exclusively formed on the basis of the militia'.[22] In fact he goes further, arguing that his basic types are more likely to be found in mixed rather than pure form.

The critics of Duverger's classification scheme are many.[23] For example, Jean Blondel wishes to describe 'caucus' and 'mass' parties as parties of 'indirect rule' and parties of 'direct rule', stressing not membership but the nature of the links between leaders and followers: 'It follows that the real distinguishing factor between mass party and party of committee is not directly related to questions of membership; the type of allegiance is the crucial problem.[24] Further, as the geographical net is cast wider, this scheme, developed on a European base begins to appear excessively bound by that one set of political experiences.

In any examination of party structure, the following factors should be considered:

1. The role of the leadership and the method of selecting it.
2. The degree of organisational centralisation.
3. The power of the leadership in relation to the rank and file; the extent of disciplinary powers; participation in decision-making and policy initiation.
4. The control of the party bureaucracy; is it the leader, the parliamentary party, or the executive committee?
5. The relationship of the parliamentary wing to the rest of the party.
6. Basis and extent of membership.

A final factor that should be considered for the development of party structures in Western Europe is the European Parliament and the possibility of cross-national party structures. Although there are few cases of attempts to create cross-national party linkages and common platforms in several European countries, political parties remain for the most part national. Over time, however, and especially if the European Parliament is able to gain greater power in relation to the Commission and the Council, there may be a need for political parties that are meaningful entities in most if not all the member states of the European Union.

Determinants of party structure

We have already seen that the ideological framework of the party is an important factor in how the party relates to the rest of the political system, and therefore will have an important bearing on the structure of the political party. If the party sees its goals as antagonistic to the existing political structures, its organisation will reflect not only the party's hostility to the prevailing norms, but also a readiness to defend itself against any repressive measures that this hostility has produced among the dominant political élites. The organisational structure of the party also responds to the existing political institutions and structures of government. A federal structure of government is more likely to produce decentralised parties; presidential elections will have different effects on the nature of the party leadership than the less individual parliamentary elections. It must be remembered, of course, that parties are not passive in this context, but, as we have seen, in their turn affect the functioning of these different structures of government.

Socio-economic factors are also important in determining party structures. The level of economic development influences the nature of the party competition and whether that competition endures and so affects the structure of the parties. There will be a different response to campaigns in urban and rural societies, and to those in which class conflict is a significant aspect of the political process.

Nationalism and religious divisions may be more important than class in forming the basis of some political parties.[25] Of course, the attitudes and values prevalent in society, the political culture, may be of vital significance in determining the types of political parties that emerge in any society. Parties with what are regarded as undemocratic structures, e.g. extreme nationalist parties, may find difficulties in electoral competition in stable liberal democratic systems.[26] The German constitution, for example, permits the outlawing of anti-democratic political parties, a provision resulting from that country's previous experience with political extremism. Even when there has been significant concern about the expansion of immigrant communities in Western European countries, more extreme nationalist politicians have found mobilising support difficult. The same has been less true, however, of extreme parties based on economic issues, e.g. anti-tax parties in Northern Europe.[27]

Historical factors are of the utmost significance in determining party structures. Parties are creations of modern political processes, and their emergence presupposes a necessary degree of urbanisation and development of mass communications; without those factors parties are little more that groups of elites or legislative factions. Parties arise when historical changes occur, and these are not subject to scientific laws. Therefore, the development of parties is more haphazard and uneven than general classifications make apparent. Certainly particular changes are necessary, such as the need for the dominant political élites to seek wider political support, and for a significant change in political attitudes.

In Western Europe the extension of the franchise forced the existing conservative and liberal parliamentary groups to form national organisations to appeal to a wider electorate in order to capture or maintain power. In Eastern Europe the political convulsions of 1989–90 led the leaders of unpopular Communist regimes to rename their parties with a variety of labels such as the Democratic Left. In Romania the Communist Party was banned and its leader Ceausescu executed, but many saw the National Salvation Front as the Communist Party in a new guise.[28] In several other cases, e.g. Slovakia, former communist parties with new labels have returned to political power.

In this context it is important to know whether the parties were extensions of groups already existing at the legislative level, or whether the parties were created outside the legislature with the aim of gaining a foothold inside. Externally created parties involve challenges to the existing dominant élites; they tend to be more centralised and are less deferential to the existing political institutions, although the British Labour Party is a powerful exception to the last point. Naturally, not all political parties originated in legislative structures. The Russian Bolsheviks had no alternative to secret, conspiratorial organisation and activities, given the hostility of the Tsarist regime. Colonial liberation movements are not given the option of constituting a parliamentary opposition to the existing government, and generally originate either as urban underground parties or as rural guerrilla organisations.[29] They can be said to grow out of crisis situations in which the legitimacy of the established political élites is no longer recognised, and new groups seek to replace them.

All these factors – ideology, structure of government, level of socio-economic development, political culture and historical 'accidents' – are interrelated. Thus, for example, American parties are primarily electoral machines, decentralised, laying little emphasis on ideological differences, exercising little disciplinary control over their members, and recruiting many of their presidential and congressional representatives from outside the party structure. For explanations for the development of parties with these characteristics, one needs to consider the federal system of government, the separation of powers, the presidential form of government, the liberal consensus, immigration and industrialisation, ethnic differences, and the extension of the franchise in the early nineteenth century before the rise of an urban working class of significance.

The decline of the traditional working class was one factor undermining the class appeal of socialist and communist parties in Western Europe. The communist parties began to abandon their highly centralised structures and organisation based on workplace cells and to repudiate many accepted communist doctrines such as the dictatorship of the proletariat; like their East European counterparts, many of them changed their names and tried to widen their appeal. For explanations of some of these characteristics, one would note the predominantly parliamentary, unitary political structures of Western European states, the extension of the franchise long after the appearance of an urban working class, the political dominance of traditional conservative and liberal élites, and the success of the Bolshevik revolution in Russia and the consequent attempt to establish a Moscow-dominated conformity on western communist parties. Naturally, the relationship of party structures to these various factors is one of great complexity, and far more analytical detail is needed for any explanation to be entirely satisfactory.

Party systems

The structures of political parties and the factors that assist in determining those structures are only one set of factors which guide us in determining how political parties function in the political system. Parties operate within party systems, and the type of system will have profound effects on party behaviour. There are various classifications of party systems but it is difficult to classify party systems according to one single criterion. The most useful factors to take into account are: (1) the number of parties; (2) the relative strength of the parties; (3) the ideological differences between the parties; (4) the structure of the parties. Using all these criteria with varying degrees of emphasis, we could arrive at the following classification:

1. *One-party systems.* The number of one-party systems has been dramatically reduced with the collapse of the Soviet empire, the changes in Eastern Europe and throughout the continent of Africa. However, China, North Korea and Cuba still offer examples of political systems in which only one party is allowed to compete and that party dominates the nomination and election processes within the system.[30]

2. *Dominant party systems.* In India the Congress Party has dominated federal politics since 1947, although its power has been waning since losing the 1977 and 1989 general elections. Likewise the Mexican dominant party, the Partido Revolucionario Institucional (PRI) never lost an election from 1917 until the 1990s, but allowed its insignificant rivals, the Partido Accion Nacional (PAN) and the Democratic Revolutionary Party (PRD) to compete in elections at every level, and is believed to give financial encouragement for this form of party competition, presumably for as long as the challenge is ineffective. The Japanese Liberal Party has won almost every general election since the end of the American occupation, but the other parties compete in what is essentially a pluralist system. Before the collapse of communist regimes in Eastern Europe, communist parties allowed a degree of competition in East Germany and Poland, but the Communist Party control of the nomination process firmly placed these systems in the one-party category.

3. *Distinct two-party systems.* New Zealand offered the best example of a system which consisted of only two major parties in the legislative assembly. The two parties, the Labour Party and the conservative National Party, achieved overall majorities in the legislature, govern alone and rotate in office. A change in the electoral law brought this party system to an end in the 1996 election. Although there are more than two parties in the Australian federal assembly, the system operates basically as a two-party system. Power alternates between a coalition of conservative Liberal Party and the National Party, supported at federal level by smaller parties, and the Labour Party.[31] The United Kingdom remains in effect a two-party system at the parliamentary level despite the existence of ten distinct groups in the House of Commons after the 1997 election. Despite not winning, over half of the votes at general elections, the Conservative and Labour Parties win the majority of seats; they have consistently governed alone since 1945 and since then have generally rotated in terms of government power. Only twice since 1945 have either of

these parties failed to win an overall majority of seats in the House of Commons.[32]

4. *Indistinct two-party systems.* The Irish Republic and the United States provide useful examples of this type of party system. The parties in the Irish Republic and in the United States lack centralised hierarchical structures and lack mass membership. Ideologically, the differences between the two major parties in each system are not clear-cut. The political divisions between Fianna Fail and Fine Gael originated in a political quarrel over the status of the British monarchy in 1922, and the Republican and Democratic Parties of the United States often have as much internal differences than inter-party differences. It is certainly difficult to place any of these four parties within a clear left–right spectrum, although the Republican Party has adopted a more clearly ideological stance on the right.

    However, to underline the difficulties of any system of classification, whilst there are only two parties represented in the American Congress or which capture control of the American presidency, the Irish party system sometimes resembles the German system. Thus Fine Gael, the second largest party, has only formed governments with the help of smaller parties and Fianna Fail has not had an overall majority since June 1989.

5. *Two-and-one-half party systems.* These are party systems in which there are two dominant parties but the larger parties rarely command an overall majority and need the support of other parties to form a government. The small German Free Democratic Party held the balance between the two larger Christian Democratic and Social Democratic Parties from 1969 to 1998. It has formed governments with first the Social Democrats until 1982 and with the Christian Democrats from 1982 to 1998. Unification has slightly complicated the party system since 1990, but the Christian Democrats with the Free Democrats controlled government until 1998. In that year a new coalition of Social Democrats and Greens took control, indicating somewhat further fragmentation of the party system. Austria provides another instance of this type of party configuration. Until 1986, the Socialist Party governed Austria with the support

of the much smaller Liberal Party (the Freedom Party). However, the Freedom Party moved significantly to the right, and after the 1986 and 1990 elections a grand coalition was constructed between the two largest parties, leaving the Freedom Party and the even smaller Green Party to form the opposition. Between 1966 and 1969, the two largest West German parties formed a similar coalition, and this was mentioned as an option when the results of the 1998 election were in doubt.

6. *Stable multi-party systems.* In this type of system the relative strength of the parties make multi-party coalitions a necessity on many occasions but the ideological differences between the parties are sufficiently muted to allow coalitions to be formed. Giovanni Sartori refers to these as 'moderate multi-party' systems.[33] Usually, coalitions are easy to form and have a long tenure. In Sweden, the Social Democrats have at times governed alone, but the party has not found it difficult to form coalitions in the past with the Centre or Liberal Parties; more recently they have been in league with the Left Party. Between 1976 and 1982 and from 1991 to 1994, the right-of-centre parties – Moderates, Liberals, Centre, and Christian Democratic Parties – generally found few difficulties in forming stable coalitions.[34] The Netherlands provides another example of a system with nine parliamentary parties after September 1989 but with a stable coalition of Christian Democrats and the two Liberal Parties. A 'purple coalition' of left and right formed after 1994 was stable for some years (a similar coalition also has survived in Finland).

7. *Unstable multi-party systems.* Italy has provided perhaps the best European example of this type of system, referred to by Sartori as 'extreme multi-party systems'.[35] Although there were over fourteen parties represented in the Italian parliament after the 1992 election, the basic problem of coalition building stemmed from the presence of Communists, constituting the second largest party to the Christian Democrats, and their exclusion from government power since 1947. Governments were unstable, lasting on average for only six months, and the Italian party system bears a strong resemblance to that of the French Fourth Republic

between 1947 and 1958; in that example both the Communists and Gaullists were unwelcome to the other parties as coalition partners.

The Italian party system has been reformed somewhat. The 1996 elections put 13 parties into parliament but several large coalitions began to function more like parties in a stable multi-party system. Further, the Communists (now the 'Communist Refoundation') have become more moderate and have co-operated in government. These changes result in part from a change in the electoral system allocating most seats to single member districts rather than to proportional representation districts.

The first two years of non-Communist rule in Poland also bore many similarities to the Italian situation, with frequent changes of government and a fragmented multi-party system.

There is no one universal system of classification of party systems, and the foregoing classification is less complex than most. However, it does illustrate both the problems of classification and the diversity of party systems. Above all it stresses the need to take into account all aspects of the system. The Netherlands and France have the same number of groups represented in the assembly, but the relative strength and ideological differences in the French party system make it perform more like a dual party system rather than a multi-party system. The two-party systems of New Zealand and the United States are distinguishable by structural and ideological considerations. The German FDP determined the fate of West German government from 1969 with only a quarter of the seats of each of the two larger parties, yet the Italian Communist Party with over a quarter of the total seats is permanently excluded from power. Moreover, all party systems are susceptible to change.

Change and party systems

The factors determining and causing changes in a particular party system are complex and difficult to isolate. There may be no perceptible changes in the party system, in spite of profound changes in other parts of the political system and deep changes in the social and economic systems. On the other hand, change may be gradual, taking place over a period of time, or the changes in the party system may be dramatic and sudden. Further, some systems may be in almost constant flux, while in other countries partisan changes may produce a party system that endures for a significant amount of time.

The party system of the United States has not significantly altered during the period of rapid growth and industrialisation of the country, and the structure of the political parties still reflects early-nineteenth-century characteristics. There have been several major realignments of the parties, but the parties themselves are relatively unchanged.[36] Few party systems demonstrate this degree of stability. Most party systems are fluid and subject to at least gradual change, and the degree of change is the factor which makes classification difficult. The British party system in the twentieth century provides a good example of this second type of change. Early in the twentieth century, the Labour Party replaced the British Liberal Party as the second largest party in the British parliament, and for a period the party system changed from a system with two major parties, the Conservatives and the Liberals, with minor parties such as Labour and Irish Nationalists, to a three-party system, with Conservative, Labour and Liberal roughly equal. The Liberals refused to die, but a two-party system – the Conservative and Labour Parties alternating as majority governments with a small Liberal Party – dominated British politics from 1945 to 1974.

The result of the two elections in 1974 revived speculations that the two-party system was no longer a feature of British politics, with the Social Democratic Party emerging as a potential alternative to the two parties in England, and more voting for nationalist parties in the Celtic parts of the country. The 1987 and 1992 elections reinforced the two-party system with even some indications of moving toward a dominant party system along Japanese lines. The election of 1997 removed the concern about the continuing domination of the Conservatives, but did tend to reinforce the two-party nature of the system. Still, the increasing support for Scottish nationalism after the adoption of a Scottish parliament is reducing

Labour domination there, and thereby threatening Labour power in the country as a whole – Scotland supplies 56 of the 419 Labour Party seats in the parliament elected in 1997.

Sudden and dramatic changes in party systems are more likely to be the consequence of political revolutions, war or foreign occupation. The emergence of a single-party system in the Soviet Union after the October Revolution of 1917 or of multi-party systems in Eastern Europe after the political upheavals of 1989 provide examples of sudden political changes that transformed the party system dramatically. These changes can be contrasted with the relatively slow political, economic and social changes that shaped the evolutionary system seen in the British example; they were the result of the forcible seizure of power by a revolutionary group or of popular revolutions.

There appear to be several generic factors that may upset the stability of party systems. One would be the emergence of new forms of political cleavage, or new sources of political mobilisation. Various new social movements such as ecology and peace have added new players to party systems. For example, the Greens have become sufficiently powerful to be a party of the governing coalition in Germany and Sweden. Likewise, the mobilisation of underlying ethnic and religious movements in a number of countries have added both new political parties, and introduced a set of new issues to the electoral process. The influence of these movements may vary according to the resources available to the groups and the opportunities presented by the party and electoral system.[37]

Thus political party systems are not static and they do change, and the causes of change are many and complex. However, one factor which is claimed to have important causal relationships with party systems is the electoral system. It is important in part because it is more manipulable than are other factors that may shape party systems.

Electoral systems and political parties

The electoral system is only one factor in the evolution of a party system, but the effects of different electoral systems can be identified in the structure, the ideology, the pattern of party interaction and in the number of parties that compete in the political system.[38] An electoral system consists of more than the methods of counting the votes cast by the voters. A full description of an electoral system would include such factors as the extent of the franchise, i.e. who is entitled to vote. It would include the rules relating to candidates and parties and those regulating the administration of elections, especially the provisions against corruption. The method of casting the vote – i.e. 'is the ballot secret?' – is part of an electoral system. Although the secret ballot may be almost universal, some aspects of electoral systems remain a characteristic of certain political systems: for example, states such as Australia enforce compulsory voting; and primary elections are a feature of the electoral system of the United States. The size and shape of the constituency is an important aspect of electoral systems: the Netherlands and Israel have one constituency for the whole country, for example. However, the aspects of electoral systems that gain the most attention are the methods of casting the vote, the ways in which these votes are counted and the translation of votes into seats.

We can distinguish between the following main types of electoral systems:

1. *Single-member constituency and single vote.* This is usually referred to as 'first-past-the-post', meaning that only a plurality of votes is required to win the seat, and provides the electoral system for countries such as Britain, Canada, and the United States. Half of the members of the Bundestag in Germany are elected in this way.

2. *Single member and second ballot.* If one candidate does not receive an absolute majority of the ballot, a second one is held, with the weaker candidates either choosing, or being required, to retire. This system is used in France with the complication of provisions for alliances of the parties at the second ballot.[39]

3. *Single member with preferential vote.* This system allows the elector to place the candidates in order of preference, the votes of the weaker candidates being distributed to the stronger ones according to second, third, etc. prefer-

ences. Australia uses this system allowing for an alternative preference vote.

4. *Proportional representation.* There are many variations of proportional representation (PR) in use throughout the world, but the essence of all the different varieties is that there is an attempt to allocate seats in close proportion to the votes cast in multi-member constituencies. The two principal types of PR are:

(a) *The list system.* The elector votes for a list of candidates presented by a political party and each party wins the number of seats in that constituency according to the votes for that party list. In Belgium, Sweden, Denmark and Italy the voter is allowed to vary the order of the candidates in the party lists. The list system is the most popular European electoral system.

(b) *Single transferable vote.* This system is used in Eire, Tasmania, Northern Ireland, and Malta. It was used for the English university seats before 1948, and was recommended for Britain by the Speaker's conference of 1917. The voters in multi-member constituencies may mark all the candidates in order of preference. When the votes are counted, an electoral quota is established, that is the minimum number of votes needed by a candidate to win one of the seats; the surplus votes are redistributed to the other candidates according to the voters' order of preference. When all the surplus votes are redistributed in this way, the weakest candidates are then eliminated and their votes are redistributed according to the voters' second, third, etc. preferences. The quota is established according to the formula:

$$\frac{\text{Total votes}}{\text{Number of seats} + 1} + 1 = \text{Quota}$$

Thus in a four-member constituency with 100,000 votes cast, the quota would be 20,001.

It is inevitable that the electoral system does affect the relative strength and number of parties in the legislature.

Dr Cheddi Jagan's People's Progressive Party was ousted from power in 1964 in what was then British Guiana by the British government changing the electoral system from single member districts to proportional representation.[40] This is not to say that proportional representation 'causes' an increase in the number of parties, but that it tends to prevent a reduction. If the 1997 British general election had been conducted with some form of proportional representation, Labour would not have obtained the landslide in the House of Commons that it did, given that it received only 43.2 per cent of the total vote. Likewise, the Liberal Democrats would have received 110 seats instead of their 46. The electoral system did its job, however, and did produce a strong parliamentary majority that can govern.[41]

Of course, a change in the electoral system could certainly change voting habits. A timely change in the electoral system under the French Fourth Republic in 1951 succeeded in its intention of weakening the legislative representation of the Communists and Gaullists, and thus ensured a somewhat longer life for the constitution. In contrast, a change to a two-ballot system in the Fifth Republic was designed to help the Gaullists who could collaborate with other parties between the two ballots.[42] The government of Northern Ireland abolished the single transferable vote (STV) in 1929, possibly to weaken dissidents in the dominant Unionist Party, and the British government reintroduced it for the June 1973 elections to increase the number of non-Unionist representatives. In the 1990s New Zealand changed from single-member districts to proportional representation (PR), and in the process created a multi-party coalition electoral system.[43]

There is little doubt that the electoral system does affect various aspects of the party system. The 'first-past-the-post' system helps the successful parties and distorts the relationship between votes and seats. A second ballot certainly reduces the number of seats held on a minority vote, and it increases the power of the local party organisations against the central organisations because of the need to bargain with other parties at local level before the second ballot.[44] The list system will increase the power of the parties over the candidates since the party decides the order of the candidates on the party list, but there is no evidence for countries such as Sweden or Italy that the list system encourages party splits or increases the number of parties. STV tends to make the voter concentrate on the individual candidate rather than the party label of the candidate and it makes it easier for smaller parties to gain representation in the assembly. In terms of the numbers of parties, a two-party system is more likely with the British and American system, and multi-party systems are more likely with PR.

Thus the electoral system is an important factor in shaping the character of the party system, and whether it distorts electoral opinion or whether it is merely a passive reflector of opinion, the electoral system plays a major role in shaping the party system.[45] It has some influence on the degree of discipline that parties can impose on their legislative representatives, and on whether parties reflect national or local interests and opinions. A list electoral system, for example, gives a great deal of power to the party to control the placement of candidates, and therefore the party can easily discipline its candidates.

Yet the electoral system is only one factor explaining the party system. Canada has a similar electoral system to that which New Zealand had when it produced the extreme version of the two party system, but federalism and ethnic politics have produced more political parties at national level.[46]

The Republic of Ireland, with STV, had only two parties before 1939 in the Irish parliament, although this electoral system tends to result in many parties. It is interesting to note that the Irish Fianna Fail party has twice been unsuccessful, in 1959 and 1968, in its attempts to change the electoral system. The change was intended to further strengthen Fianna Fail and to weaken the electoral chances of the Labour Party, the third strongest in the legislature.[47] The 1997 election in Ireland produced a parliament with seven parties, reflecting an increased number of cleavages in Irish politics (a Green Party reflecting a growing environmental movement, for example) as well as an electoral system that makes it easy for parties to gain seats.

The arguments over the consequences of electoral systems are firstly factual ones: does a particular set of electoral laws have certain effects or not, and what is the relevance of these effects to other social, economic and historical factors, with regard to the nature of the party system? Secondly, there are evaluative considerations, such as whether the stability of governments is a more desirable aim than is an attempt to faithfully represent public opinion. Like many other aspects of politics, there are multiple and conflicting values involved in the choice of electoral systems, and indeed in the development of political party systems.

Summary

Political parties and interest groups are usually considered a crucial element in democratic politics, and that certainly is true. These organisations are the means for connecting citizens with government, and for providing government with information about what the public wants. Political parties also provide the personnel for governing directly, especially in parliamentary systems. Political parties also can be the mechanisms for rewarding and punishing performance of governments in office, as they will re-elected or not based on that performance. Parties and interest groups can also function as a source of new policy ideas for governments, and can influence government to move in directions that might not be expected without the energy brought by parties and their members.

Parties and interest groups are, however, also important for non-democratic systems. They fulfil some of the same functions of linking government and society as do parties and groups in democracies, although much of the emphasis in non-democratic systems is on conveying the wishes of the governing groups to the public, rather than on representing the demands of the public. Parties and officially created interest groups also become mechanisms for controlling the public in non-democratic systems, chanelling their participation through avenues acceptable to the government. Although these mechanisms are far from fully democratic, they may yet link the public and the political élite and may be a means for leaders in non-democratic countries to understand what the 'demands' of the public might be were citizens free to express them.

Notes and references

1. S. Bowler, *Demanding Choices: Opinion, Voting and Direct Democracy* (Ann Arbor: University of Michigan Press, 1998).
2. A classic argument on this point is W. Kornhauser, *The Politics of Mass Society* (Glencoe, IL: The Free Press, 1959). For a more recent discussion, see Ian Budge, *The New Challenge of Direct Democracy* (Oxford: Polity, 1997).
3. The Cuban and North Korean regimes also have strong Communist parties but also have strong elements of personal leadership as well.
4. N. Harvey and M. Serrano, *Party Politics in an Uncommon Democracy: Political Parties and Elections in Mexico* (London: Institute of Latin American Studies, 1994).
5. J.A. Schumpeter, *Capitalism, Socialism and Democracy* (London: Harper, 1961) p. 279.
6. Sir Lewis Namier, *The Structure of Politics at the Accession of George III* (London: Macmillan, 1959), has strongly argued for the rejection of the party labels of Whig and Tory in the mid-eighteenth-century Houses of Parliament.
7. During the past several decades American political parties have been realigning, with the Republican Party taking more and more of the Southern conservative vote, and the Democratic Party becoming confined largely to the inner cities dominated by minority groups, as well as some rural areas with large minority populations.
8. Peter Mair, *Party System Change: Approaches and Interpretations* (Oxford: Oxford University Press, 1997), ch. 5.
9. The concept of interest aggregation comes from Gabriel Almond and G. Bingham Powell, *Comparative Politics: A Developmental Analysis* (Boston: Little, Brown, 1967).
10. Some parties, such as the BNG in Galicia, act as catch-all parties*within* the context of regiomal politics, but to the extent that they are relevant in national politics they are certainly a single-issue regional party.
11. See S. Henig (ed.), *Political Parties in the European Community* (London: Allen & Unwin, 1979) ch. 4, for an outline of this feature of French political parties.
12. A. Bullock, *Hitler: A Study in Tyranny* (London: Harper, 1952) pp. 64–5.
13. See P. Norris, *Passages to Power: Legislative Recuitment in Western Democracies* (Cambridge: Cambridge University Press, 1997).
14. Herbert Kitschelt, *The Logics of Party Formation: Ecological Parties in Belgium and West Germany* (Ithaca, NY: Cornell University Press, 1989).
15. R.A. Dahl, *Democracy in the United States,* 4th edn (Boston: Little, Brown, 1981) p. 207.
16. See Peter Mair, *The Changing Irish Party System* (London: Pinter, 1987).
17. R. Kindersley, *In Search of Eurocommunism* (New York: St Martin's, 1981).
18. For a description of the Portuguese system, see T.C. Bruneau, 'Continuity and Change in Portuguese Politics: Ten Years After the Revolution of 25th April, 1974', *West European Politics*, 7, 2 (April 1984) pp. 72–83.

19. M. Duverger, *Political Parties*, 2nd edn (London: Macmillan, 1962) pp. 17–40.
20. In the 1996 election the Democratic Party revived.
21. Robert Blake, *The Conservative Party from Peel to Major* (London: Arrow, 1998).
22. Duverger, *Political Parties*, p. 37.
23. See Klaus von Beyme, *Political Parties in Western Democracies* (Aldershot, 1985) pp. 159–253.
24. J. Blondel, 'Mass Parties and Industrialised Societies', in *Comparative Government*, ed. J. Blondel (London: Unwin, 1969) p. 121.
25. See, for example, the party systems in Belgium, Switzerland, and several in the newer democracies of Eastern Europe.
26. H.– G. Bet, *Radical Right-Wing Populism in western Europe* (New York: St Martin's, 1994).
27. These are the various 'Progress' parties in Denmark, Norway and Sweden. See Paul A. Taggart, *The New Populism and the New Politics* (London: Macmillan, 1996).
28. Jonathan Eyal, 'Why Romania Could Not Avoid Bloodshed', in G. Prins (ed.), *Spring in Winter* (Manchester: University of Manchester Press, 1989) pp. 157–60; E. Behr, *'Kiss the Hand you Cannot Bite': The Rise and Fall of the Ceausescus* (London, 1991) pp. 240–2.
29. One other option is as groups of intellectuals who later adopt more specfically political goals.
30. For the Chinese party system, see S. White *et al.*, *Communist and Post-Communist Political Systems*, 3rd edn (London: Macmillan, 1990) pp. 161–74.
31. See P. Loveday, A. W. Martin and R. S. Parker, *The Emergence of the Australian Party System* (Sydney: Hale & Ironmonger, 1977).
32. The Wilson government did not have an overall majority between the February and October elections of 1974, and the Callaghan government lost its overall majority as a result of by-elections between 1976 and 1979.
33. Giovanni Sartori, 'European Political Parties: The Case of Polarized Pluralism' in J. La Palombara and M. Weiner, *Political Parties and Political Development* (Princeton: Princeton University Press, 1966).
34. See A. H. Thomas, 'Social Democracy in Scandinavia', in *The Future of Social Democracy*, ed. W. E. Paterson and A. H. Thomas (Oxford: Oxford University Press, 1986) pp. 172–222.
35. Sartori, 'European Political Parties', *op.cit.*
36. Theodore J. Lowi, *A Republic of Parties?* (Lanham, MD: Rowman & Littlefield, 1998).
37. See D. Rae, *The Political Consequences of Electoral Laws* (New Haven: Yale University Press, 1967). See V. Bogdanor, 'Conclusion: Electoral Systems and Party Systems', in *Democracy and Elections*, ed. V. Bogdanor and D. Butler (Cambridge: Cambridge University Press, 1983) pp. 247–61.
38. See D. Goldey and P. Williams, 'France', in V. Bogdanor and D. Butler, *Democracy and Elections* (Cambridge: Cambridge University Press, 1983), pp. 71–83. The Socialist government of 1981–5 changed the French

electoral system from the second-ballot to the list system in an attempt to reduce the size of the Right's victory in the 1985 elections, and the Chirac government reversed that decision for the next election.

39. P. G. J. Pulzer, *Political Representation and Elections in Britain*, 2nd edn (London: Allen & Unwin, 1972) pp. 55–6.

40. See Anthony King *et al.*, *New Labour Triumphs: Britain at the Polls* (Chatham, NJ: Chatham House, 1998).

41. Philip E. Converse and Roy Pierce, *Political Representation in France* (Cambridge, MA: Harvard University Press).

42. J. Vowles, 'The Politics of Electoral Reform in New Zealand', *International Review of Political Science* 16, pp. 95–115.

43. See V. Wright, *The Government and Politics of France*, 3rd edn (London: Hutchinson, 1989) pp. 165–8.

44. See R. Taagapera and M. S. Shugart, *Seats and Votes* (New Haven: Yale University Press, 1989).

45. The 1997 election in Canada produced a rather extreme regional split, with the ruling Liberals having only one seat west of Ontario, and the major opposition party – Reform – having no seats east of Manitoba. The Parti Quebecois is concentrated in Quebec and the Progressive Conservatives in the Maritime provinces.

46. It is often noted, however, that Irish politics is as much about personal relationships with the member of the Dail as about party and ideology. See N. Collins and C. O. Raghleigh, 'Ireland' in F. F. Ridley and A. Doig, *Sleaze* (Oxford: Oxford University Press, 1995).

47. For some advantages of the present British electoral system, see J. A. Chandler, 'The Plurality Vote: A Reappraisal', *Political Studies*, 30 (1982) pp. 87–94; P. Hain, *Proportional Misrepresentation: The Case Against PR in Britain* (Aldershot, 1986). Also R. Plant, 'Criteria for Electoral Systems: The Labour Party and Electoral Reform', *Parliamentary Affairs*, 43, 4 (October 1991) pp. 549–57, provides an excellent framework for the discussion. The arguments are all summarised in the Jenkins Report,

6

Pressure Groups

'Pressure groups are social aggregates with some level of cohesion and shared aims which attempt to influence the political decision-making process'.[1] Of course, this brief definition presents certain empirical and conceptual problems. Farmers' organisations, trade unions or civic amenity groups can be readily identified as pressure groups, but some groups do not conform to the definition as easily. Thus government organisations such as the civil service or the military may attempt to influence the policies which they themselves implement and therefore possess many characteristics of a pressure-group. Pressure groups sometimes contest elections to gain representation in the assembly and in these circumstances are similar to certain types of political parties, especially those that concentrate on a single issue, never seeking or hoping to achieve government office; many nationalist and environmentalist parties fall into this category.[2]

In spite of these definitional complications, pressure groups can be identified in all political systems. Many pressure groups devote all or most of their activities to influencing government policy. This is especially true for groups formed around particular ideas rather than around an economic interest: labour unions, for example, spend a good deal of their time protecting the interests of their members in labour–management negotiations. Other pressure groups may only rarely seek to influence broader government policies and they concentrate mainly on other more particularised activities – for example, a local nudist group seeking permission to use a stretch of the coast for its activities.

Pressure group analysis

There is much dispute among academics over the problem of terminology and definition: various terms are used, such as lobby, political group, organised group, pressure group and interest group, to describe organisations that attempt to influence public policy. None the less, it is useful to employ the term *pressure group* as the broad generic term and then subdivide pressure groups into interest groups and attitude (or promotional) groups. Thus, *interest groups* can be said to be those groups whose members share attitudes resulting from common objective characteristics – for example, all the members of the group are farmers, business people or plumbers – while the members of an *attitude group* hold certain values in common irrespective of their objective background – for example, all the members of a society for prevention of cruelty to animals oppose maltreatment of animals whether they are business people or trade unionists. The distinction can be useful in terms of analysing the membership, the intensity of group solidarity, cross-pressures on members and the degree of political influence wielded by the group.

In particular, the members of interest groups have some reason to remain members even if the leadership may not do exactly as the members might like. Members of attitude groups, on the other hand, would receive few benefits other than the political activities of the group and hence would want the political stances to be in closer conformity; if not, they lose nothing by leaving and joining another group. Indeed, members of attitude groups might consider themselves to be denying their own values if they remained members of a group that did not correspond to their values.

Pressure groups are certainly not a new phenomenon in politics, but the academic recognition of pressure groups is more recent. The first systematic study was Arthur Bentley's *The Process of Government*, published in 1908, but widespread academic interest really dates from 1945, and David Truman's *The Governmental Process* is the classic statement of interest group theory from that period.[3] The study of organised groups has now been incorporated into wider analyses of the distribution of political power and the nature of the state, with some contemporary network theories arguing that the interactions of interest groups are the crucial element for understanding governance.[4]

We have already noted in Chapter 2 that pluralist approaches to political power place particular emphasis on the role of pressure groups in liberal democracies. The pluralists argue that competing group interaction determines the outcome of many political conflicts, provides wider avenues of political participation, and ensures a wider distribution of power in those democracies than there would be without those interest groups. The state is sometimes regarded as neutral in pluralist theories, holding the ring for the contending groups. Some pluralists argue that the state intervenes on behalf of the weaker or less privileged groups, thus levelling the playing field that otherwise might be skewed, as argued by the élitists such as Schattschneider.[5]

Marxists also agree that organised groups are important political actors. However, the Marxist view holds that the capitalist state is far from neutral and that there are great imbalances in terms of political power between the groups. Thus not only will the state in liberal democracies favour business interests against those of organised labour, but there will also be wide disparities of resources between the two; this is what Miliband calls 'imperfect competition'.[6] The Marxist view has somewhat less to say about the wide range of interest groups, other than business and labour, that attempt to influence policy-making, although again their basic prediction is that business will dominate.

A third view of the role of pressure groups is held in different variants by both Marxist and non-Marxist writers. They argue that many liberal democracies are at least partially characterised by corporatism. Thus Schmitter argues:

Corporatism can be defined as a system of interest representation in which the constituent units are organized into a limited number of singular, compulsory, hierarchically ordered and functionally differentiated categories, recognised or licensed (if not created) by the state and granted a deliberate representational monopoly in exchange for observing certain controls on their selection of leaders and articulation of demands and supports.[7]

Schmitter goes on to contrast state-centric corporatism with society-centric corporatism, the former being characterised by the role of government in initiating the relationships between state and society, and sometimes assisting the formation of groups – a pattern of corporatism more common in authoritarian regimes. The latter form is characterised by the autonomous creation of groups in society. In both cases, however, there are strong formal links between state and society that are crucial for the formation of policies.

Liberal corporatism as found in many contemporary political systems should not be confused with the fascist concept of the corporate state.[8] The main argument of those who apply the corporate thesis to liberal democracies is that increasing state interventionism, especially in the field of economic management, has led to the need to incorporate certain essential groups into the decision-making process. Thus the state needs the co-operation and advice of certain crucially placed groups such as business and labour. Some versions of corporatism, sometimes called corporate pluralism, extend interest group involvement to include a wide variety of groups.[9] Also, a few political systems (Ireland, Bavaria and formerly Hong Kong) have chambers of their legislatures composed of corporate representatives, rather than representatives of geographical areas.

The emphasis, then, in corporatism is on the functional representation of certain important groups in the policy-making process, and in return for easier access to this process the state gains greater social control. Government can use the trade-union leadership, for example, to curb any militancy from the rank and file.[10] Some corporatist theorists see liberal democracies as full-blown corporatist societies, but most theorists regard corporatism primarily as a useful tool of analysis for dealing with organised groups in political systems (see Table 6.1). Panitch and Jessop, for example, both argue that although there are many barriers to corporatism, cyclical resurgence or development of corporatist forms can be expected in most liberal democracies.[11]

Finally, scholars have begun to think of interest groups not as free-standing entities but as members of 'networks' or 'communities'.[12] Interest groups have proliferated and demo-

Table 6.1   Degree of corporatism in twelve European countries

	Monopoly of associations	Centrality of organisations	Total
Austria	1[a]	3	1
Norway	5	1.5	2
Denmark	8	1.5	4
Sweden	5	4.5	4
Finland	5	4.5	4
Netherlands	2	9	6
Belgium	3	9	7
Germany	9	6	8
Switzerland	7	14	9
France	10	14	13
United Kingdom	13	12	14
Italy	13	14	15

[a] 1 = maximum

Source: Klaus von Beyme, 'Der liberale Korporatismus als Mittel gegen dir Unregierbarkeit', in U. von Alemann, (ed.) *Neokorporatismus* (Frankfurt: Campus, 1981), p. 139. By permission.

cratic governments find it more and more difficult to restrict access to policy-making, legally or politically. For example, while an agricultural ministry may have had to pay attention only to farmers' organisations, they must now also allow environmental groups, consumers, health advocates, and a variety of other organisations to have at least some access. This naturally increases the complexity of policy-making, but also may improve co-ordination of polities as well as enhance the overall quality of the decisions being made.

These conceptualisations reflect an important reality in government, but also present problems for understanding how groups have an impact on policy. In particular, these models are not good at explaining how these various, and often conflicting, perspectives on policy can be reconciled. It is fine to say that there are these broad communities surrounding each policy area, but it is still difficult to see how each group can have an influence.[13] It may be that these networks actually disguise more conventional pluralist or élitist patterns of influence, and that all the participation actually allows government decision-makers to choose policies that they want.

Determinants of pressure group methods

Methods used by pressure groups in liberal democracies to realise their aims vary according to:

1. The political institutional structure.
2. The nature of the party system.
3. The political culture.
4. The nature of the issue.
5. The nature of the group.

The institutional structure affects the activities of pressure groups in various ways. For example, Britain has a unitary system of government with concentration of political power at the centre and in the hands of a relatively strong executive, and therefore pressure groups will deservedly regard their efforts as more successful if they gain access to ministers and their civil servants than if they are only able to influence MPs in the House of Commons.[14] America has a bicameral legislature in which the Senate and the House of Representatives are of roughly equal political importance, and with the separation of powers, pressure groups can aim at the administration and the legislature, playing off one or sections of one against sections of other institutions. Moreover, the existence of a strong committee system in the United States Congress makes these a focus of attention for various pressure groups. This division of power between different centres may increase the opportunities to groups, but it may emphasise the opportunities to frustrate, not to propose.

France during the Fourth Republic had a 'parliamentary-centred' structure, and although influence at the administrative level was regarded as important, there were many more opportunities to frustrate hostile policies and legislation at the parliamentary level than is the case in Britain. The constitutional changes brought about in France by the Fifth Republic of 1958 have tended to shift the attention of the pressure groups from the National Assembly to the administration. French prime ministers are now much stronger in relation to the legislature, and need not discuss certain matters there at all; thus pressure groups are now more eager for direct consultation with the administration.[15]

Federalism provides another interesting example of the effects of different political structures on pressure group activity. American pressure groups can operate at state level to defeat federally entrenched rivals, or concentrate at federal level to win concessions denied to them in the states. Small retailers successfully fought state by state to impose numerous state taxes on the larger chain-stores in the 1920s and 1930s in spite of powerful chain-store influence in Washington,[16] and the National Association for the Advancement of Colored People by-passed the influence of the strong white segregationist elements in the states and won concessions at federal government level – operating largely through the court systems, however, rather than through the more politicised institutions.[17]

Relations between pressure groups and political parties and the effect on pressure group activity of different party systems provide other variables in pressure group politics. The largest British trade unions are formally affiliated to the Labour Party, and they provide the Party with the bulk of its money and membership.[18] The link between groups and parties in the United States is much weaker, although the AFL–CIO (American Federation of Labor–Congress of Industrial Organizations), and especially some constituent unions such as the American Federation of Teachers, have close ties to the Democratic Party and expect better treatment when the Democrats control the presidency or Congress. Unions tend to channel their money into the Democratic Party through political action committees, or as in the 1996 election may engage in their own 'political education' campaigns that in essence are part of the Democratic campaign.[19]

French pressure groups illustrate how close the ties between groups and parties can be. French trade unions are divided into three main sections, depending on whether they support the Communists, Socialists or are independent of party. The most powerful union, the CGT (*Confédération Générale du Travail*), is an excellent example of a close relationship of a pressure group to a political party, in this case the Communist Party. This has had important repercussions on the strength and influence of French trade unions, since not only are they divided ideologically but the strongest is a satellite of a political party that has been effectively excluded from power for most of the period since 1947. The Roman Catholic Church provides an example of these ties between parties and groups: the church has had close links with the strong Christian Democratic Parties in Germany and Italy.

The type of party system and the structure and ideology of the parties have significant effects on pressure group activity. American Congressmen, given the weakness of party structure, the need to raise huge amounts of campaign funds, and the absence of strong ideological differences between the parties, are easy targets for pressure groups, especially if those groups are based in the legislator's own constituency: Congressmen are very sensitive to local pressures.[20] The two-party system in Britain, with the absence of comparable local pressures, allows greater resistance to group activities. Cross-voting is rare in the House of Commons, so groups must pay heed to party alignments. Multi-party systems provide a more fertile field for pressure group activity, especially at legislative level, even if the emphasis here is on preventing what is disliked rather than on encouraging what is preferred. This difference is often expressed as the difference between promotional groups and defensive groups.

The third variable is the political culture. In the first instance membership in groups of all sorts varies across different political cultures and this support or hostility for membership helps explain the relative success of interest groups. As shown in Table 6.2, there are pronounced differences in the levels of group membership of the public, even among the more developed countries. If we had data from a wider range of countries we would see that many of the less-developed countries have markedly lower rates of membership. Thus, the basis for interest group influence is based in the ability of groups to form and to maintain membership.

There may be greater hostility shown to particular types of group activity in certain countries: trade unions are usually regarded with greater suspicion than their counterparts, employer associations, and much trade union activity is directed towards persuading their own members of the wisdom of certain policies and towards improving the image that trade unions have with the general public in order to better their

Table 6.2   Group membership in industrialised democracies (percentage of survey respondents who supported membership or active membership of one or more voluntary organisations)

	Memberships	Active memberships
Australia	61	27
Belgium	43	21
Canada	58	33
France	27	15
Great Britain	53	20
Ireland	52	21
Italy	26	18
Japan	30	13
N. Ireland	67	27
Netherlands	63	25
Norway	62	23
Spain	31	22
Sweden	68	26
United States	73	32
West Germany	49	21

Source: J. Curtis, E. G. Grabb and D. E. Baer, 'Voluntary Association Membership in Fifteen Countries: A Comparative Analysis', *American Sociological Review*, 57 (1992) pp. 139–52.

bargaining position *vis-à-vis* the government. Direct action and resort to violence may be more common in some political cultures than in others, even in democratic political systems. French farmers have a well-established reputation for blocking roads with farm produce and machinery to support their demands against the government. The activities of the French students and trade unionists during the political troubles of May 1968, and then again in the autumns of 1995 and 1998, provide further examples of French attitude-group activities. The tradition of the authoritative state in Germany may explain the relative weaknesses of attitude groups there. The religious divisions in Northern Ireland have made it difficult for pressure groups to act independently of either religious group; the civil rights movement from its beginnings in 1968 became increasingly identified as pro-Catholic and this made it more difficult to influence the Protestant-based Unionist government. Thus in various ways the political culture determines the shape, intensity and direction of pressure group activity.

The nature of the issue is another factor in the analysis of pressure group activities. Strategies must be very different for issues that provoke interest from a wide number of groups as compared with those in which a few groups dominate. Also, pressure groups have to respond differently in particular circumstances although the aims of the group may be unchanged. British industry has long acted through such groups as Aims which undertake extended campaigns of educating the public and attempt to ensure the return of Conservative governments. However, dissatisfaction with the Conservative government's economic policy led the leader of the Confederation of British Industry (CBI) to threaten 'a bare-knuckle fight' with the government in 1980, a rare breakdown of business-government relationships in British politics. Also, the Labour Party has changed its stances on a number of issues so that business interests are almost as friendly with their governments as with the Conservatives.

The fifth factor that influences the methods used by pressure groups is the nature of the group itself. Thus the aims of the group will affect how the group attempts to realise those aims. Groups with aims hostile to important policies or institutions of the existing political system cannot hope to exert influence on the administration and legislature in the way that legitimated business groups would do – thus the Pro-Life groups' attempts to realise their aims through influencing the selection of candidates in the American Republican Party and educating public opinion through their publications, as well as more confrontational methods. The type of sanctions that the group possesses will affect its methods. Groups with powerful political sanctions will not have to resort to national campaigns and programmes of civil disobedience. Further, governments will need the active co-operation of some groups if policies are to be implemented; a refusal to co-operate would be a powerful weapon in the hands of the group in any negotiations with the government. The medical profession provides a good example of a group whose co-operation is often needed in carrying out government policies.[21] Trade unions are often regarded as being very powerful in liberal democracies, but the number and strength of their sanctions is often over-estimated: trade unions are usually forced to spend a great deal of their resources in creating a more favourable climate of public opinion because of the political weaknesses of the unions. Sanctions include not only the ability to withhold co-operation from governments, but also the ability to influence the number of votes in a general election – the Christian right in the United States is beginning to use this electoral strategy very effectively. An emphasis on sanctions tends to exaggerate the power relationship of governments and groups, but it is important to remember that both groups and governments generally prefer co-operation to conflict. There are other aspects of the group itself that affect the methods used by the group. The nature of the group's organisation – whether it has a large and permanent bureaucracy, the type of leadership the group enjoys, and the degree of internal democracy – influence the ways in which a group operates. Membership is very important; here one should examine the degree of commitment of the members, the size of the membership in relation to the potential membership, and the type of members in regard to such factors as class, age, sex and perhaps heterogeneity. Small élite groups can be more effective than much larger groups whose members lack money, organisational skills, and political contacts. Finally, the wealth of the group has an important bearing on its methods; groups such as unions that can employ real sanctions over their own members in order to collect dues have a real advantage over more voluntary groups.

Levels of pressure group activity

Pressure group methods in liberal democracies are mainly concerned with influencing the decision-making processes at the executive and the parliamentary levels, and the attempted emphasis at a particular level will partly depend on the three variables of the political institutions, the party system and the political culture. As a general rule, with the increase in executive power and area of responsibility in the twentieth century at the expense of the legislatures, pressure groups are concentrating their activities at administrative levels, but obviously activity at one level certainly does not preclude activity at another.

It is the most powerful economic interest groups that are more likely to have access to governments and their civil servants, although the Howard League for Penal Reform in Britain is an example of an influential attitude group which has regular channels of communication with ministers. It is co-operation that should be stressed at this level of consultation: governments want advice, technical information and most of all co-operation from strong interest groups.

In America the administrative agencies have substantial independence of the president and Congress and are therefore targets of pressure group influence, but the groups can and are used by the agencies in their political struggles with other agencies, other pressure groups and Congress. The American Farm Bureau, representing the wealthier farmers, is an interesting example of agency–clientele relationships. The Bureau was formed indirectly out of federal government initiative in 1919, and its successfully close relations with the Department of Agriculture have generally allowed it to overshadow its rivals, the National Farmers Union and the Grange.[22] While these 'iron triangle' relationships among interest groups, agencies and congressional subcommittees have become somewhat less structured than in the past, they still can provide a good basis for understanding policy-making in the United States.[23]

In many countries the advisory role of interest groups with administrative organisations is well institutionalised. For example, in the Scandinavian countries and to some extent in Germany and the Netherlands each administrative organisation will have an advisory committee composed of representatives of all relevant interest groups.[24] In Britain groups influence policy through a wide variety of permanent advisory committees on which sit group representatives alongside civil servants, e.g. the National Advisory Council on the Training and Supply of Teachers. In France. pressure group representation has been institutionally organised for some groups at this level since 1924 and now includes Chambers of Commerce and Industry, Chambers of Agriculture, Chambers of Trade and the Social and Economic Council, which is composed of trade unionists, employers and government representatives. However, emphasis on formal relations should not lead to an underestimation of informal contacts, and pressure group spokesmen are often selected for their ease of contact with government representatives – former members of parliament make excellent candidates.[25]

Pressure group activity at parliamentary level is generally more spectacular and less secretive, but it is doubtful whether the publicity it receives is always commensurate with its importance. This is particularly true at Congressional level in the United States: the Congressional lobbyists are more professionalist than their British counterparts, and an emphasis on personal contacts with legislators has been reinforced by greater reliance on public relations campaigns and electoral assistance to sympathetic candidates. Technical advice and information are less important to American legislators than they are to most European legislators, who are poorly served with legislative aids.

Groups working at the parliamentary level attempt to establish contacts with individual representatives to gain their support, but usually they are successful only when the representative is already sympathetic to the aims of the group. Most lobbyists know who their most likely targets are, and waste little time on those whose ideological or constituency characteristics would preclude them from agreeing with the lobbyists' positions. For example, as lobbyists attempt to exert influence at the European level they may work on their national representatives as well as on a functionally specialised Directorate General.[26] However, the secrecy that accompanied the activities of one particular lobby helped it to suceed; the more publicised attempts to influence legislators by mass lobbying and bombarding representatives with petitions, letters and telegrams bear out the generalisation that noise tends to indicate political weakness.

At the extreme, bribery is still used by some interest groups. This is usually thought to be characteristic of less-developed systems, but sometimes also is reported of more-developed systems. In the 1960s and 1970s about a hundred large American corporations are reported to have made improper payments over several years to governments and representatives of foreign legislatures. When the most notorious of these payments were revealed, those by Lockheed, Gulf and Exxon, several governments and political parties were shaken by the allegations. Means of preventing this sort of influence are being implemented, albeit slowly, by the American Congress.[27] In other national countries what would be considered bribery in most settings would be considered relatively normal forms of political influence.[28]

National campaigns are the most conspicuous method of pressure group activity, but unless accompanied by activity at other levels they may be an indication of political weakness. The Campaign for Nuclear Disarmament illustrates this point. However, although their public campaigns failed to stop particular pieces of legislation or the implementation of certain policies, they did have significant influence on policy over the longer time period. With the increasing availability of media, national campaigns have a greater chance for success. In the United States the highly successful media campaign against President Clinton's health reform proposals in 1994 was in large part responsible for those proposals never reaching the floor of Congress for a vote. Nevertheless, public campaigns often indicate total and open hostility to government policies, and there lie the seeds of failure. The more successful pressure groups over the longterm appear capable of working less directly, and of compromising and co-operating with government to achieve their ends.

One other important area is open to pressure groups: in America, unlike other liberal democracies, pressure groups have more opportunities for attempting to influence the judiciary. American federal constitutional courts have wide constitutional powers to overrule the executive and the legislature and to interpret the meaning of legislation in more politically significant ways. Pressure groups will attempt to influence the selection of judges who may have a background of political activity; they can also use test cases and undertake public campaigns to influence particular decisions.[29] They offer the courts technical services and use a device known as the *amicus curiae* briefs, which allows a party not involved directly in a case before the court to present legal arguments because it can claim that a decision would affect it in some way. But although American courts, and especially the Supreme Court, are firmly part of the political process, the traditions of the courts, the security of tenure of judges and their non-accountability to an electorate provide some defence against pressure group activity. Moreover, it could be said that, until recently, the federal courts have tended to favour poorer and minority groups.[30]

Pressure group activity in the liberal democratic sense is almost absent from autocratic and socialist systems. In some autocratic systems it is the low rate of economic development, poor communications and lack of technological advances that are strong barriers to pressure group activity. In some, the emphasis on nationalism often brings embryo pressure groups into a nationally, not sectionally, orientated value system, and of course there is the emphasis on coercion. It is interesting to note the role of the military in autocratic systems, since in many developing countries the army is often composed of the best educated and technically competent elements. Given the nature of autocratic systems it is difficult to ensure the legitimisation of pressure group politics, and groups not completely subservient to the government are forced to take a more hostile attitude towards the very basis of the regime.

By the end of the 1980s reform processes in the USSR and certain East European states had blurred the differences between pressure group politics in liberal democratic and socialist states. Both Poland and Hungary had large numbers of groups functioning with a degree of official toleration. The introduction of *glasnost* in the Soviet Union, followed by the first multi-candidate parliamentary elections in 1989, saw the proliferation of 'informals', so called because although operating openly, these groups were not formally registered with the authorities as had been required in the earlier regimes. A number of these informals transformed themselves into political parties after the removal of the 'leading role of the Party' from the Soviet Constitution in spring 1990.[31] None the less, other regimes, such as the Romanian or Albanian, remained highly hostile to any sign of organised activity outside the framework of the Communist Party and extremely repressive of any perceived dissent.

Determinants of pressure group influence

It is difficult to measure precisely the influence exerted by pressure groups, but some generalisations can be made. The government's own policy will be an important factor, especially the emphasis that particular policies receive from the policy-makers. But governments and pressure groups operate within a web of political values and attitudes and these provide other variables to determine group effectiveness. In Britain, groups to promote the welfare of animals will have more public sympathy than, say, a society advocating some form of euthanasia. Nevertheless, the nature of the sanctions a group can use and the usefulness of the group to governments and legislatures are very important factors which make interest groups generally more powerful than attitude groups. The nature of the group's organisation, the identification of the rank and file with the initiatives of the leaders, the degree of participation by the members, and the size of the group's purse are other variables. Thus the Roman Catholic Church is the dominant religious institution in many political systems, but there are divisions between the Church leadership and followers on matters of abortion, birth control and divorce. As a result of these internal divisions the Church is often defeated by its opponents. The absence of internal democratic procedures often prevents more liberal values being articulated within the organisation.[32] These may be factors tending to offset the large membership of the organisation. Money is another important factor in the success or failure of pressure groups, especially in view of the emphasis placed on public relations campaigns, but the example of the wealth and large membership of the German DGB (Federation of German Trade Unions) not being translated into commensurate political influence is a warning that they are only two variables among many.

The degree to which a group maximises its potential membership and the extent to which similar interests are divided between rival organisations are important variables. The National Farmers Union has nearly 80 per cent of all farmers in England and Wales as members, but we have noted the three major divisions of farmers in the United States. In several

European countries there are separate trade unions affiliated with communist, socialist and Christian democratic parties. Miners' trade unions often display a near-maximum membership, a result of geographical concentration which strengthens their position in other ways, i.e. influencing elections and ensuring that a miners' representative is returned to the legislature.

There are important barriers to pressure group effectiveness besides the faults of a group's own internal organisation and lack of political skill. Group activity takes place in a wider political society, and to maximise its influence a group will try to identify its aims with what is described as the national interest. No group can be successful and still be identified with the ruthless pursuit of its own aims. However, this view of countervailing societal pressures must be treated carefully. Some groups are identified with national values and yet are pursuing aims that are as 'self-centred' as their opponents'. Thus business interests may claim that a strike by trade unionists is damaging the country's valuable export drive, and so disguise their disquiet at the damage done to their interests as businessmen.[33] It is possible, of course, to feel that the two are inseparable – 'What is good for General Motors is good for America.'

Perhaps a more important obstacle to pressure group influence is the overlapping membership of groups, which may moderate the extremism and particularism of their demands. Again, this problem is particularly relevant to Anglo-American and Scandinavian pressure group politics, where groups, especially attitude groups, are more numerous and may be less ideologically orientated. This limitation on pressure group effectiveness depends at least in part on the degree to which the leadership is representative of the members, and on the efficiency of the communications within the group. The overlapping membership of the pressure group leaders may be far more important in reducing the sectionalism of group demands than that of members. On this point of unrepresentative leadership, trade unions are particularly criticised because some form of representative democracy is expected of such organisations, but the same criterion is not applied to all groups: no one expects the same degree of participation by all members of the Roman Catholic Church, and therefore the legitimacy of the group's demands is not affected.

The secrecy surrounding much pressure group activity is an aspect contributing to suspicion and exaggeration of the power of pressure groups. This is sometimes a factor allowing one group to infiltrate another and disguise its real demands. This may be relatively open, as with the 'anti-cruel-sport' element in the British Royal Society for the Prevention of Cruelty to Animals, but it may be far more sinister, as when the American Asphalt Company infiltrated the American Farm Bureau in the 1930s, a move that was disclosed in 1935 by a Congressional committee investigating the Farm Bureau's campaign for better roads. Another strategy used to disguise pressure group activity – the use of vague names such as The Campaign for the American Way – also invites suspicion and appears deceptive to many citizens.

The American Federal Regulation of Lobbying Act of 1946 was an attempt to curb and publicise the activities of groups lobbying the American Congress. It stipulates registration, declaration of sources of funds and a list of the legislation that the lobbyists were employed to oppose or support, but its application is limited and even such a powerful group as the National Association of Manufacturers has not registered. There have been no major equivalents in other liberal democracies, representing in part the negative attitude that Americans have about the influence of interest groups.

The permanent civil service, competing parties and the desire of governments for electoral success may balance the representative aspects of pressure groups. The government is often the only countervailing force against farming interests, which are not effectively balanced by direct opposing interests; consumer and environmental groups generally are too weak to provide meaningful opposition. Moreover, by encouraging wider political participation, pressure groups are said to extend the liberal democratic concept of representative government, and in some instances groups provide the only source of opposition to the united front of the political parties.

Notes and references

1. A. R. Ball and F. Millard, *Pressure Politics in Industrial Societies* (London: Macmillan, 1986) pp. 33–4.
2. Ecological parties have, however, taken seats in several European governments, and the Spanish government depends upon the Catalan party for its majority. It seems that once an interest group begins to act like a party, it may be taken seriously and made part of coalitions.
3. David Truman, *The Governmental Process* (New York: Knopf, 1951).
4. R. A. W. Rhodes, *Understanding Governance: Policy Networks, Governance Reflexivity and Accountability* (Buckingham: Open University Press, 1997).
5. E. E. Schattschneider, *The Semi-Sovereign People* (New York: Holt, Rinehart & Winston, 1969).
6. R. Miliband, *The State in Capitalist Society* (London: Weidenfeld & Nicolson, 1973) ch. 6.
7. P. C. Schmitter, 'Still the Century of Corporatism?', *Review of Politics*, 36 (Jan. 1974) pp. 93–4.
8. A. Cox and N. O'Sullivan, *The Corporate State: Corporatism and the State Tradition in Western Europe* (Aldershot: Edward Elgar, 1988).
9. Stein Rokkan, 'Votes Count but Resources Decide', in R. A. Dahl (ed.), *Political Oppositions in Western Democracies* (New Haven: Yale University Press, 1967); Johan P. Olsen, *Organized Democracy* (Oslo: Universitets-forlaget, 1987).
10. See L. Panitch, 'The Development of Corporatism in Liberal Democracies', in *Trends Towards Corporatist Intermediation*, ed. P. Schmitter and G. Lehmbruch (London: Sage, 1979) pp. 119–46.
11. See Panitch, ibid, pp. 86–7. Also L. Panitch, 'Trade Unions and the Capitalist State', *New Left Review*, 125 (Jan.–Feb. 1981) pp. 21–43; and B. Jessop, 'The Transformation of the State in Post-War Britain', in *The State in Western Europe*, ed. R. Scase (London: Macmillan, 1980) pp. 23–93.
12. R. A. W. Rhodes and D. Marsh, *Policy Networks in British Government* (Oxford: Clarendon Press, 1992).
13. Keith Dowding, 'Model or Metaphor?: A Critical Review of the Policy Network Approach', *Political Studies*, 43 (1995) pp. 136–58.
14. A. G. Jordan and J. J. Richardson, *Government and Pressure Groups in Britain* (Oxford: Clarendon Press, 1987).
15. See V. Wright, *The Government and Politics of France*, 3rd edn (London, 1989) p. 279; also A. Stevens, *The Government and Politics of France* (London: Macmillan, 1992) pp. 272–82.
16. See H. Zeigler, *Interest Groups in American Society* (Englewood Cliffs, NJ: Prentice-Hall, 1964) pp. 44–6.
17. The most famous example is the Supreme Court ruling in *Brown* v. *Board of Education of Topeka* (1954) that was the beginning of the end of legal segregation in the public schools.

18. See M. Pinto-Duschinsky, *British Political Finance, 1830–1980* (Washington: American Enterprise Institute, 1981) chs 6, 8.
19. Unions and business in the United States are forbidden from making other than nominal contributions to candidates so a variety of mechanisms such as politic action committees (PACs) have been developed.
20. See M. P. Fiorina, *Congress, The Keystone of the Washington Establishment,* 2nd edn (New Haven: Yale University Press, 1994).
21. The medical profession obviously must co-operate with programmes for public health care provision, but also usually is empowered to license and regulate doctors as well.
22. See G. K. Wilson, *Special Interests and Policy Making: Agricultural Policies in Britain and the United States, 1956–70* (New York: Wiley, 1977) pp. 76–80.
23. See B. Guy Peters, *American Public Policy*, 5th edn (Chatham, NJ: Chatham House, 1998).
24. See Johan P. Olsen, *Organized Democracy* (Oslo: Universitetsforlaget, 1997).
25. See W. Grant, 'The National Farmers Union: The Classic Case of Incorporation?', in *Pressure Politics: Interest Groups in Britain,* ed. D. Marsh (London, 1983) pp. 129–43; in the United States almost any former Congressman who wants to can get a position lobbying his or her former colleagues.
26. S. Mazey and J. J. Richardson, *Lobbying in the European Union* (Oxford: Oxford University Press, 1993).
27. See G. K. Wilson, *Interest Groups in the United States* (Oxford: Basil Blackwell, 1981) pp. 62–4.
28. S. H. Alatas, *Corruption: Nature, Causes, Consequences, Functions* (Aldershot: Avebury, 1990).
29. This has been seen in a number of high-profile cases such as *Roe* v. *Wade* establishing abortion rights, as well as in the role of the NAACP in a number of civil rights cases.
30. See R. Hodder-Williams, 'Constitutional Legitimacy and the Supreme Court', in *Developments in American Politics,* ed. G. Peele *et al.* (Basingstoke: Macmillan, 1992) pp. 138–64. Public enquiries of a quasi-judicial nature are also important in many political systems. For information on the role of these enquiries in the field of environmental pressure group activities, see Ball and Millard, *Pressure Politics in Industrial Societies,* pp. 183–8.
31. For a discussion of pressure groups in the USSR and Eastern Europe before the reforms of Mikhail Gorbachev, see Ball and Millard, *Pressure Politics in Industrial Societies.* On the recent changes in the USSR and Russia, see P. Duncan, G. Hosking and J. Aves, *The Road to Post-Communism* (London: Pinter, 1992).
32. See Ball and Millard, *Pressure Politics in Industrial Societies,* pp. 235–9.
33. For a discussion of the dominant ideology that supports the demands of business groups in liberal democracies, see C. Lindblom, *Politics and Markets* (New York: Free Press, 1977).

7

Representation, Elections and Voting Behaviour

Political parties, interest groups and social movements are the primary means for conveying public demands to government, and of representing social and economic clusters. Political parties and groups do not exist in isolation but rather are, at least in part, a function of the legal and political rules and institutions within which they operate. They also reflect the social cleavages in their societies; it is difficult to mobilise the public about issues that do not divide them and which are not perceived as being politically relevant. Political party systems rarely reflect directly every cleavage or every source of disagreement among the public, but they must find some means of balancing the need to reflect differences with the need to accommodate those differences in order to provide governance to their society.

We assume that most issues of democracy will be decided in so-called 'representative institutions', especially legislatures and parliaments. There are, however, alternatives that permit the public to choose laws directly, and to dismiss incumbent officials. Direct democracy has had appeal for many theorists of democracy, but it is difficult to make this work in practice. The complexity of modern political systems and the complexity of the issues with which they deal may make the assumptions of direct democracy, primarily that the citizens can and should make good policy choices through voting in referenda, increasingly questionable.

Theories of representation

We have seen that political parties and pressure groups represent interests, attitudes and values in the political system, but there is often confusion over what is meant by the term 'representation'. Adolf Hitler once said that he had the greatest claim to be called representative of his people, and this claim must be based on different grounds from those of liberal democratic systems which demand periodic and competitive elections. Rather than elections, it was based on his (presumed) capacity to reflect the true wishes and feelings of the German people at the time. The British House of Commons is said to be a representative assembly, but this does not mean that it mirrors the geographical, class, sex, age and religious distribution of the British population.[1] Numerous scholars have attempted to determine the extent to which parliaments, bureaucracies and other political institutions are representative of their society.[2]

Direct democracy is difficult to implement in modern states, and some form of representative system is found in all states, except for a few conservative-autocratic systems. Naturally, there are wide variations in the form of representative government and the selection processes of the representatives: President Hastings Banda of Malawi claimed that he did not have to submit to re-election because the people 'selected' him to be president for life. However, most political systems share two basic concepts of representation: first, that sovereignty resides with the people and therefore the government is responsible to the people; and second, that the will of the majority is more important than that of minorities. Neither of these two concepts has any real meaning until they are amplified, and the applied within different political systems, and neither has any meaning unless expressed in terms of particular governing structures. But we shall see that basically the two principles do provide the foundations of modern systems of representation.

Yet there are the problems in all democratic systems of defining the 'people' and deciding how their will should be expressed. Rousseau's answer was direct participatory democracies in small decentralised states:

Sovereignty, for the same reason as makes it inalienable, cannot be represented; it lies essentially in the general will, and does not admit of representation: it is either the same, or other; there is no intermediate possibility. The deputies of the people, therefore, are not and cannot be its representatives: they are merely its stewards, and can carry through no definite acts. Every law the people has not ratified in person is null and void − is, in fact, not a law. The people of England regards itself as free; but it is grossly mistaken; it is free only during the election of members of parliament. As soon as they are elected, slavery overtakes it, and it is nothing.[3]

The European medieval basis of representation was closely bound with the concept of corporate hierarchies. The 'people' were not individuals but rather groups in society, these groups being based on occupation and status. Thus medieval representative assemblies were assemblies of estates, each with responsibilities, duties and rights and arranged according to a natural order of authority: the early English parliament had three estates, of peers, church and commoners, of which the House of Commons and House of Lords (containing the Lords Spiritual) survive. The secularisation of Western European societies and the rise of personal powerful monarchies saw the decline in some areas of the medieval assemblies, and the king was to become the representative of the people according to God's law. That having been said, some remnants of the older, corporate theories of representation persist in corporate legislative bodies in Ireland and Bavaria, and in Social and Economic Councils in a number of countries, as well as in the European Union.[4]

These corporate conceptions on representation are important because the break with the past is not a dramatic one, and many of these older theories remain in operation, intertwined with modern theories of representation. Emphasis on intermittent lines of continuity in representation is necessary for understanding. Thus, the American revolutionaries rejected the sovereignty of the British crown and the British parliament, and were willing to quote John Locke as frequently as their opponents, but they only reluctantly placed that sovereignty in the hands of the people, and then only with massive institutional safeguards that had an extremely conservative impact. In fact, it is difficult to talk about theories of representation with the two underlying concepts of popular sovereignty and majority rule in modern terms before the nineteenth century. It will be convenient to group modern theories under two broad headings for further examination: (1) liberal democratic theories of representation; (2) collectivist theories of representation. Neither category can be completely isolated from the other, for as we shall see they both have common intellectual origins, and moreover we shall find several different approaches under these common headings.

Liberal democratic theories of representation

There are a number of alternative theories that can be grouped under this heading;[5] however, it is possible to isolate the essentials of liberal democratic theories of representation. Firstly, there is the emphasis on the importance of individual rights, especially the inviolability of the individual's property, and the necessity of limiting the powers of government to protect those rights. The justification for these individual rights was to be found in the theories of natural rights, rights that were beyond the competence of any government interference. Thus the American Declaration of Independence of 1776 claimed: 'We hold these truths to be self evident that all men are created equal, that they are endowed by their Creator with certain inalienable rights, that among these are Life, Liberty and the pursuit of Happiness.' Thus, liberal democracy implies not only an extension of the franchise but an equality of voting rights. The representative represents individuals, their opinions and their interests, and therefore he or she is elected according to geographically demarcated constituencies, not according to classes, occupational distinctions or distinct interests.

Secondly, there is within liberal democratic theories of representation a rationalist strand. Humans are argued to be creatures of reason; they are able to identify their own interests and their own opinions, and are aware of the wider claims of the community. The individual will therefore use his vote in an intelligent fashion and is consequently entitled to share in the selection of representatives. Thomas Jefferson laid clear emphasis on the importance of an educated majority as a prerequisite for American representative government,[6] and this view was echoed by the classic English liberals of the mid nineteenth century. Human reason was thought to be superior to historical tradition or hallowed custom, and therefore political institutions and practices are to be judged empirically.

This rationalism leads to the third characteristic of liberal representation theory, that of the sovereignty of the people, which was to be expressed through universal suffrage. The British reformist tradition in the nineteenth century measured its success by the successive Reform Acts which increased the size of the electorate, attempts to equalise the size of constituencies, the introduction of the secret ballot, the attack on corrupt electoral practices, and the weakening of the unrepresentative House of Lords in 1911. The implicit goal of 'one person, one vote, one value' has yet to be achieved fully, given the marked variations in the size of constituencies[7] as well as the continuing powers of the House of Lords. The impact of this theory of representation can be seen more clearly in the legal challenges to unrepresentative practices in the United States. In a series of cases the Supreme Court has demanded that electoral districts be as closely as possible equal in population and impact.[8] This liberal, egalitarian view of representation then conflicted with something of a reassertion of corporate conceptions, arguing that districts should be drawn in ways to ensure some legislative representation for minority groups.[9]

One can see that in this framework the representative has a particular role to play: he is responsible to his electorate, but he is not its delegate; he represents a geographical collection of opinions, but is not required to surrender his own. Liberal democracy emphasises the role of the representative assembly as a protection against the encroachment of executive power, especially encroachments on the liberties of the individual. However, there is the problem of the tyrannical majority, for if the representative assembly reflects the opinions of the electoral majority, can that popular majority interfere with the 'inalienable rights' of individuals? The problem was outlined by Alexander Hamilton during the debates on the American constitution in 1788: 'Men love power . . . Give all power to the many, they will oppress the few. Give all power to the few, they will oppress the many. Both therefore ought to have power, that they may defend itself against the other.[10] The extension of the British franchise aroused similar fears of mob democracy amongst the liberals. John Stuart Mill, fearing the uneducated majority, suggested limiting the vote to the literate and increasing the vote of the people with certain superior qualities.[11] The pessimism of the liberal doubters seemed to have been justified with the extinction of liberal democracy in Germany in the 1930s. The majority of the electorate rejected liberal democratic candidates pledged to support the Weimar Republic to vote for totalitarian parties intent on destroying German liberalism.

The potential conflict between the sovereignty of the majority and the protection of the rights of the individual may be seen in terms of Robert Dahl's concepts of Madisonian and populistic democracy.[12] Dahl defines the first in the following way:

> What I am going to call the 'Madisonian' theory of democracy is an effort to bring off a compromise between the power of majorities and the power of minorities, between the political equality of all adult citizens on the one side, and the desire to limit their sovereignty on the other.[13]

It is this term of 'Madisonian' that Dahl applies to the American political system with its constitutional checks and balances.[14] His definition of populistic democracy is 'that it postulates only two goals to be maximised – political equality and popular sovereignty', and hence may be open to majority domination of minorities.[15]

There are other variations within the representative theories of liberal democracy: the utilitarian demand for representatives to constitute an exact social mirror of the electorate presents one enduring aspect of these theories; the English idealists' partial reaction against nineteenth-century individualism in their belief that the system of representation should allow common interests to emerge after a process of discussion, is another strand. However, these representative theories, taken as a whole, have managed to accommodate themselves to the rise of the mass party and the growth in executive power. They have done this in two ways: first by the emphasis on the doctrine of the mandate, i.e. that the government programme is the implementation of election promises that have received the consent of the electorate. This is a partial reiteration of the rationalist element in liberal democratic representative thought, and as we shall see later, it is difficult to sustain in view of what knowledge we have of the way in which voters decide which party to vote for.

Given the weaknesses of the mandate theory, there has been a second accommodation in a reversion to the theory that at election times voters are deciding which competing team of political leaders to support, and representative liberal democracy must be compatible with the existence of political élites. As Rose has pointed out, it is difficult to maintain that electors can choose policies, but they certainly can choose groups of élites.[16] The most compelling version of this approach is that voting is retrospective.[17] The argument is that there is not enough information to make rational choices about alternative governments in advance of their election. Therefore, voters are better advised to vote on the basis of what the incumbent government has done, or perhaps also on the basis of what each group of élites vying for office had done in their last period of incumbency.

Collectivist theories of representation

Collectivist concepts of representation were developed in modern form largely by the nineteenth-century European socialists.[18] These ideologues rejected the individualism underpinning representation of the liberal theorists and emphasised the importance of class conflict within society and the middle-class liberals' use of the state as an instrument of class oppression. Therefore, the socialists argued that assemblies should be representative not of individuals and opinions but of the majority class whose interests have been subordinated by middle-class parliaments. Here we find an emphasis both on the sovereignty of the people and on the will of the majority. Thus, the *Communist Manifesto* of 1848 states: 'All previous historical movements were movements of minorities. The Proletarian movement is the self-conscious, independent movement of the immense majority, in the interests of the immense majority.'[19]

The claim of the Soviet Union to a distinctive and more democratic type of representation was always undermined by the acclamatory nature of elections, with choice limited to endorsement or (rarely) rejection of a single candidate. Several East European states experimented at various times with greater choice than that offered by the USSR,[20] but only in 1989 did Gorbachev try to rejuvenate the representative institutions. He attempted to foster greater accountability to the electorate with the introduction of multi-candidate elections in the Soviet Union. The result was a shock to the Soviet élite that had been insulated from the public. Although the Communist Party easily retained its pre-eminent position in the new Congress of People's Deputies, a number of party bosses suffered resounding defeats, especially in the key cities of Moscow and Leningrad. In a number of republics local communist leaders began to jump on to the nationalist bandwagon in an effort to retain electoral credibility.[21] Even before the collapse of the Soviet Union, that country was moving rapidly to accept most principles of the liberal theory of representation, including that of multi-party competition.

Functions of elections

Elections are universally a means of choosing representatives, though other functions of elections vary with the type of political system. One feature of the 1980s and 1990s has been a general increase in electoral choice. Previously, one could distinguish between multi-party elections, multi-candidate elections in a hegemonic system, and single-candidate elections. Within these categories there were considerable variations – for example, the Kenyan electorate had a choice of candidates from the single party, but it regularly rejected incumbents deemed to have done too little for their constituencies. The single-candidate elections in a number of socialist states have all but vanished; even North Korea provides a limited choice of candidates. All the East European states now permit multi-party competition, and some (Poland and Estonia for example) have developed party systems with a large number and wide variety of parties. In Africa, too, multi-partyism is firmly on the agenda, but there is wide variation in the success to which this goal is being achieved, and in ways that the choice is to be exercised.

Elections do allow voter participation in the choosing of their representatives. However, we have already noted the distorting effect of the various types of electoral system in the competitive elections of liberal democracies. The successful candidates may be the choice of the minority, or the system may give the parties control over which candidates are presented to the electorate. Voters under the single transferable vote have a greater choice over which candidate should represent a particular political party than voters under the British electoral system. In the highly controlled nominal multi-party systems of the former communist states, the Communist Party determined the total allocation of parliamentary seats to different parties.

The diversity of arrangements for choosing representatives is matched by a similar diversity in regard to candidate selection. This draws attention to questions of how parties select candidates and what are the opportunities for the electors to influence that choice. In single-party states like the Soviet Union before 1990, the Communist Party issued directives regarding the composition of representatives in terms of age, gender, occupation and the like; the Communist Party also exercised a *de facto* veto over the candidates, who were formally selected by so-called social organisations such as trade unions. In the United Kingdom the political parties are the key agents of candidate selection. In the United States, however, primaries are held where the voters elect their candidates for the forthcoming elections; this system serves to undermine party control of the nominating process.

Choosing a representative does not mean that the elected representative is responsible to, or controlled to any degree by, the voters. Parties present policy choices to the electorate but elections are rarely fought over a single dominant issue; therefore the failure of the elected representatives to fulfil their promises to their voters on one issue may be blurred by claims of success on other promises. Of course, there are exceptions. The East European elections of 1990 were seen as plebiscites on the continuation of communist rule. Umbrella organisations such as Solidarity in Poland or Civic Forum and Public against Violence in Czechoslovakia won massive victories because of their records of opposition to the old regime.

Of course, referendums are a means of allowing voters to directly influence the decision-makers in terms of specific policies. Referenda are a common means of making policy in Switzerland at both the national and cantonal level.[22] Thus referendums have been held in Sweden on alcohol, in the Irish Republic on abortion, on tax-cutting in California and many other American States, and political devolution in Scotland and Wales. In 1992, a New Zealand referendum decided on significant changes to the electoral system, and in the same year the Danes voted against and the French voted for the Maastricht Treaty in their respective referendums.

Referendums, however, are not necessarily the populist democratic device that their supporters sometimes claim. Referendums are not always binding on the government and the timing and the nature of the question or questions asked are important in determining the outcomes.[23] Citizens have at time passed referenda with contradictory purposes in the same election. The discrepancies in the resources available to competing groups in a referendum campaign may prevent equal presentation and dissemination of competing opinions. Finally, referenda force complex policy questions to be reduced to simple yes or no answers, and therefore may produce inferior public policies.[24] Generally, referendums are conservative devices and the results tend to uphold the status quo.[19]

Elections do not necessarily decide which government takes office. In single-party systems the result is a foregone conclusion even though the electorate may influence the composition of the government by preferring one candidate to another from the same party. Few African governments outside South Africa have lost office as a consequence of an election. Even in the liberal democratic states of Western Europe, the relative strengths of the political parties in coalition government decides the nature of the government, and the bargaining of the parties is as important as the election that produced the varying party strengths. Until 1998, for example, governments in Germany have been the consequence of the decision of the Free Democrats over whether to support the Christian Democrats or the Social Democrats.

We have already noted that electoral corruption may distort the people's choice, both in terms of which representative is elected to the assembly and which government takes office. The corruption may be mildly amusing, as in a Corsican election when a Socialist alliance polled 4,965 votes and the Gaullists polled 4,260 votes with only a total registered electorate of 4,303,[25] but it becomes more serious when it is claimed that Kennedy's victory over Nixon in 1960 was achieved by the manipulation of vital votes in the Democratic stronghold of Cook County, Illinois.[26] The corrupt practices of President Marcos of the Philippines led directly to his fall from power in 1986. The problem of electoral corruption in newer democracies is particularly crucial; establishing norms of fairness and equal access in elections early in their history becomes a means of institutionalising an open democratic system.[27]

Yet elections have functions other than those concerned with the choice and accountability of representatives or governments. Elections allow a degree of communication between the rulers and the ruled; the latter can educate the former on what are perceived as the main political issues. Above all, elections are a means of legitimising the right of the rulers to govern. Even in one-party regimes with little choice available to the voter, the authorities seek to maximise the turn-out and often exaggerate the actual number who take part in the election to demonstrate popular support of their regime.[28] This legitimising process both mobilises the people for support of the regime and helps to engender positive attitudes among the governed, and, in the process of legitimising the status quo, produces a degree of political stability constantly sought by those who hold political power.

Voting behaviour

We have already noted the role of political parties and the electoral system in deciding the result of general elections in all those political systems that hold elections, whether competitive or non-competitive. Another important area of inquiry is the field of voting behaviour. Obviously, this form of inquiry is more important in those political systems in which the voter has some sort of choice, no matter how limited. Unfortunately for the student of politics, there is little agreement among political scientists on the reasons why voters prefer one individual or party to the alternatives.[29] Therefore, we are faced with numerous, though not always conflicting, theories and models that purport to explain electoral behaviour.

Some of these disagreements stem from political changes that tend to render former certainties about behaviour outdated. Thus, increasing secularisation of society may lessen the impact of religion on voting behaviour, or the class structure may change over a period of time, and complicate theories on the relationship between membership of a social class and voting preferences; the embourgeoisement of the working class has tended to reduce the relevance of class for voting.[30] Changes in gender roles have reduced, but not eliminated the differences among men and women in their voting behavior.

There are, however, important methodological problems in the analysis of voting behaviour. At first glance voting behaviour studies appear more susceptible to a scientific approach than many other areas of inquiry, given the vast amount of quantifiable data the political scientist has at hand, yet the acquisition of these data is beset with numerous problems. First, every elector cannot be asked questions concerning past and future intentions and therefore the sample must be chosen with care; for example, if surveys are conducted by telephone, compensation must be built into the sample, since working-class people are less likely to possess telephones than the middle class. Secondly, the nature of the questions asked is very important. Potential support for the Liberal Democrats in the 1992 British general election was higher in polls such as Gallup that prompted the respondent by naming the Liberal Democrats than in those polls that simply asked which party the elector intended to vote for. Third, there are problems involved in the interpretation of the material. This is very important in cross-national comparisons, for if there are different conceptual uses of key terms such as social class, floating voter or church membership, then the conclusions are seriously flawed. Thus although the British Labour Party in the 1992 general election scored well on several important issues such as health and education, the Conservatives won a decisive victory. In fact, the failure of all the opinion polls in this election to indicate the correct result has thrown grave doubts on their reliability as predictors.[31]

Within this complex arena of voting behaviour studies, three broad approaches stand out. First is the party identification model: voters cast their vote primarily out of long-term loyalty to a particular political party; second the rational choice approach, with the electorate rationally deciding which way to vote on the performance and promises of the candidates or parties; third, the sociological approach which emphasises the correlation between voting behaviour and the voter's class, religion, age, or group memberships. None of these broad approaches provide a complete explanation of voting behaviour, and there are many divergent currents within each of them. However, each approach may be briefly examined.

The party identification model was the most popular interpretation of voting behaviour in the 1950s and 1960s. In most liberal democracies stability, not change, characterised the behaviour of the electorates and surveys revealed a high level of allegiance to specific political parties. Changes occurred as a result of the behaviour of small sections of the electorate, often labelled 'floating voters'; but stability was the outstanding characteristic of voting patterns. Whether this stability reflected relative economic prosperity, or whether the investigatory methods were deficient is not clear, but the interpretation of stability was very clear.

In the 1990s, it is obvious that voting behaviour based on loyalty to political parties is no longer a persuasive explanation. Political scientists now speak of 'partisan dealignment', that is the weakening of the voters' loyalty or attachment to specific parties (see Table 7.1). Electorates in industrial liberal democracies are now more volatile; they are now more likely to

Table 7.1   Dealignment: declining identification with political parties
(percentage saying strongly attached to a political party)

	1980	1985	1992
Belgium	19	22	22
Denmark	32	34	28
Finland	37	33	30
France	19	18	16
Germany	32	34	28
Ireland	35 .	26	24
Italy	39	37	31
Netherlands	33	31	28
Norway	36	30	31
United Kingdom	37	30	41
United States	31	29	24

Source: European Commission, *Eurobarometer*; US National Election Survey, various years.

change their voting behaviour in each election. There has been the rise of the genuinely independent voter, particularly in American elections.[32] These independent voters are not necessarily the politically ignorant or apathetic voters, but those who vote independently of party labels and may vote for candidates with different party labels for different political offices on the same day, a behaviour termed 'ticket splitting'.[33] Although the independent voter is the hero of the civics book, we also know that political party loyalty is often a good cue for voters, and hence the independent voter may actually be less informed than more partisan voters.

This is not to imply that parties are not important in explaining patterns of electoral behaviour. The personality of the candidate, particularly in French and American presidential elections, is significant, but partisan identification is a crucial factor. Although party control of the nomination process has been weakened in American elections by a number of populist reforms, parties are generally crucial in this respect. The presentation of issues, the mobilisation of the vote, and the organisation of election campaigns are of the utmost significance; the inept electoral performance of the British Labour Party in 1983 certainly increased the Conservative majority.

The second approach, stressing rational choice, was developed first by Anthony Down's influential work published in 1957.[34] Downs likened political choices to economic choices; in the market place, the consumer will compare products in terms of costs and quality and purchase those goods which it is economically sensible to buy. Likewise, in the political market place, the voter will cast his or her vote for the party that is most likely – given the information available – to serve the ends of the voter. Social position or party loyalty are less important factors than the rational search for the party or candidate that will best serve the individual interests (often defined in economic terms) of each voter. This approach is not necessarily incompatible with party loyalty, but it does emphasise the importance of issues in elections. Electors may deem certain issues such as defence or education to be of such importance that it determines the direction of the vote. The importance of certain issues may lead to continual voting for the same party:

> For many electors . . . certain issue areas will be very important, regardless of what macro-issues dominate the campaign. . . . Such electors as a result of their permanent preoccupations will vote for the same party all the time – often as part of a cohesive social group concerned with the same issue.[35]

Thus in a wider sense this approach may allow aspects of the party loyalty and sociological approaches to be included within its explanation. The rational choice approach allows the voter to vote on the record of the government, making a retrospective judgement, and thus to ignore the promises of candidates and parties. Certainly, there is strong evidence that the state of the economy at the time of the election is a powerful determinant of electoral behaviour; the American presidential election of 1992 and the German election of 1990 appear to underline the importance of the economy. Moreover, there is evidence from many liberal democracies that issue voting is on the increase, with voters attempting to match their own preferences with the likely behaviour of candidates.[36]

The sociological approach has more supporters among students of voting behaviour, but it should not be forgotten that the theoretical divergences within this approach are many and the arguments diverse. Broadly, the sociological approach stresses the group membership of the voter and gives prominence to the voter's social class, religious adherence, regional or ethnic loyalties and the age and sex of the voter. Of course, these characteristics may overlap – e.g. the voter may be a middle-class, church-going female voting in Italian elections – or they may conflict – e.g. a middle-class, Catholic, Irish immigrant voting in England. It is important to remember that the sociological approach merely identifies correlations between social cleavages and voting behaviour; it does not claim that there is a causal connection behind those correlations.

There is no doubt that class is a powerful indicator of voting intentions. Generally, the working class is more likely to support a left-of-centre party and the middle classes more likely to vote for a right-of-centre party. It matters little to this explanation that for most of the electorate the terms 'right' and 'left' have little meaning.[37] What is important is that there is a strong correlation between class and voting behaviour. Thus in the French presidential election of 1988, over two-thirds of businessmen, professionals and farmers voted for the conservative candidate, Chirac, while 70 per cent of the manual working class voted for the Socialist candidate, Mitterrand.[38] Even in the United States where voting along class lines is less pronounced, blue-collar workers were more likely to vote for the Democratic Party nominees in the 1984 and 1988 presidential elections, whilst the Republicans, Reagan and Bush, won more white-collar support.[31]

However, if all social classes voted along class lines, conservative parties, particularly in Western Europe, would be in permanent opposition since the working classes generally outnumber the middle classes. The British Conservative Party has enjoyed long periods of dominance because sufficient numbers of the working class have refused to vote along class lines. Thus in the 1992 election, only 38 per cent of skilled manual workers voted Labour, while 41 per cent supported the Conservatives. At the same election, it was estimated that 20 per cent of the middle-class voters supported the Labour Party.[39] With the numerous scandals among the Conservatives, and a Labour leader that could calm any fears of a return to the 'tax and spend' policies of the past, Labour was able to win over a quarter of middle-class voters in the 1997 election.

In all industrial liberal democracies, there has been a weakening of the relationship between class and voting over the last twenty years, and this has produced an argument among political scientists as to whether this weakening correlation is the result of voters simply ceasing to vote along class lines (class dealignment) or whether the class structure itself in these societies is in a process of change.[40] Certainly, the traditional manual working class has declined in industrial liberal democracies and there has been a significant growth in white-collar occupations. This in turn has affected the nature of trade union membership, which in the past was associated with voting for left-of-centre parties. Further, general economic growth means that most manual workers can enjoy what might appear to be a middle-class life-style.

The British general election result of 1983 led many observers to use social class in a different way. The working class were more likely to vote Conservative if they owned their own houses as opposed to renting them from the local council; working-class employees in state employment, whether white- or blue-collar workers, were more likely to vote for the Labour Party than employees in the private sector; those dependent on the state, such as pensioners or social security recipients, were more likely to vote Labour.[41] Of course, the definition of social class that is used in the investigation of voting patterns is of crucial importance.[42]

The correlation between social class and voting behaviour may be reinforced or weakened by the other factors. Thus if one class predominates in a particular geographic area, it is plausible to argue that there is greater conformity in voting patterns; in a white-collar suburb, white-collar workers would have their conservatism reinforced, while the tendency of manual workers in this suburb to vote socialist would be weakened. Studies of European communist parties have drawn attention to the party sub-culture in explaining the underlying solidarity of the communist vote: the working-class family transmitted communist values to the children and these values were reinforced by membership of leisure and social groups which were organised by the communist parties themselves. Thus communist sub-cultures were established among certain sections of the electorate, illustrated by the famous 'red belts' in areas surrounding large cities in Italy and France.[43]

Religion is still an important indicator of voting patterns although its impact has declined. In predominantly Catholic countries such as Italy there is strong support for the Christian Democrats, and even in the Netherlands and Germany, where Protestantism is as important as Catholicism, there are clear correlations between religious allegiance and voting for religious or confessional parties. However, cross-cleavages are important; thus in the Anglo-Saxon democracies such as Australia, Britain and America, Catholics are more likely to vote left-of-centre as a result of ethnic and class disadvantages. In the United States, Jews voted almost 80 to 20 in favour of Clinton, and white 'born-again' Christians again voted overwhelmingly for the Republican candidate, Bush, in the 1992 presidential election. However, there is the problem of defining membership of a church, for different churches may define their membership in various ways, i.e. regular attendance, baptism, family membership, etc.[44] Moreover, membership of a church, whatever the method of calculation, may strongly correlate with social class status; thus Anglicans in England, and Episcopalians and Unitarians in the United States, are more likely to be middle class, whilst Baptists in both countries and particularly in the United States are more likely to be lower-middle and working class.

Women are more likely to be regular church attenders than men, but independently of religious adherence, women have traditionally tended to support right-of-centre parties. However, this correlation appears to be weakening, and this trend is more pronounced in the more secular liberal democracies of Britain and America than in those with a Catholic heritage such as France, Italy and West Germany.[45] In the United States in recent elections, however, women have tended to vote more for the Democratic Party than for the Republican. This pattern appears to result from the women's greater interest in programmes such as social welfare, and especially education, and their lower level of concern about higher taxes.

Age, too, is a complex variable in explaining voting behaviour. Older people clearly have a tendency to vote for conservative parties but one has to take care that this tendency is not partly a result of predominance of women, or even the middle class, among older voters as a consequence of demographic trends. It may be the case that conservative voting does not necessarily dramatically increase as the voter gets older, but that the apparent voting patterns of the elderly may be a consequence of the hardening of voting habits that were formed in a different historical period. Thus a seventy-year-old American Democratic voter in the 1980s may be reflecting an attachment for the party, an attachment established during the economic depression of the 1930s when the individual voted for the first time and voted Democratic.[46] There have been some noticeable inter-generational shifts in voting, especially in the appeal of Green and other alternative parties to younger voters.[47]

There are other variables in the sociological approach to studying voting patterns. There are many regional and nationalist parties throughout Europe in systems with competitive elections such as the Scottish and Basque nationalist parties or the Tyrolese separatist parties of Italy. In some political systems, the majority parties split along ethnic or linguistic lines, reflecting English–Boer animosities in South Africa or Walloon–Flemish differences in Belgium. In the United States, black voters give their support overwhelmingly to Democratic candidates, but here one must note a correlation between colour and economic deprivation.

Thus, approaches to studying why people cast their votes in the way they do are varied and complex and subject to many qualifications. However, as we have seen, the different approaches are not necessarily exclusive of contrasting approaches. All the approaches must struggle with methodological problems, especially those of defining concepts, and the societies they analyse are not static. Long-term structural changes and sudden crises such as war or economic depression complicate the area of study; there may be more volatility within the electorate than the aggregated figures betray. These structural changes lead to partisan realignments and dealignments, and to the formation of new sociological cleavages. It is a field where excessive dogmatism should be avoided and all conclusions must be tentative.

The role of the mass media

One factor of increasing importance in the determination of election results is the role of the mass media, and especially that of television. However, there is little agreement on how important the effects of the mass media really are in individual electoral behaviour. The question is undoubtedly of great importance to students of politics, since there is now general agreement that in industrialised liberal democracies the major source of political information is the mass media, and that the importance of this source is growing. These issues become all the more important as television faces the need to balance its information role with its entertainment functions.[48]

Newspapers used to be the chief source, but with the growth of television, and increasingly the Internet, their relative importance has declined. Yet newspaper readership remains still very high in most systems with competitive elections, especially in Germany and Great Britain where over half the adult populations read the political news in a newspaper every day. Newspapers also may be more important in shaping élite opinion than in shaping the views of the mass electorate. Ownership of newspapers is very concentrated in some political systems; Axel Springer owns nearly all the Sunday newspapers in West Germany, and the ownership of British newspapers is similarly in few hands, with Rupert Murdoch increasing his share of readers over the last decade both in terms of the number of newspapers and in terms of the number of readers.[49] Even in the United States where there are fewer national newspapers, syndicated columns by well-known journalists partly bring the United States into line with Britain and Germany.

Newspapers in most liberal democracies show clear political biases, and these political biases appear to be increasing. In 1992 only three of seventeen British national newspapers gave any support to the Labour Party, although there were major defections by the time of the 1997 election. The German Springer empire consistently supports the right-of-centre parties. On the other side of the political spectrum, the Australian Liberal and Nationalist parties complained bitterly of the pro-Labour stance said to have been shown by the majority of newspapers and television stations in the 1987 election. American newspapers make more of an issue than most others in separating their editorial views from their presentation of the news, but in most cases biases in the selection of news items and in reportage appear to be increasing.

Television strives to take a more neutral stance with regard to political issues, partly because outside the United States it is more likely to be controlled by public corporations, and even where privately owned, television is subjected to more controls than the newspapers. In Germany, the Constitutional Court in its supervision of television has successfully resisted private ownership. In countries such as Britain where television is partly in private hands and in the United States where the public service is minute, there is often an overlap between ownership of television stations and newspapers, with the possibility that some communities may have only a single source of media.[50]

Television now takes the major share in political advertising and election campaigns are increasingly fought through the television screens. This makes any accusation of political bias all the more sensitive. Television, whilst striving to be politically objective, does, in fact, provide less political information than the newspapers. It stresses personalities and images to the detriment of informed political analysis. Television because of its increasing pre-eminence in the dissemination of political information becomes more open to political interference on the part of governments. The bias in favour of the government of the day shown by French television has long been the subject of comment, and the splitting up of the monopoly public corporation into six regions and the attempted reforms proposed by President Mitterrand in 1982 have failed to significantly change the situation. British governments increasingly attempt to force television to provide a more favourable image of the party in power. These attempts became more overt and less subtle when Kenneth Baker, the Home Secretary, warned the

BBC during the 1992 election campaign to be 'very careful indeed' or it would suffer repercussions from the next Conservative government.

Yet despite this heavy reliance on the media, and especially television, for political information on the part of the electorate, there is no agreement among observers on the effect of the media on political attitudes or voting behaviour. It is argued by some that the media merely reinforce existing party loyalties and political opinions. It is the more politically committed that spend more time reading, watching or listening to analyses and comments on political matters. Others argue that the media influence opinion and importantly set the political agenda; they decide what political issues are to be important.[51] It may be, however, that both views are correct. The media may reinforce pre-existing opinions when they exist, but can shape opinion when there are not already firmly held values.

Those holding the first view claim that the media merely increase political awareness and do not significantly affect public opinion. Thus an analysis of the quadrennial television debates between presidential candidates in the United States have tended to find that the effect on viewers was less than expected.[52] Election debates are different from news coverage of political events, and in Britain the Glasgow Media Group studies of television reporting of political issues claim to have detected persistent bias against groups such as trade unions and in favour of established political élites.[53] In the United States conservatives claim that the media has a liberal bias, despite the large majority of ownership by conservative individuals and corporations. In many countries, even democratic countries such as France, the media is dominated by public ownership and there are claims of bias in favour of the incumbent parties.

Yet even if the political effects of media distortion of political messages are slight, whatever bias there is may be becoming more important, given the increasing electoral volatility in liberal democracies. If voters are no longer as firmly anchored to party loyalties and if class and religious membership become less significant in terms of identifying electoral trends, then the media and particularly television become more important in defining issues and shaping trends. Even if the evidence for short-term influence, such as influencing votes in a particular election, is difficult to obtain, there is the importance of long-term formation of political attitudes; much of the public's scepticism about government may be attributable to the media and the consistently negative reporting. The media cannot be ignored as significant political actors, and their influence, especially that of the broadcast media, must be understood in order to understand the ebb and flow of contemporary politics.

Summary

Voting and elections are crucial components of the democratic process, and far from unimportant for non-democratic systems. The choice of the way in which those elections are conducted will have an important effect on their outcomes, as well as their meaning for the participants. The designers of constitutional systems must decide whether they want the system to be strictly proportional and to represent all interests according to their magnitude, or whether the system be designed to produce majority rule. Those designers must also be cognisant of the capacity of elections, properly run, to build legitimacy, especially in newly democratic systems.

As well as being concerned with the nature of electoral institutions, we need to understand why people vote as they do, and how public opinion is constituted. Voting decisions may reflect the impact of socio-economic factors, or the decisions may be made simply on the basis of long-term identification with a party, and even established political allegiances in a family. Voters also may be swayed by the personal appeal (or repulsion) of a candidate. Public opinion also may be shaped by conscious efforts of political élites and the media. One of the convenient myths of democracy is that voters make rational choices of candidates, but in reality voting may be not so calculating or instrumental, but may only be a means of expressive support for the system, or emotional attachments to certain symbols.

Notes and references

1. See A. H. Birch, *Representative and Responsible Government* (Toronto: University of Toronto Press) pp. 13–17, for a discussion on the different usages of the term.
2. S. C. Selden, *The Promise of Representative Bureaucracy* (Armonk, NY: M.E. Sharpe, 1997).
3. *The Social Contract* (Everyman's Library edn, London, 1913) p. 78.
4. In some instances these operate almost as third bodies of the legislature, with major legislature being sent for discussion, if not formal ratification. See B. G. Peters and C. Hunold, *European Politics Reconsidered*, 2nd edn (New York: Holmes & Meier, 1999), ch. 6.
5. See Birch, *Representative and Responsible Government*, for an outline of British theories of representation. For the development of the American liberal consensus, see L. Hartz, *The Liberal Tradition in America* (New York: Harcourt Brace, 1955).
6. See R. Hofstadter, *The American Political Tradition* (New York: Knopf 1962) pp. 26–32.
7. The average constituency in England has some 90,000 voters while that in Scotland has closer to 70,000 voters.
8. The landmark case was from Tennessee: *Baker* v. *Carr* (1962).
9. The Court eventually limited that conception of equality. See *Reno* v. *Shaw* (1993).
10. Quoted in R. A. Dahl, *Democracy in the United States* (Chicago: Rand McNally, 1976) p. 73.
11. J. S. Mill, *Representative Government* (Everyman's Library edn, London, 1910) pp. 280–90.
12. R. A. Dahl, *A Preface to Democratic Theory* (Chicago: Rand McNally, 1956).
13. Ibid, p. 4.
14. See W. T. Gormley, 'The Bureaucracy and Its Masters: The New Madisonian System in the US', *Governance*, 4 (1991) pp. 1–18.
15. Ibid, p. 50.
16. Richard Rose, *The Problem of Party Government* (London: Macmillan, 1976).
17. M. P. Fiorina, *Retrospective Voting in American National Elections* (New Haven: Yale University Press, 1981).
18. For an account of these early socialist theories, see G. Lichtheim, *The Origins of Socialism* (London: Weidenfeld & Nicolson, 1968).
19. *The Communist Manifesto* (Penguin Books edn, Harmondsworth, 1967) p. 92.
20. See R. Furtak (ed.), *Elections in Socialist States* (London: Harvester, 1990).
21. On the 1989 elections, see S. White and G. Wightman, 'Gorbachev's Reforms: The Soviet Elections of 1987', *Parliamentary Affairs*, 42 (October 1989) pp. 560–81; also P. Lentin's 'Reforming the Electoral System: The 1989 Elections to the USSR Congress of People's Deputies', *Journal of Communist Studies*, 7 (1 March 1991) pp. 69–94.

22. K. W. Kobach, 'Switzerland', in D. E. Butler and A. Ranney (eds), *Referendums Around the World* (London: Macmillan, 1994).
23. I. Budge, *The New Challenge of Direct Democracy* (Oxford: Polity, 1998).
24. Ibid.
25. *Time Magazine*, 16 February 1970.
26. See L. Lewis *et al.*, *An American Melodrama* (New York: Viking) pp. 230 and 509.
27. Various international organisations are used to monitor elections to attempt to ensure fairness and openness, and President Jimmy Carter and the Carter Center have become something of the gold-standard in election monitoring.
28. See M. Harrop and W. L. Miller, *Elections and Voters: A Comparative Introduction* (London: Macmillan, 1987) pp. 21–4.
29. For an overview, see F. U. Pappi, 'Political Behavior: Reasoning Voters and Multi-Party Systems', in R. E. Goodin and H.-D. Klingemann (eds), *A New Handbook of Political Science* (Oxford: Oxford University Press, 1996).
30. See A. Heath, *Understanding Political Change: The British Voter 1964–1987* (Oxford: Pergamon, 1991).
31. See Peter Kellner, 'The Invisible Voters who Fooled the Pollsters', *The Independent*, 1 May 1992.
32. This point is not without its doubters, who emphasise the continuing impact of party identification. See B. E. Keith, *The Myth of the Independent Voter* (Berkeley: University of California Press, 1992).
33. See M. P. Wattenberg, *The Decline of American Political Parties 1958–80* (Cambridge, MA: Harvard University Press, 1984).
34. A. Downs, *An Economic Theory of Democracy* (Chicago: Rand McNally, 1957).
35. I. Budge and D. Farlie, *Explaining and Predicting Elections* (London: Allen & Unwin, 1983) p. 41.
36. For American evidence, see B. Cain, 'The American Electoral System', in *Developments in American Politics*, ed. G. Peele *et al.* (London: Macmillan, 1992) pp. 37–47. Also M. P. Wattenberg, 'From a Partisan to a Candidate-Centred Electorate', in *The New American Political System*, 2nd edn, ed. A. King (London: Macmillan, 1990) pp. 139–74. For Britain, see H. Himmelweit *et al.*, *How Voters Decide* (London, 1981), and A. Heath *et al.*, *Understanding Political Change: The British Voter 1964–1987* (Oxford, 1991) p. 36.
37. D. Fuchs and H.-D. Klingemann, 'The Left-Right Scheme', in M. K. Jennings and Van Deth (eds), *Continuities in Political Action* (Berlin: De Gruyter, 1990).
38. See F. Platone, 'Public Opinion and Electoral Change', in *Developments in French Politics*, ed. P. Hall *et al.* (London: Macmillan, 1990) p. 74.
39. See NOP, *The Independent*, 12 April 1992.
40. R. J. Dalton, S. Flanagan and P. A. Beck, *Electoral Change in Industrial Democracies: Realignment or Dealignment?* (Princeton: Princeton University Press, 1984); Dalton, *Citizen Politics*, 2nd edn (Chatham, NJ: Chatham House, 1996).

41. See P. Whiteley, *The Labour Party in Crisis* (London, 1983) pp. 94–107. See also, Dunleavy *et al.*, *British Democracy at the Crossroads* (London: Allen & Unwin, 1985) pp. 121–46.
42. See Heath *et al.*, *Understanding Political Change*, ch. 5.
43. See A. Kriegel, *The French Communists* (Chicago: University of Chicago Press, 1972). This effect appears to have persisted even after the general decline of communist voting, and the renaming of the party at least in Italy.
44. See A. R. Ball and F. Millard, *Pressure Politics in Industrial Societies* (London: Macmillan, 1986), pp. 211–16, for a discussion of the problems of calculating and defining church membership.
45. See D. McKay, *American Politics and Society*, 2nd edn (Oxford: Martin Robertson, 1989) p. 104. Also see W. L. Miller, 'Voting and the Electorate', in *Developments in British Politics*, ed. P. Dunleavy *et al.* (London: Macmillan, 1990) pp. 42–68.
46. See Dalton, *Citizen Politics*.
47. Regrettably, these alternative parties also can include those of the extreme right such as neo-fascists.
48. J. Langer, *Tabloid Television: Popular Journalism and the 'Other News'* (London: Routledge, 1998).
49. See R. Negrine, *Politics and the Mass Media in Britain* (London: Routledge, 1989), pp. 69–78.
50. There are Federal communications laws attempting to prevent excessive domination of the media, but increasing concentration in the industry makes that more and more difficult to enforce.
51. On the role of newspapers, see J. J. Mondak, *Nothing to Read: Newspapers and Elections in a Social Experiment* (Ann Arbor: University of Michigan Press, 1995).
52. The one major exception may have been the Nixon–Kennedy debate in 1960. This was the first major debate of this type and perhaps the novelty produced a greater impact than subsequent debates.
53. See Glasgow University Media Group, *Really Bad News* (London, 1983). This is the third book in the series, the first being published in 1976. See also P. Dunleavy, 'Fleet Street: Its Bite on the Ballot', *New Socialist*, January 1985, pp. 24–6.

PART THREE

Structure of Government

8
Assemblies

We will now look at the formal institutions of government. This was the traditional focus of political science and to some extent remains so. In order to understand how governments go about the business of governing we must understand the institutions that make, implement and adjudicate policies. That having been said, the usual assignments of functions to particular institutions – legislatures making law, for example – were entirely too simple and most institutions perform a variety of tasks. The public bureaucracy, for example, makes many more rules in almost any political system than does the legislature.[1] Those rules may only be filling in the details of the broader pieces of legislation made by an assembly or parliament, but the sheer volume of rule-making in bureaucracies, and by political executives, overwhelms the activity of legislative bodies.[2]

The first of the formal structures we will investigate are assemblies, or the bodies of officials elected to represent the public and, in most political system, also charged with making primary legislation. This will be followed by a discussion of political executives, the public bureaucracy, and finally the judicial system. We will discuss each of these institutions separately, but in some ways the most important aspects of governing involve interrelating the different institutions to create an effective pattern of decision-making.

The nature of assemblies

The traditional emphasis on constitutional law in the study of politics has tended to confuse the discussion of assemblies, with the result that there has been exhaustive accumulation of detail on procedural matters, but less consideration of the wider relationship with the total political system. The usual term 'legislature' is one indication of the exaggeration of the law-making function of assemblies. This function is important in some political structures, but historically assemblies have emerged from the executive's need for advisory bodies, a need which in the example of the British parliament later provided a means of limiting the power of the executive. Legislative functions were neither historically anterior to, nor are they necessarily more politically important than, other functions of modern assemblies.

The emphasis on the doctrine of the separation of powers in liberal democracies provides a useful guide to the distribution of legislative and executive powers, but interpreted too rigidly and applied universally it leads to misconceptions rather than enlightenment. Legislatures also perform other important functions in controlling the executive, and in reducing the opportunity for malfeasance on the part of political executives and bureaucracies. Perhaps most importantly, legislatures are the clearest link between the people and government – even in systems in which there is also a directly elected president. The smaller size of legislative constituencies, and the local roots of legislators in many systems, makes legislatures the natural democratic link between the rulers and the ruled.[3]

There are wide variations in status, powers and functions even between states whose constitutional frameworks lead to expectations of conformity rather than difference. Nelson Polsby, for example, distinguishes between 'arena' and 'trans-formative' legislatures.[4] At one extreme we find the National People's Congress, the Chinese assembly, as an 'arena' legislature. This assembly has wide powers according to the 1982 constitution, but has a huge number of delegates (almost three thousand), meets infrequently, and sees most important decisions made by the party. Therefore, its role as an independent law-making body is slight at best.[5] At the other end of the spectrum, the United States Congress exercises real power in respect to various decision-making processes, and it offers a far more potent political challenge to executive power than its counterparts in most parliamentary systems.[6] The US Congress is a transformative legislature, capable of transforming the proposals of executives into proposals of its own, or capable (with sufficient majorities) of legislating even in the face of executive resistance expressed through the veto.

These differences among assemblies depend on several variables. The constitutional structure of the state may provide for a federal structure, and this, as in the case of the German Bundesrat, may exalt the importance of a second chamber. The transition from a parliamentary to a 'semi-presidential' type of government by the French under the Fifth Republic reduced the power of the National Assembly.[7] British governments with majority party support in the House of Commons have been immune from major adverse votes of confidence in the House since 1885, thereby limiting the real importance of the legislature as an institution for controlling the executive.[8] The party system was the major factor explaining the weaknesses of assemblies in the former communist states, while the political importance of the Italian parliament and the post-communist Polish parliament is enhanced by their confused party systems.

The system of representation also leads to many variations among assemblies; we have seen in Chapter 7 that socialist states reject the liberal democratic view of representation but that even in liberal democratic systems there are significant differences. For example, the American Congressmen with their identification with local constituency interests offer a contrast to the British MPs, who can afford to take a wider national view of political priorities and who are not so tightly tied to local interests. The linkage to constituency is even less when parties control the placement of candidates on lists in proportional representation elections.[9] There are other variables which affect the position of assemblies in the political process. The level of socio-economic development and the importance of regional differences are significant for the functioning of the national assembly. The political culture and the historical development of the political institutions in a given political system are other important variables explaining in part the role and power of assemblies.

To examine these functions more systematically, we may classify them under the following broad headings:

1. Relations with the executive.
2. Legislative functions.
3. Representative functions.

Assembly–executive relations

In parliamentary governments the political chief executive is selected by the assembly in that the strongest party in the assembly provides the necessary political support for its leader to emerge as prime minister, chancellor, etc., and to select the majority of the members of his government from his party represented in the assembly. Of course, the process differs according to the type of party system that exists in the parliamentary regime. In two-party or dominant party systems the process of selection is straightforward, and the next prime minister is known immediately after the general election.[10] In multi-party systems the process of selecting a prime minister may be more complex, and difficulties in the bargaining procedures between the parties may lead to internal party splits. The process of bargaining to form a new government may require months in systems such as the Netherlands with a number of parties represented in the assembly.[11] Even in those cases, however, the probable prime minister tends to be known, with the bargaining being largely over the distribution of the whole range of ministries available.[12]

Once a government has been chosen by the assembly its relationship with the executive is far from over. The next question is whether the assembly will use its powers to dismiss the executive, and how frequently it will do so. For example, in the nineteenth century the House of Commons in Britain could 'make' and 'unmake' governments with frequent ease. The French Republic of 1946–58 was characterised by instability and the ability of the National Assembly to limit the lives of successive governments; between 1947 and 1958 the National Assembly defeated twenty-one governments. The Italian parliament since 1946 has succeeded in restricting the average life of Italian governments to nine months. In the Scandinavian case, however, the tradition has been that, once selected, governments tend to survive the entire life of a parliament, even if they become small minorities.[13] In 1999 the European parliament began to assert its powers over the Commission, with the result that the entire Commission resigned after a parliamentary report on corruption.

In presidential systems the chief executive is usually elected directly by the mass electorate, yet in some the assembly shares the powers of executive appointment. In the Philippines, the Congress must confirm any presidential nomination of a vice-president in the event of a mid-term vacancy and the nominee must be a member of Congress. The American Senate must confirm all 'political' appointments of the president – and refused to confirm a number of major appointments made by President Clinton.[14] Also, although it cannot defeat the president even in the theoretical terms of parliamentary governments, Congress may use the power to impeach a president. In 1974 the start of impeachment proceedings in the House of Representatives led to the resignation of President Nixon, and in 1998–9 the long debate over impeaching President Clinton substantially weakened his presidency. The constitutional power of the Senate to 'advise and consent' on the appointment of justices to the Supreme Court, for example, provides an opportunity for the legislature to influence the policy of the judiciary at federal level.

The power to influence executive policies is more important than the power to appoint and remove the political head of state. In Italy, for example, the power to defeat governments so frequently is essentially a negative power, to prevent, not to promote – the politics of 'immobilism' as it has been called.[15] Influencing the decision-making process may be achieved in various ways. Debates and questions may have some effect on the government and certainly serve to inform the government about opinion within the assembly. Even in the most stable party-dominated assemblies, debates may set a chain of events in motion which leads to a change of government.[16] Debates may also present real opportunities to improve legislation, although in parliamentary regimes it may be difficult for a government to accept changes at the floor stage of the proceeding, even if they might improve the legislation.[17]

But even without the drastic consequences of a government falling, the knowledge that in parliamentary regimes a government will have to explain and defend some of its policies in the assembly does lead to some circumspection. This is true even of countries where the government cannot be brought down by an adverse vote in the assembly: in Switzerland the federal council cannot be forced to resign in this way, but a clash with the assembly may still lead to a modification of government policy. The American president frequently consults Congressional leaders to secure support and prevent adverse criticism. For example, President Bush consulted widely with Congressional leaders before embarking on the Gulf War, and President Clinton consulted, albeit less widely, on his various military involvements.

'Semi-presidential' systems such as France and Finland constitute a mixture of the presidential and the parliamentary logics.[18] In France there is a president elected directly by the people as well as a prime minister elected by the National Assembly. Each of these officials has constitutionally prescribed realms of action, and even when they have been members of different political parties – called cohabitation[19] in France – these respective powers appear to have been largely respected. There are elaborate devices for the co-ordination of policy between the two executives and in practice the system appears to have functioned as well when divided as when more unified.[20] The Finnish case is not dissimilar, although in the coalition governments common in Finland the historical dominance of one presidential figure – Kekkonen – has made cohabitation less visible.

Assemblies conduct investigations into government policies, and these can act as a brake on the government motor. These investigations may be carried out by committees of the assembly: the House of Commons Select Committee on Public Accounts in Britain provides an example, consisting of fifteen members and chaired by a leading member of the Opposition. The Committee has no executive power and merely reports back its findings to the House of Commons, but it has acquired a fearsome reputation and governments dread adverse reports. Committees of investigation have been developed more thoroughly in the American Congress. Some are appointed specially, e.g. the Senate Committee led by Senator Ervin, investigating the Watergate affair, while in other cases the standing committees of the Senate and House do the job, e.g. the House Judiciary Committee and the investigations following the Starr Report on President Clinton.

Even when there is not a formal investigation through a committee, or even the legislature as a whole, parliaments engage in some form of oversight. One of the more popular of these forms is the use of questions by members of parliament to the executive on the floor of the legislature. Question Time in the British House of Commons has been made famous by television, but similar procedures are used in most parliamentary bodies.[21] In most cases this form of control is useful primarily as a means of ventilating the issues that concern members and their constituents – few if any governments now fall because of questions posed by ordinary members – and the need to avoid embarrassment can be a spur to better internal controls in government.

Supply of money for government spending has been a traditional weapon in an assembly's arsenal in seeking to exercise some control over government policies; in fact the English House of Commons owes its origin to the need of medieval kings to tax their wealthier subjects. The supply of money may be broken down into several stages, such as the assembly's authorisation to raise revenue, permission to spend money, and as we have seen with the Select Committee of the House of Commons on Public Accounts, legislative post-audits to determine how the money was spent.[22] The details of financial control can be of daunting complexity; the real importance of these powers is found in their use to influence the policies of the government that necessitate spending money – that is, almost any policy of consequence.

Again the United States Congress provides the extreme example of this form of control and influence. Even though the president now proposes the budget, no money can be spent without the approval of Congress; lack of appropriations acts shut down the federal government twice during the 1990s. Further, the Congress has developed the Congressional Budget Office as a means of counteracting the expertise that the Office of Management and Budget has in public expenditure issues.

Even though the president is Commander-in-Chief and has a central position in foreign and defence policy, Congress has been able to influence extensively American defence policies by its control over appropriations; Congress limited further American government aid to the rebels in Nicaragua in the 1980s by using the power of the purse.

Yet the restrictions on influencing policy by means of financial control are obvious even in the most independent of assemblies. Complexity of procedure, the amount of money involved in modern government spending, the lack of time and specialised information and the inability of assemblies to match executive speed of action and united leadership, all these militate against much effective influence. These observations on financial control also have a wider bearing on assembly–executive relations: the increasing power of executives to initiate and realise their own policies is a fact of the twentieth century, and this is particularly true for foreign policy. The United States Congress's constitutional powers in regard to the declaration of war have been eroded by the simple failure of the government actually to declare war in the last three major conflicts: Korea, Vietnam and the Gulf War. The War Powers Act of 1973, passed partly as a result of Nixon's misuse of power in illegally invading Cambodia in 1970, is an attempt to reassert more power over the president in the use of American armed forces.

Of course there is nothing incompatible between strong government and the increased ability of assemblies to influence the political executive: it may be argued that the French Fifth Republic was not so much an attempt to establish a more dictatorial executive against a democratic National Assembly, as a search for a more balanced legislative–executive relationship in place of the ineffective and self-stultifying powers of the Assembly in the Fourth Republic. Likewise, the Bundestag in Germany appears to be a well-organised and effective legislature relative to many in parliamentary regimes but the German government has certainly been effective relative to many others in Europe.[23]

It must also be borne in mind that many assemblies in liberal democratic systems lack the procedural weapons of even the British House of Commons. Questioning the executive on the floor of the assembly is rare in most European parliaments; the French National Assembly introduced immediate oral answer questions for the first time in April 1970. Some assemblies, such as the German Bundestag, rarely make use of the committee of inquiry and there is no provision for votes of confidence without electing a new Chancellor. On the other hand, other assemblies in parliamentary systems have found ways to counteract the powers of the executive and to have an independent impact on policy; the powers of the Danish parliament *vis-à-vis* a whole range of policies (perhaps most interesting, European Union policy) is a prime example.[24]

However, it is impossible to consider the relations between the assembly and the government without emphasising the importance of the party system. Even in the United States Congress, with less party discipline than most of its European counterparts, party membership still remains the most reliable indicator of Congressional voting.[25] Contrary to many fears expressed at the time of the appearance of mass parties at the end of the nineteenth century, power has remained with the parliamentary wings of the parties in liberal democratic systems, not with the mass organisation outside the assembly. Therefore the advent of mass parties has not weakened the power of assemblies as it was assumed it would, and this has allowed parliamentary representatives to behave more in conformity with the liberal democratic ideas of representation that were discussed in the last chapter. Thus, the key to the power structure in most modern assemblies lies in the party system in the assembly itself. This is where the parliamentary leadership and executive support emerges, and this determines the degree of control and influence the assembly exercises.

A final point to be made here is that even quiescent legislatures do have the latent power to exert control over the executive. This became most apparent in 1999 when the European Parliament voted to dismiss the entire European Commission. One of the conventional criticisms of the European Union has been that there is a 'democratic deficit' with the public having little or no real control over the executive – the Commission. The willingness of the parliament to force this resignation may in retrospect be seen as the beginning of a more genuine democratic system at the European level.

Legislative functions

The law-making functions of assemblies may be seen as an extension of the function of influencing the executive. In this area, again as a consequence of administrative complexity and party organisation, the government's initiative is substantial. The capacity of the government of the day to dominate legislation does vary, however, across country and across time (see Table 8.1). In Britain all important and controversial legislation emanates from government sources, and the very few exceptions to this rule need pronounced government support. There is provision for private members' legislation, but this is severely restricted and may, as in the period 1945–51, disappear completely. In the 1979–80 session of parliament 71 government bills were successful, but only ten of 152 private members' bills received the royal assent. In the United States

Table 8.1   Sources and success of legislation

	Government bills as % of total	Government bills passed (percentage)	Private bills passed (percentage)
Austria	65	96	50
Belgium	23	100	7
Denmark	59	84	6
Finland	48	100	1
France	22	82	80
W. Germany	74	100	58
Greece	87	77	1
Ireland	90	10	NA
Italy	29	51	9
Luxembourg	94	100	24
Netherlands	98	85	16
Norway	90	99	12
Portugal	70	14	48
Spain	5	88	11
Sweden	NA	99	1
United Kingdom	92	92	10
AVERAGE	58	86	17

Source: Based on data from the Inter-Parliamentary Union, *Parliaments of the World* (New York: Facts on File, 1992).

Congress almost 80 per cent of the bills considered come from the executive, and the presidential initiative has now become permanent and institutionalised, as illustrated. In other countries (Austria, Germany), however, legislation often comes from individual members or from minority parties, and a good deal of legislative activity is outside the direct control of the government.

The legislature may, in addition, be constitutionally barred from making laws on certain matters: Article 34 of the French 1958 constitution defines the subjects on which the National Assembly can make laws, and those which are the prerogative of the executive. But it is usually the more fundamental constitutional laws that are placed beyond the legal competence of the assembly, and most states provide special procedures for constitutional amendments; for example Belgium requires the election of a special assembly to consider constitutional revisions. Even when legislatures can make changes in the basic law there are requirements for extraordinary majorities, and legislative approval may be only the first step in a long process.

Executives are often armed with powers to veto legislative proposals; this is really only of importance in presidential systems such as the United States where presidential vetoes are rarely overridden by Congress.[26] In parliamentary regimes there is the threat of the dissolution of the assembly, but this is rarely used to discipline the assembly, especially in the more stable party systems of Britain, and was a dead-letter throughout the history of the French Fourth Republic. Most European governments survive for the whole life of the parliament, the main exceptions being those of Italy and Finland. In some countries, e.g. Sweden and Norway, the practice is not to dissolve parliament, preferring to function with minority governments, often very small minorities, rather than create instability through dissolutions.[27]

Most assemblies have provisions for bringing discussion on bills to an end. Closures, guillotines and adjournment debates are devices which can be used to prevent undue delay and obstruction by opposition parties, while still maintaining the rights of minority parties to criticise the sitting government. These devices are firmly entrenched in the constitution of the French Fifth Republic, and they are used quite extensively in the crowded timetable of the British House of Commons. However, they are not universal: the Netherlands, Sweden, Denmark and Norway either have no provision for terminating debate at all, or they simply are not used. This is in part because the consensual nature of these governments permit the parties to negotiate the allocation of time among the parties. The United States Senate provides a good example of unlimited discussion: here it requires the difficult process of petition of sixteen senators backed by two-thirds of those senators present and voting to end a debate, and the ability of a senator to maintain the floor as long as he or she is able – the filibuster – has been the death of many legislative proposals.

In spite of these various obstacles, the legislative activities of assemblies are important. The procedures are a fundamental means of the legitimisation of rules in a society, they provide for some oversight of government activities, and they allow interest groups to operate through their parliamentary representatives. Of course, the extent of the assembly's power in the rule-making process will depend on the strength of the government, the scope of its legislative programme and the immediacy of a general election, but in most liberal democracies it is rare for a government to emerge from the legislative process with its programme unscathed. The Conservative governments after 1979 suffered setbacks in spite of large majorities; in 1986, for example, 70 Conservative MPs voted against the government's Shop Bill to ensure its defeat. In the Spring of 1999 even the massive majority held by Blair's Labour government came into question over a social policy bill, and the long honeymoon in parliament appeared to be over. The government continued to dominate parliament but the renewed understanding that revolts were possible may lessen that domination.

Representative functions

Walter Bagehot once described the functions of the House of Commons as elective (maintaining the government), expressive, teaching, informing and legislative,[28] and it is the expressive, teaching and informing functions that are most relevant to the representative aspects of modern assemblies.

There are elections in the vast majority of modern states, and although the resulting representative assemblies differ in status and power, they share, in varying respects, the function of providing some form of link between government and governed. They are one, but only one, means of channelling demands from below and providing information and explanation from above. Bernard Crick has enlarged Bagehot's description of the functions of the House of Commons: 'The most important actual function of Parliament does not (and normally should not) consist in the threat to overthrow governments or of passing, refusing or amending legislation, but in the need to put relevant facts and fancies before the electorate which does sit in judgements upon governments.[29] The need for governments to be accountable to legislatures, meaning literally to render some account of their actions in a public forum, and the opportunity of the opposition of the legislature to scrutinise that record, are crucial elements in democracies increasingly dominated by the power of the executive.[30]

The seemingly meaningless rituals of much of the procedure that most representative assemblies utilise in the passage of legislation, or the granting of public money, are not explicable in terms of efficiency. Rather, they are better understood in terms of the roles that assemblies play in the legitimation and authorisation of government policy, the resolution of conflicts between groups represented, and the need to speak to a wider political audience than that of the assembly itself. These are important functions in the working of the whole political system and work towards the stability of the system. Further, the rituals provide a means of controlling potential conflict among groups within the assembly by reminding them of the dignity assumed to be involved in their roles.

The place of communist parties in Western European assemblies illustrates the legitimation function of parliaments. These parties have largely been denied participation in governing, and in theory may be aiming at the overthrow of the parliamentary regime, but the fact of their being represented at legislative level in a number of political systems is a safety valve and is a support for the structural status quo. Congressmen in the United States may perhaps cynically work for the defeat of a bill by devious means in order to prevent their having actually to record a vote against the measure and thus anger interests in their constituencies, but what is significant here is the recognition of the link between the representative, legislative activities, and the electorate.

At a more individual level representatives reinforce these links with the public by helping or advising particular constituents. This assistance may only involve guidance in the field of administrative legal rights, and placing some pressures on the bureaucracy for benefits,[31] but the 'social welfare officer' role does become more personalised when the representative seeks to satisfy patronage-seekers looking for government positions; in fact, certain rewards may have already been mortgaged to individuals as the price for supporting and furthering the representative's election to the assembly.

Internal organisation

The manner in which modern assemblies perform these tasks of influencing the executive, legislating and representing wider interests and opinions depends on their organisation and internal procedure. We have already noted that efficiency may not be the goal of assemblies, in that they seek to implement more quickly government policies, especially in regard to legislation; therefore these three separate functions may conflict with each other, and this potential conflict should be remembered when proposals of reform are advanced.

The number of times an assembly meets in a given period and whether the representatives regard their attendance as a full-time occupation or as an addition to some other form of employment, are important aspects of an assembly's effectiveness. The demotion of the French National Assembly under the Fifth Republic was underlined by a reduction in the length of its sessions. We have seen that the Supreme Soviet met very infrequently, and in fact claimed that infrequency was an advantage of the Soviet representative system in that the members of the assembly were not set apart from their electorates. The British House of Commons attempted to extend morning sittings in 1967, but abandoned the experiment because of the hostility of some MPs who argued that involvement in extra-parliamentary employment was a vital aspect of their role as representatives, and certainly the traditional view of the 'amateur' MP remains a significant aspect of parliamentary politics in Britain.

West European assemblies are still vastly inferior to the United States Congress in regard to sources of information and research facilities. This is partly due to American political life being less secretive, but it is also easier for American Congressmen to carry out their duties, especially that of influencing and controlling the executive, because of their separate offices, a vast library, Congressional professional staff and adequate funds to hire personal assistants. The average member of the US Congress will have several dozen employees while legislators in most other systems are fortunate if they have one or two staff members.

The use of committees also may be vital aspects of the internal organisation of assemblies. Using committees has the advantages of division of labour, with its speed and specialisation, a lower degree of formality and a mitigation of the sometimes unreal partisan conflicts that take place on the more publicised floor of the assembly. However, committees provide a most controversial aspect of assembly organisation because the arguments over the advantages and disadvantages of an extended committee system are at the heart of the discussion of what the proper functions of assemblies and the relations of the assembly with the executive are.

Committees, in the main, have two broad functions: that of assisting (in some cases dominating) the legislative process, and that of inquiring into particular problems. Both functions have been developed more thoroughly in the United States than in any other assembly. The committees in the Senate and the House of Representatives monopolise the legislative procedures: bills begin in committee, are discussed and examined there and can be killed in committee without the inconvenience of a formal vote on the floor of either house. At an even greater extreme, legislative committees in Italy are able to pass minor pieces of legislation (*leggine*) on their own. In other cases, e.g. France, the role of committees is limited severely, with only a few committees with little power permitted to exist – the National Assembly is limited to six committees.

The investigatory powers of legislative committees are of great importance. In the American Congress committees specialise in a particular field such as foreign affairs, finance, defence and armed services. Committees also can create a number of subcommittees that can further specialise. Membership on committees and subcommittees varies according to which party has the majority of members, the largest party always supplying the committee chairman and a majority on the committee. The committees, however, have increased their influence *vis-à-vis* the once dominant committee chairmen. Developments during the 1970s and 1980s, such as the weakening of the seniority system as a basis for the selection of chairmen, have tended to fragment further the distribution of power in Congress.[32]

The considerable power of Congressional committees results in part from the lack of Congressional party unity, the absence of centralised leadership, and the immense pressures for local benefits exerted on Congressmen from their constituencies. Critics of the committee system base their arguments on the apparent inefficiency of the legislative process that results from committee dominance, and the ability of Congressional minorities to frustrate majority wishes.[33] It should be remembered that the present committee system is ideal for the reconciling of conflicting interests in American politics. Further, the committee system can enhance the deliberative abilities of Congress and its ability to be a truly transformative legislature.

Committees have emerged as power centres in the German Bundestag: all the important legislative work of the assembly is done in committee, and committees have developed some of the specialisation of their American counterparts. However, a cabinet system (ministers and civil servants have the right to attend committee meetings), the existence of disciplined parties, the lack of information and professional staff, and the failure to develop investigatory powers, have prevented these Bundestag committees from fully rivalling the powers of Congressional committees. Likewise, the Committee on the Constitution in the Swedish Riksdag has rather broad powers to investigate government activities and policies. Another important example of legislative committees organised to monitor and oversee the executive can be found in Denmark, especially in supervising that country's relationships with the European Union.[34]

The committee system of the British House of Commons may be seen as in contrast to that of the American Congress. British committees lack specialisation and are involved in only a limited part of a bill's progress through the House. There have been various attempts since the 1960s to strengthen the committee system of the House of Commons. Following the 1979 election, fourteen select committees were added to the main survivor of the old system, the prestigious Public Accounts Committee. These new committees were an innovation in that they mirrored existing government departments: thus there are now committees on Agriculture, Defence, Transport, etc., and they were given increased powers to hire staff and to call witnesses.

It is still too early to judge how successful these committee reforms are, but they have certainly increased the amount of valuable information to MPs and thus strengthened the Commons in its role as watchdog of the executive.[35] Critics of the new system point to the extra burden on the civil service in preparing evidence for committees, and there are still the old fears that specialised committees interfere with ministerial responsibilities. It is difficult to show where the committees have influenced particular government decisions, even if they do contribute to the climate of informed opinion. In Canada the committee system in the Senate has undertaken some of the same functions as the select committees in the UK parliament,[36] and assemblies in a number of other countries have sought to develop more effective committee systems, especially for the function of controlling the executive.

The argument over committees in representative assemblies is basically that of deciding what the main functions of assemblies are. If members are to rival the executive's sources of information, detail and speed of decision, and seek to pierce the secrecy of the increasingly complex machinery of the administrative process, it would seem that the development of an effective committee system is the only answer. But if the emphasis is on the electoral battle, on publicity rather than on direct policy influence, and on the legitimisation of government directives, then the development of committee systems in modern assemblies is not necessarily the first priority.

Second chambers

So far we have discussed the functions and organisation of assemblies without particular emphasis on whether they are bicameral or unicameral. Most modern assemblies have two chambers, the most prominent exceptions being New Zealand, which abolished the upper house in 1950, and Denmark, which did likewise in 1954, while Sweden followed in 1970.[37] The defence of second chambers rests on two foundations. First, a second chamber widens the basis of representation, or provides for a second form of representation, and second an additional chamber may prevent hasty action by the first, acting as a conservative stabiliser and assisting the first in its many duties.

The argument based on widening the representative basis of the assembly (see Table 8.2) may be readily seen in federal states: the American Senate has two representatives from each of the fifty states, irrespective of population; the Australian Senate has ten members from each of the six states; and the same pattern is followed in other federal states such as Switzerland. In Germany and in Austria, however, representation in the Bundesrat is roughly proportional to population; further, in Germany, the representatives are appointed by the state government rather than being elected.[38] In non-western systems the patterns of representation are roughly the same, with territorial representation being widely spread among these countries.

The Republic of Ireland has a second chamber, in theory based on a type of functional representation, members being elected by different occupations and professions, but the Irish party system modifies this type of representation into a somewhat more partisan institution. In most unitary and parliamentary regimes the second chamber is either appointed or elected indirectly; in contrast, in Norway a single elected chamber divides in two to form a bicameral legislature for a limited number of issues. Also, the second chamber in Japan is

Table 8.2 Size and representative basis of legislatures

	Lower House	Upper House
Algeria	380	144 (1/3 appointed; 2/3 elected by local authorities)
Argentina	259	72 (3 per province)
Bahrain	30	
Belgium	150	71 (25 from Flanders, 15 from Wallonia, 21 from community councils, 10 coopted)
Canada	301	104 (appointed by Governor General)
Denmark	179	
France	577	319 (electoral colleges in *départements*)
Germany	672	69 (appointed by *Land* governments)
Russia	450	198 (2 per constituent unit)
South Africa	400	90 (10 per province, elected by provincial assemblies)
United Kingdom	659	1,213 (26 bishops, 752 hereditary peers, 409 life peers, and 26 Lords of Appeal)
United States	435	100 (2 per state, general election)

elected much as is the lower house of the Diet, but with sixty per cent from constituencies and forty per cent in the country as a whole.

However, widening the representative basis of assemblies in this way is only valid if the second chamber has sufficient power and utility in regard to its supposed functions; but as the Abbé Siéyès once remarked: 'If the second Chamber agrees with the first it is unnecessary: if it disagrees it is pernicious.'

The lower house is usually the more representative chamber measured by the yardstick of majority rule, and it is usually given the predominant role, being allowed ultimately to over-rule the obstruction of the second chamber and also being held responsible for selecting and dismissing governments. However, given the executive origins of the bulk of legislation the obstruction of legislation is often aimed directly at the government, rather than being strictly an issue of enhancing the quality of the legislation.

Certainly second chambers can assist the lower house with the legislative programme, initiating and amending bills, but the real basis for a defence of second chambers is political: second chambers act as a more conservative force in the political system, and must be seen as indicating a fear of liberal representation in the populistic sense. Ironically, the United States Senate, which was not elected directly until the early years of the twentieth century, being previously elected by the state legislatures, has become generally less conservative than the more directly representative House, which is elected *en bloc* every two years. This is in part because cities, and their large minority populations, figure very heavily in the election of senators.

With the major exception of the United States Senate, which is the constitutional equal of, and indeed has more political prestige than, the House of Representatives, most second chambers are politically unimportant, and attempts to increase their powers, as with the Senate in the French Fifth Republic, have failed. There are occasions when the pattern of power in the political system will increase the political importance of the second chamber in parliamentary systems. The power of the House of Lords increased after the 1974 election because the relative strengths of the parties in the British House of Commons had been significantly altered, i.e. no party has a strong independent majority over all the others.[39] It was then again reduced after the 1997 election with its large Labour majority who began to consider eliminating or reducing the power of Lords, although Lords did defeat a 1998 bill on changes in European elections.

The Australian political crisis of December 1975 illustrated this latent power of second chambers; the Senate's opposition to the Labour government's budget led to the Governor General's dismissal of the government and the ultimate defeat of the Labour Party in the ensuing general election. However, occasions on which second chambers are decisive are rare, and, indeed, second chambers are often an embarrassment in that efforts to reform their composition and powers inevitably raise the question of representation and for what purpose second chambers need certain political powers. It would seem that in the absence of the development of some effective form of functional representation – as noted for the Irish Senad – a federal structure provides the greatest relevance for second chambers.

The decline of assemblies?

With the development of mass disciplined parties and the increasing scope and complexity of executive powers in the twentieth century, it is fashionable to talk of the decline of assemblies. However, it must be asked whether the development of parties and the increased power of modern governments have been entirely at the expense of assemblies. In some instances governments need the legitimating capacity of the assembly to make difficult policies. Governments may not be strong enough to resist the various group pressures, and they need parliament to establish links with the electorate to help justify policies, such as cuts in welfare state programmes in Europe in response to entering the Economic and Monetary Union.

Part of the problem is the excessively rosy view of nine-teenth-century liberal representation and the myth of the sovereignty of assemblies. To the extent that this was true the outcome was often stagnation rather than good government. Assemblies have never really 'governed', even in pre-sidential systems such as the United States where there was not such an intimate link between legislative and executive powers as in parliamentary systems. Further, if legislatures did lose power during part of the post-war period they have been organising themselves to control governments more effectively. They have remodelled committee systems (especially by adding more or less permanent committees shadowing ministries), created more staff positions, and generally sought to make themselves more worthy institutional opponents for the political executive.

We therefore return to the representative functions of assemblies and their role as the links between governments and governed. Jean Blondel has pertinently argued that 'While the "decline of legislatures" may be apparent to some – limited – aspects of rule making, the decline of assemblies as communicating mechanisms can scarcely be substantiated.[40] It is a question therefore of whether assemblies can become more efficient in this communicating process. They can be at a disadvantage in this function as well; legislatures are often divided while executives tend to be more unified and capable of presenting a common perspective on policy. In contrast, however, legislators often have very close links with their constituents and are able to communicate better with citizens than can executives.

Notes and references

1. C. Kerwin, *Rulemaking*, 2nd edn (Washington, DC: CQ Press, 1998); R. Baldwin, *Rules and Government* (Oxford: Clarendon Press, 1995).
2. For a comparative discussion of political executive and their rule-making, see J. M. Carey and M. S. Shugart, *Executive Decree Authority* (Cambridge: Cambridge University Press, 1998).
3. See, for a classic study, R. Fenno, *Homestyle: House Members in Their Districts* (Boston: Little, Brown, 1978); also, J. D. Huber, *Rationalizing Parliament: Legislative Institutions and Party Politics in France* (Cambridge: Cambridge University Press, 1996).
4. N. W. Polsby, 'Legislatures', in F. I. Greenstein and N. W. Polsby (eds), *Government Institutions and Processes* (Reading, MA: Addison-Wesley, 1975).
5. See L. Holmes, *Politics in the Communist World* (Oxford, 1986), pp. 154–5; also S. White *et al.*, *Communist and Postcommunist Systems* (London: Macmillan, 1992) pp. 120–2.
6. See C. J. Bailey, 'Congress and Legislative Activism', in *Developments in American Politics*, ed. Gillian Peele *et al.* (London: Macmillan, 1992) pp. 115–37. See also J. E. Owens, 'Congress in the 1980s', *Politics Review*, 1, 3 (February 1992).
7. Huber, *Rationalizing Parliament*.
8. A. Adonis, *Parliament Today* (Manchester: University of Manchester Press, 1990) pp. 93–4.

9. At the extreme, the entire country is a single constituency in several smaller European democracies.
10. Disraeli established the precedent in Britain of offering his resignation immediately after his election defeat instead of awaiting defeat in the House of Commons.
11. K. Gladdish, *Governing from the Centre: Politics and Policymaking in the Netherlands* (London: Hurst, 1993).
12. See pp. 214–15.
13. See Kaare Strom, *Minority Government and Majority Rule* (Cambridge: Cambridge University Press, 1990).
14. Some of these rejections were for partisan reasons, while others were because of real or alleged improprieties by the nominee. The President furthered the poor relations with Congress by appointing the same people on a 'temporary' basis.
15. See Mario Caciagli and D. I. Ketzer, *Italian Politics: The Stalled Transition* (Boulder: Westview, 1996).
16. The famous May 1940 debate in the British House of Commons on Chamberlain's handling of the war led to the fall of his government.
17. The existence of a second house of the legislature, whether elective or not, often provides a locus for accepting amendments. Likewise, government may be able to accept amendments in committee without appearing to have conceded excessively to the opposition. The above having been said, consensual parliamentary systems (as contrasted with the majoritarian Westminster systems) find it easier to accept amendments to legislation.
18. This term was coined by Maurice Duverger, 'A New Political System Model: Semipresidential Government', in A. Lijphart (ed.), *Parliamentary Versus Presidential Government* (Oxford: Oxford University Press, 1990).
19. J. V. Poulard, 'The French Double Executive and The Experience of Cohabitation', *Political Science Quarterly*, 105, pp. 243–67.
20. Roy C. Pierce, 'The Executive Divided Against Itself: Cohabitation in France', *Governance*, 4 (1991), pp. 270–94.
21. See M. Wiberg, *Parliamentary Control in the Nordic Countries: Forms of Questioning and Behavioural Trends* (Jyvaskyla: Finnish Political Science Association, 1994).
22. In most countries auditing is a legislative activity; see A. Gray, B. Jenkins and B. Segsworth, *Budgeting, Auditing and Evaluation* (New Brunswick, NJ: Transaction, 1992).
23. T. Saalfeld, 'The West German Bundestag After 40 Years', *West European Politics*, 13, 3 (1989) pp. 68–89.
24. See Thomas Pedersen, 'EU Policy Coordination in Denmark', in H. Kassim, B. G. Peters and V. Wright, *Coordinating European Policy at the National Level* (Oxford: Oxford University Press, 1999).
25. Party cohesion in Congress has been increasing to levels almost equal to European parliaments, especially among Republicans. See Dean McSweeney and J. E. Owens, *The Republican Takeover of Congress* (New York: St Martin's, 1998).

26. This has been true even when there is a 'divided government' and the president and Congress are of different political parties. The requirement for a two-thirds majority presents a very high barrier to an override.

27. These governments do have the capacity to dissolve parliament but rarely exercise that right.

28. Walter Bagehot, *The English Constitution* (London: Fontana, 1963) pp. 150–4. Also see J. Obler, 'Legislatures and the Survival of Political Systems', *Political Science Quarterly*, 96, 1 (Spring, 1981) pp. 127–39, for a criticism of the functional approach to the study of legislatures.

29. B. Crick, *Reform of Parliament* (London: Weidenfeld & Nicolson, 1968) p. 238.

30. Peter Aucoin, 'Accountability in Public Management: Making Performance Count', in B. G. Peters and D. J. Savoie (eds), *Revitalizing the Public Service* (Montreal: McGill/Queen's University Press, 1999).

31. Morris Fiorina and others have argued that constituency service is crucial for the electoral fortunes of Congressmen. See his *Congress: Keystone of the Washington Establishment*, 2nd edn (New Haven, CT: Yale University Press, 1987).

32. See N. W. Polsby, 'Political Change and the Character of the Contemporary Congress', in *The New American Political System*, 2nd edn, ed. A. King (Washington, DC: American Enterprise Institute, 1990) pp. 29–46.

33. C. J. Deering and S. S. Smith, *Committees in Congress* (Washington, DC: CQ Press, 1997).

34. T. Pedersen, 'EU Policy Coordination in Denmark'.

35. But see M. A. Jogerst, *Reform in the House of Commons: The Select Committee System* (Lexington, KY: University Press of Kentucky, 1993); Matthew Paris, 'The Corridors of Power', *The Times*, 26 June 1998.

36. B. O'Neal, *Senate Committees: Role and Effectiveness* (Ottawa: Library of Parliament, 1994).

37. The majority of the smaller countries of the world have unicameral legislatures; there is little or no reason in these systems for a second chamber that reflects territorial differences.

38. U. Thaysen (1994) *The Bundesrat, the Länder, and German Federalism* (Washington, DC: American Institute for Contemporary German Studies).

39. For a discussion on the role of the Lords, see D. Shell, *The House of Lords* (Hemel Hempstead: Philip Allan, 1992).

40. J. Blondel, *An Introduction to Comparative Government* (London, 1969) p. 390. Also, see J. Blondel, *Comparative Legislatures* (Englewood Cliffs, NJ: Prentice Hall, 1973) pp. 140–2.

9

The Political Executive

Although assemblies have many functions, including those of
law- or rule-making, we have argued that their main function
is that of providing a link between governments and governed.
When we turn to governments and political executives, we find
similar overlapping functions ascribed to the various components of the governmental machine. The political executive is
responsible for executing the law, but increasingly the executive has taken responsibility for making law as well. Especially
in presidential regimes the executive also has a representative
function. As noted in the preceding chapter, many legislatures
have become subservient to the governments drawn from it,
and may be little more than rubber-stamps for the government, and particularly the chief executive.

Area of study

Traditionally a distinction has been made between making
policy and subsequently putting that policy into operation –
rule-making and rule application – and it also has been
customary to distinguish between the different roles of the
political executive and the professional administration. Thus,
according to liberal democratic theory (or at least the Westminster version) the minister made policy and was responsible
to the parliament for that policy-making and also for the policy
implementation of his department, while his or her civil
servants, although not necessarily completely anonymous, were
certainly not politically responsible to the assembly in this way,
only indirectly through the minister.

The distinction between the executive in this political sense,
and the administration in the permanent sense, is difficult to

sustain in practice. It does point to some important differences of status and function, but even in political systems where the dividing line between politicians and civil servants is clearer, it is impossible to see top civil servants without any degree of policy initiative, especially given the increasing complexity and scope of the policy-making process in modern 'welfare' states. Civil servants have a far greater degree of independence and wider powers of policy initiation than constitutional myths will allow; they are as firmly a part of the political process as are parties and pressure groups.[1] The breakdown of the traditional allocation of functions within the political system has progressed further in that not only are bureaucrats seen to trespass into the judicial field, as we shall see later with administrative courts,[2] but the judiciary itself has become equally part of the rule-making and rule application processes.

In some states the distinction between politicians, responsible ultimately to an electorate and owing their political position to a process of party recruitment, and civil servants, trained and selected on the basis of special skills, and ready to implement the commands of their political overlords, is very thin indeed. Unlike British civil servants, their French counterparts are allowed to take part in political party activities, and are less concerned to avoid party labels. In the French Fourth Republic over half the ministers came from civil service backgrounds. Between 1959 and 1988, 80 per cent of foreign ministers, 80 per cent of defence ministers, 75 per cent of finance ministers, 70 per cent of education ministers and all prime ministers came from civil service backgrounds.[3] In the 1990s over a third of all members of parliament in France have civil service backgrounds.[4] Much the same is true of the upper reaches of the German civil service who have partisan affiliations and may be 'politically retired' when there is a change in government.[5] In many other regimes the civil service is a natural source of talent for inclusion in cabinet, especially in crucial economic posts.[6]

In the former USSR it was always difficult to distinguish between 'politicians' and 'bureaucrats'. The communist system was based on the interaction of two huge bureaucracies, that of the Communist Party and that of the state administration. Senior personnel moved easily from one hierarchy to the other and their functions were often blurred, although according to the 1977 Constitution the CPSU was the superior body, playing a leading role for society. One major role of the party *apparat* was to monitor and control the state bureaucracy. Gorbachev's reforms attempted to reduce day-to-day interference of the state bureaucracy in the economy and strengthen the representative institutions; these reforms in turn reduced the Party bureaucracy's supervisory functions and threatened its power and privileges.[7]

As countries that formerly were dominated by the Soviet Union have gained their independence they have had to cope with the tradition of political domination of the bureaucracy, while attempting to implement liberal democracy. This problem is complicated by the relative lack of administrative talent that is not compromised by involvement with the former regime. In some of these countries, as alternation in office has begun to occur, governments have become more concerned with ensuring that the bureaucracy will be in agreement with the intentions of the political leaders.

The dividing lines between political policy-making and bureaucratic implementation are often confused in developing countries. Policy implications are present in all significant administrative behaviour, and in political systems where the development of party systems and other coherent power centres may be lacking, the bureaucrats are less likely to be the passive pawns of political leaders. This was especially true when there were strong cultural differences between the nationalist politicians and the ex-colonial trained civil service. As the public bureaucracy has become more indigenous, however, the tendency to use patronage to control bureaucracy (as well as a means of providing jobs for supporters) has increased, further blurring the line between policy and administration. The argument has been that developing societies require 'committed bureaucracies' in order to propel programmes into society that often impose costs on different segments of that society, but that has been a ready excuse for politicising the bureaucracy.

The extent to which civil servants have trespassed into 'political' areas even in liberal democracies has been emphasised by Richard Rose in relation to British government.[8] He has argued that British political parties are not capable of monopolising the important positions in the machinery of government, and that there is a lack of continuity in the positions that are occupied by party politicians. British government, he argues, does not tend to select politicians with the necessary expertise and experience to rival that of permanent administrators, nor with the encouragement to develop long-term political solutions: the result, argues Rose, is government decision-making by civil servants.[9] That view was formed before both Mrs Thatcher and Mr Blair had demonstrated that leadership from the top can change policy dramatically. Still, in the day-to-day business of running a Department, the civil servants may retain substantial influence.

Thus, it is difficult to make clear-cut distinctions between the career bureaucracy and the political executive composed of prime ministers, chancellors, presidents, and their cabinets in regard to their functions. It will be particularly difficult to distinguish between political executives and their immediate staffs who may, or may not, be members of the 'permanent' civil service but whose task is to serve those at the very summit of government power.[10] Nevertheless, some distinctions can be made, and even at the risk of methodological confusion, it is convenient to separate a discussion of political chief executives of state and their bureaucratic assistants. We will discuss the career service and their role in administration, in Chapter 10.

Chief executives

Terminology presents certain difficulties in discussing chief executives. The terms 'prime minister', 'chancellor' and 'president' mean different things in different political structures: there are substantial variations in the political significance of the presidents of France, the United States and Germany in relation to the distribution of political power in their respective countries. In some political systems there is a distinction between the political head of government and the ceremonial head of state; there is always the division in liberal democratic parliamentary regimes, but in presidential systems such as the United States the roles are fused in one person.

Chief executive powers may not be vested in one person, but dispersed between two or more individuals. In the Soviet Union from the fall of Khrushchev in 1964 up until 1990, when Gorbachev introduced a strong executive presidency, power was concentrated in the hands of the Politburo of the CPSU. The Fifth French Republic allowed the president to exercise more real power than the prime minister, but with the same constitution the 1985 election forced President Mitterrand to concede more power to prime minister Chirac as France entered a period of cohabitation.[11] Constitutional frameworks often hide more than they show about the distribution of political power with regard to chief executives. Richard Neustadt has illustrated the possible divorce between constitutional rights and political power with the anecdote of President Truman contemplating the election of General Eisenhower as his successor in 1952: 'He'll sit here,' Truman would remark (tapping his desk for emphasis), 'and he'll say, "Do this! Do that!" *And nothing will happen.* Poor Ike – it won't be a bit like the army. He'll find it very frustrating.[12]

The generalisation is often made that the twentieth century has seen an increase in the power of chief executives, but even allowing for some historical distortion, we are back to the question asked in the second chapter: power in relation to whom or what?[13] Decision-making by governments and administrations may not be synonymous with the power of chief executives, and we may be in danger of crediting modern governments with a more monolithic nature than they in fact possess. Nazi Germany, far from being a hierarchical pyramid of power relationships, dominated by Hitler, resembled in fact a feudal regime in which the barons fought and intrigued against each other for the attention and favours of the Fuhrer, and the power to cultivate their own private empires away from their leader's interest.[14]

Chief executives in liberal democracies may be divided into prime ministerial and presidential types, although there are exceptions, such as Switzerland with its Federal Council acting almost as a collective presidency. In presidential systems both the political and ceremonial functions of head of state are vested in one man. The American president is elected for a four-year term of office and is limited to only two successive terms by the Twenty-Second Amendment to the Constitution. He is elected directly by the people (by means of the Electoral College), not by Congress, and is not responsible to Congress in any formal manner. Although Congress may control the supply of money, veto nominations and investigate aspects of government machinery and policy, the office of president is far from the Jeffersonian concept of the president as chief servant to implement the will of Congress.

The president and Congress are elected by different constituents at different times, and often a different party controls the presidency and the legislature with no serious consequences for American government.[15] Advisers and cabinet members are chosen with a large degree of political freedom by the president, and modern presidents show an even greater tendency to choose their executive assistants from outside Congress. It has been estimated that whereas in the period 1861–96 37 per cent of cabinet appointments were from Congress, between 1941 and 1963 this figure had dropped to only 15 per cent.[16] Carter, Reagan and Bush continued the tendency to recruit from non-political backgrounds, although the Clinton administration did contain more appointments from Congress. Still, the overwhelming majority of Cabinet appointees come from universities, business and law; few had ever won elective office.[17]

A president or a hereditary monarch may be the ceremonial head of state in parliamentary–cabinet systems of government. The British monarchy monopolises the prestige as formal head of the executive but has a minimum and decreasing degree of political power. The monarch nominally chooses the prime minister, but in reality that decision is made by the political parties and their selection of their own leaders. That task constitutes a major function of other formal heads of state such as the Italian president, and in many political systems that must form coalition governments. The possibility that the 1992 election in Britain might not have produced a clear majority raised the possibility that the Queen would be able to exercise some independent judgement in selecting a prospective prime minister, but that possibility did not materialise. Similarly, the royal assent is necessary before a law can be put into effect, but by convention that is never denied, nor are requests from a prime minister to dissolve parliament and call new elections.

The British prime minister is elected to the House of Commons in the same way as any other MP; he or she must obtain a majority in the lower chamber before forming a government, and that government is, with very few exceptions, chosen from amongst members of both Houses of Parliament. The prime minister and cabinet are 'responsible' to the House of Commons; they must explain and defend their policies in the Commons,[18] and if the Commons withdraws its support of the government, the prime minister either resigns or advises the monarch to dissolve parliament in order to seek fresh support through a general election. The British prime minister dominates the House of Commons far more effectively than the American president does Congress. The reason, however, may lie only partly in the formal constitutional differences and may owe more to the differences in the British and American party systems; even when the president and Congress are from the same party the president cannot depend on support in the legislature.

The communist systems provided illustrations of different types of leadership relations. Formally, executive power was vested in a government or Council of Ministers responsible to parliament. In practice the Communist Party Politburo functioned as the equivalent to a cabinet in a parliamentary democracy. Despite a theoretical commitment to collective leadership, individual leaders often became dominant. From the 1930s Stalin was the subject of a massive programme of campaigns glorifying his role and his achievements, later denounced by his successors as the cult of personality. In Romania, Ceausescu was the object of similar manipulated adulation from the late 1960s; because of the nepotism practised by Ceausescu, the system in Romania was laughingly referred to as 'socialism in one family'. A similar description could have been applied to the regime of Kim Il Sung in North Korea, where the leadership cult was carried to grotesque extremes, and is being continued by his son Kim Jung-Il. However, there are also examples of collective leadership. Hungary under Janos Kadar (1956–88), Poland under Edward Gierek (1970–80), Czechoslovakia under Alexander

Dubcek in 1968, and the USSR during the Andropov–Chernenko 'caretaker' period, following the death of Brezhnev in 1982, are all cases where the leadership was oligarchic rather than individual.

Autocratic systems present more difficulties in the attempts to discuss executive heads. Conservative autocracies such as Saudi Arabia illustrate the exercise of executive chief of state functions by a hereditary monarch, although certain offices common to other systems, such as a prime minister, may exist even if only as figureheads. The relationship between these types of ruling monarchs and their prime ministers resembles the British system in the eighteenth century, or that of Bismarck and the German emperor at the end of the nineteenth century. That is, the prime minister or chancellor is dependent on the support of the monarch, not of any representative assembly, for his continuation in office even where elections take place. Of course, the concentration of executive power in one man may be legitimated through elections; the domination of France between 1851 and 1869 by Louis Napoléon is a most interesting European example of plebiscitary dictatorship. The Portuguese dictator Salazar monopolised executive power between 1932 and 1968, holding only the office of prime minister legitimated through elections.[19]

Military juntas provide a different type of executive structure, and the former Greek dictatorship of the army colonels, 1967–74, is an example of this type of political executive operating within the former formal constitutional structures. Usually the leaders of successful coups or revolutions wish to legitimise the new power structure: the Spanish dictator Franco reintroduced the monarchy in an attempt to stabilise the existing structure after his death. The Brazilian army seized control in 1964 and suspended certain constitutional rights, but secured the election of successive generals as Brazilian presidents, and in the face of opposition passed an emergency act in December 1968 closing Congress and giving almost limitless discretionary power to the president. The Portuguese military junta held a series of elections after the coup of April 1974 to legitimise the new regime, and in an apparently genuine desire to find an alternative form of government.

Origins and stability of chief executives

Chief executives, whether constitutional monarchs, civilian presidents or military dictators, are rarely representative in that they reflect the numerically dominant social classes, ethnic groups, etc., in society. They are produced by powerful groups such as the church or the army, or they are recruited by the major political parties. Armies supply the chief executives in many developing political systems not only because of their monopoly of physical force, but also from the concentration of technical and administrative competence in the armed forces, and sometimes their ability to cut across tribal and other social divisions. Archbishop Makarios, president of Cyprus, provided an interesting example of one source of recruitment, not as common in modern states; and the origins of South African prime ministers before the end of apartheid were determined through the political dominance of one of the two white minorities. But usually, political parties based on a wide franchise have forced traditional élites in society to widen the avenues for political recruitment and promotion. In communist systems the political party becomes the sole source of recruitment, and these states were generally more successful than other authoritarian regimes in resisting army coups.[20]

In liberal democracies executives are recruited from established political élites working through the political parties. Thus, in Britain, Labour prime ministers often have an almost identical social background to that of Conservative prime ministers, and Ramsay MacDonald may be said to have been the only prime minister of working-class origins, although Wilson, Callaghan, Heath, Thatcher and Major were lower middle class in origin. A similar position is found in Germany, although without the same concentration on a few schools and universities as in Britain. The German top political leadership continues to come from the top social strata.[21] The United States provides one of the best examples in a liberal democratic system with options for recruitment of chief executives outside the ranks of the political party professionals. President Eisenhower, who was sought after by both political parties as a presidential candidate, and who is credited with the remark that he did not in fact like politics, was the most recent of the long list of American presidents who were nominated and elected on the basis of non-political achievements. The federal system has provided a training ground for executives, with Presidents Carter, Reagan and Clinton having been state governors.[22]

The processes of achieving the position of chief executive are varied. In socialist regimes the emphasis has been on the manoeuvring within the single party: Stalin achieved supreme power by his control of the party bureaucracy and his subsequent ruthlessness in dealing with party rivals.[23] In these systems there tend to be few autonomous structures for a prospective leader to use as 'opportunity structures' for gaining experience. This places a premium on being able to operate successfully within the party, and to follow the many twists and turns of doctrine. It may also place a premium on patience, as leaders such as Fidel Castro and Mao Tse-Tung have demonstrated remarkable staying power.

In liberal democracies not only is the intra-party battle usual, but there is also the necessity of defeating rival political party leaders in competitive elections, if not always to gain power, at least to retain it. There are also what can be termed the various extra-constitutional means of achieving chief executive power, such as coups and civil wars and perhaps imposition by a foreign power. However, it is difficult to classify some means of achieving executive control as constitutional and others as not. General de Gaulle was invested with chief executive powers in 1958 by the president of the Fourth Republic, but the potential army revolt in Algeria could not be ignored in their decision-making. Hitler was invited to become German chancellor by President Hindenburg in 1933, but since 1930 successive governments had been ruling by emergency decrees, and although the strict letter of the constitutional laws was observed with Hitler's succession, the political situation in Germany made it something of an academic question.

The European Union represents (as it so often does) a unique case in the selection of the executive. The European Commission is selected by national governments, with each country having one or two members depending upon size. In those countries with two representatives the pattern has emerged of having one member from the ruling party or coalition and another from an opposition party.[24] Members of the Commission, despite their national, and political, origins take an oath to place the interest of Europe ahead of national interest. The Commission had been an extremely stable executive prior to 1999 when concepts of parliamentary control began to be realised and the Commission resigned en masse.[25]

The stability of the chief executive varies. Lord Bryce once remarked that 'the problem of constructing a stable executive in a democratic country is indeed so immensely difficult that anything short of failure deserves to be called a success',[26] and this was Bryce's view of the office of American president. The term of office of a president of the United States has only been interrupted by the death of the president, with one exception, Nixon's resignation, and furthermore the nomination for a second term of office of an incumbent is seldom denied to him by his political party. There were signs that the former stability was being threatened by electoral volatility. Ford, in 1976, was the first president since Hoover in 1932 not to be returned to office by the electorate, although he was not originally elected to the presidency. Carter was decisively defeated in 1980 and Bush was defeated after only one term in 1992.

In regard to parliamentary liberal democracies, the examples of France and Italy have been frequently quoted to illustrate the instability of executive leadership, but Sweden, Japan and to a lesser extent Australia, show not only the long domination of government by one party, but the stability of the governments those parties have supported. In Britain since 1945, Attlee in 1951, Home in 1964, Wilson in 1970, Heath in 1974 and Callaghan in 1979 suffered reversals in general elections while holding the office of prime minister, although Conservative dominance from 1979 until 1997 emphasises the stable elements in British cabinet government. In British government the governing party's support for its leader and prime minister is very consistent. No Labour prime minister has been forced out of office by his party, and only Balfour in 1905, Chamberlain in 1940 and Thatcher in 1990 can be said to have lost office through declining support in their own party.[27]

Of course, it is very difficult to discuss the stability of chief executives in liberal democratic systems without reference to the party system and the electoral system; more fractious party systems tend to produce greater political instability, as Italian politics illustrates clearly. The numerous parties and their shifting coalitions have limited the durability of governments in Italy to an average of just over one year. Furthermore, the degree of stability of all these various governments is very similar to the durability of chief executives in authoritarian regimes. Salazar, Mussolini and Hitler held power for thirty-six, twenty-one and twelve years respectively, and Franco ruled for over thirty years. Still, Margaret Thatcher remained in power for twelve years, Helmut Kohl did so for sixteen, and Tage Erlander in Sweden for twenty-three years.

The Soviet Union provided an example of stability and change in socialist systems. Stalin died in 1953 after having monopolised all sources of executive power of the Party and the state. His immediate successor Malenkov became both chairman of the Council of Ministers, the equivalent of prime minister, and chief secretary of the Central Committee of the Communist Party, the most influential position inside the Party. In the ensuing struggle for power with Khrushchev, Malenkov relied on the state executive machinery as opposed to the control of the Party, and his replacement as first secretary of the Party in October 1953 by Khrushchev was followed in 1955 by Bulganin, Khrushchev's ally, replacing Malenkov as chairman of the Council of Ministers. The seal was put on Khrushchev's victory by the expulsion of Malenkov and other opponents from the governing bodies of the Party, the Central Committee and the Presidium, in 1957. In 1958 Khrushchev replaced Bulganin as chairman of the Council of Ministers, and appeared to have followed Stalin's example of concentrating Party and state sources of executive power in his own hands. Khrushchev was successful in his leadership struggle because his political abilities and his career within the Communist Party apparatus enabled him to secure support within the top levels of the Party hierarchy.

Despite the example of Khrushchev, however, the absence of a clear process of succession meant that it was very difficult to remove the leader; consequently, the tenure of leaders was very lengthy indeed. Only Poland saw frequent leadership changes partly because of factionalism within the Communist Party and partly because of the assertiveness of its working class, whose protests were vital in the political upheavals in 1956, 1970, 1980–1 and 1988–9. In the USSR, Gorbachev tried to assure the institutionalisation of leadership in a new presidency, elected by Parliament and subject to a maximum of two five-year terms of office. In the then Soviet republics, direct election of presidents, including Boris Yeltsin in Russia in June 1991, facilitated the transition from republic to independent statehood following the failed coup of August 1991.

Functions and powers of chief executives

Putting on one side the ceremonial functions of the formal head of state or the formal functions of the political executive, the most important function of the chief political executive is that of providing policy-making leadership to the government, and this gives rise to definitional boundary problems. The traditional areas of executive action, such as foreign policy, defence and internal policing, have been joined by the crucial roles modern governments play in the management of the economy and in attempting to satisfy demands for social welfare. It is these additional functions that have increased the complexity of the decision-making process and increased the size of modern bureaucracies, with the political executive having to ensure co-ordination throughout the whole government machine. A nineteenth-century British prime minister such as Robert Peel could participate in all the decision-making of central government, but modern chief executives must delegate in ways that allow, for example, such an important piece of legislation as the 1944 Education Act to weave its way through the House of Commons without once being considered by the cabinet.

The increased scope of modern governments has been partly the result of technological changes, but a significant factor in the twentieth century in major political systems has been the totality of modern wars. As A. J. P. Taylor has pointed out: 'Until August 1914 a sensible law-abiding Englishman could pass through life and hardly notice the existence of the state beyond the post office and the policeman.[28] For Americans the Cold War ended a pattern of the state retreating after military conflicts, so that there was a continuing presence of government in a way never before experienced. Even for many minor military powers the expense of modern weapons and their potential for destruction impose very large fiscal and organisational costs on those governments.

One area in which the chief executive is most active is that of foreign policy. The degree of freedom in this sphere is due partly to reduced electoral considerations and partly to the need for speed and secrecy of action. The Cuban missile crisis of 1962 is an illustration of the speed of response and personal decision-making by Kennedy and Khrushchev. There was little opportunity to consult and win approval of other power centres in the American system on the part of President Kennedy, although he was constantly explaining his actions in public.[29] The episode underlined the comments of Woodrow Wilson in 1908, four years before he became American president: 'One of the greatest of the President's powers . . . [is] his control which is very absolute, of the foreign relations of the nation.' The power of the American president in 1962, or in relation to the Vietnam war, can be paralleled in parliamentary systems by the power of the British prime minister during the Suez and Falklands crises of 1956 and 1982, and by the Israeli prime minister during the various crises sustained by that country.[30]

A significant area of chief executive responsibility is that which demands emergency action in the constitutional sense. All modern executives have developed a degree of freedom in defining emergencies and an increase of power to deal with them. The British government was granted dictatorial powers by the Emergency Powers Act of 1940, which passed through all its parliamentary stages in a single day, and gave unlimited power in practice to the government over citizens and their property. Article 16 of the French constitution of 1958 reads:

When there exists a serious and immediate threat to the institutions of the Republic, the independence of the Nation, the integrity of its territory or the fulfilment of its interna-

tional obligations, and the regular functioning of the constitutional public authorities has been interrupted, the President of the Republic takes the measures required by the
circumstances, after consulting officially the Prime Minister,
the Presidents of the Assemblies and the Constitutional
Council.

This was used in 1961. Gandhi declared a state of emergency
in India in 1975, and in Poland Jaruzelski declared martial law
in 1981. Executive pronouncements of 'states of emergency' are
far more common in third world states of South America and
Africa than they are in liberal democracies.

Chief executives and the political process

The claim of decreasing control of governments and increasing
scope of administrative activity is not necessarily to be equated
with the increased power of governments or chief executives.
Certainly presidents, prime ministers and chancellors are at the
centre of government activity and their power to appoint the
rest of the members of the government is a very real power
indeed. However, as Richard Neustadt has observed in a
perceptive analysis of the power of the American presidency,
the process of influence must go further than the mere power to
appoint and dismiss; it must be a continual ability to personally affect the behaviour of those he has appointed. Thus
President Truman's dismissal of General MacArthur during
the Korean War, far from being an example of presidential
power, was in fact a confession of weakness: Truman had failed
to influence events by other means, and the dismissal of such an
important figure as MacArthur, with the severe political
consequences that it entailed, was a last resort on the part of
the president.[23]

Chief executives rarely have a free hand in the selection and
appointment of members of their governments; electoral considerations, the party balance of power, and the danger in
leaving outside the government prominent rivals who could
become a centre for discontent, act as restraints. The ability to

survive is not a true indication of executive power, but a number of concessions have to be made to ensure the internal party (or coalition) support that makes survival possible. Harold Macmillan dismissed a third of his cabinet in 1962, and this, it could be argued, was an illustration of the power of the British prime minister, but the dismissals were partly dictated by the fall in the electoral popularity of the government; they lessened the scope for further changes, and they may have been connected with the willingness of Macmillan to resign in 1963. Likewise the systematic devaluing of the 'wets' in the Conservative Party by Mrs Thatcher reduced the appeal and the talent pool for Cabinet.

The office of chief executive, whether prime minister, president, etc., does invest the individuals concerned with authority that they do not possess as politicians, and this strengthens their position against potential rivals. Moreover, the publicity and the opportunities to exploit the mass media are important factors: Charles de Gaulle was a master in the utilisation of television, and his carefully staged press conferences were designed to create the impression of aloof royalty unsullied by the real world of political bargaining and compromise. With political recruitment falling more and more into the hands of political parties, it is rare for a head of government to reach the top position without the ability and personality for political advancement: political parties in both socialist and liberal democratic systems provide thorough selection processes, and the party is the key to executive stability in these systems.

An important aspect of the power of chief executives is the relationship with other members of the government. Observers of the British prime minister's relations with the cabinet have stressed the interdependence of the two and have emphasised the complexity of the relationship.[31] A significant aspect of the chief executive's position *vis-à-vis* other members of his government is the growth of the leader's personal secretariat, which is drawn from outside the ranks of the party and the professional civil service. It provides individual advisers and a barrier between the leader and the rest of the government.

There is the President's Office in France and the Prime Minister's Office in Britain, but the most developed is the

American president's White House Office.[32] The American president has a formal cabinet which since the Eisenhower presidency has infrequent full meetings. Far more important is the Executive Office of the President, created in 1939, of which a principal part is the White House Office. It consists of personal advisers who are directly responsible to the president and who assist with co-ordination within the administration, relations with Congress, speech-writing, press relations and policy advice. This 'praetorian guard', as it has been called, is successful in even protecting the president from his own cabinet; the careers of Donald Regan with President Reagan, and John Sununu with Bush, provide good examples of this protection.[33] However, the danger of any personal body of advisers is that they may insulate the leader too effectively from outside political pressures, which may result in party or electoral disaster.

There are various bases of support that a modern government leader must secure to ensure his retention of office: the distribution of power within the political party; relations with the assembly; electoral connections with public; and the co-operation of powerful pressure groups, such as business, labour or the church. The loyalty of the armed forces is a factor for preserving a leadership position in some political systems. But apart from these 'external' considerations, the most difficult problem is to ensure effective control and overseeing of the whole administrative structure of government; this is the most subtle, and the hardest to paint in black and white. A leader can organise and reorganise the structure of the administrative machine and the political controls, and he may have full constitutional powers of appointment and dismissal and wide opportunities for patronage, but the complicated machinery of the modern state may still defy him. Richard Neustadt has summed up aspects of this approach to executive power when commenting on the power of the British prime minister:

> The P.M.'s hold on ministers at most times is so great that he can have his way with them in matters of this sort if he is determined to. On the other hand his hold on civil servants is tenuous, and that's the real separation of power in the British system, as I understand it.[34]

Cabinets

As well as the leading players in the drama of government, there are a number of supporting actors. Even in presidential regimes the chief executive has a cabinet composed of other political executives, each of whom generally is responsible for managing a department of government. Also, it is probably inappropriate to refer to these as supporting players, given that each tends to be a powerful political actor in his or her own right. Even when it is clear that the prime minister is more than *primus inter pares*, as the convention in Britain once was deemed to be, the cabinet represents not only the executive power in government but also a number of political fiefdoms, the power of which must be reckoned with by any successful prime minister.

Forming a cabinet is one of the most important things that a prime minister will do during his or her term of office.[35] The membership of a cabinet represents a number of different considerations that must be balanced. In coalition governments the most important consideration will be allocating portfolios among parties in a way that will secure all their participation in the government. Often small parties that are crucial for the coalition are able to ext more important positions than their relative size might appear to merit. For example, during the long tenure of the Kohl government the Free Democrats were able to hold the Foreign Ministry; the tradition was continued in the Social Democratic-led government formed in 1998 with the Greens being allocated the Foreign Ministry.[36] In some cases the cabinet may have to be expanded in order to accommodate all the parties and their representatives.

Even in single party governments there is usually a need to balance a variety of considerations. Most parties sufficiently large to form a government will have a variety of factions that will need to be accommodated. Failure to take into account the variety of opinions within a party may lead to the eventual demise of a political leader; Mrs Thatcher's drive to eliminate the 'wets' within the Conservative Party reduced her overall base of support. Parties may also want to produce a regional balance in the party – any Canadian government will require ministers from Ontario, Quebec, the Maritimes and the West. Governments may also have to balance according to ethnicity, gender and a host of other socio-economic factors.

Once selected for office ministers generally find they have taken a nearly impossible job. In addition to their first jobs as members of parliament, and the representative of a constituency, a minister must take responsibility for policy and management in what may be an extremely large and complex department. In some cases a department may be the largest single organisation in the country; although not a ministerial department, the National Health Service is a part of government and is the largest single organisation in Europe. A minister is also a member of the collectivity of cabinet, and must participate in its meetings, and in the meetings of numerous cabinet committees.[37] He or she must also meet with a number of interest groups attempting to influence public policy. All these duties add up to the simple fact that many ministers report a tremendous workload and difficulties in meeting all the requirements of their job.

The use of committees as a means of structuring the cabinet provides advantages and disadvantages, especially when the political goal is some form of collective decision-making. On the one hand, committees constitute yet another set of responsibilities for ministers, and take that much more time. On the other hand, committees do allow ministers to make policy and budgetary trade-offs among themselves and to reach compromises across a range of policy areas. This has been most apparent when committees are heavily involved in setting budgetary priorities, as in envelope budgeting in Canada.[38]

Given the above problems, some governments have attempted to find ways for ministers to be able to manage their departments more effectively. Most of these methods depend upon reducing the time that the minister must spend on parliamentary duties. In France and Norway when a member of parliament becomes a minister he or she must leave the parliamentary seat (generally in favour of a pre-specified alternative).[39] In Austria and Sweden, and in some instances in Germany, ministers are co-opted from outside parliament, providing both substantive expertise and more time to do the job. Other governments provide ministers with ample personal staff to assist in doing the job, and particularly in controlling the bureaucracy within the department. For example, French and Belgian ministers have substantial *cabinets* to assist them in both making and implementing policy. The concern about losing policy-making authority to the bureaucracy has prompted a number of other countries to consider providing more personal staff to ministers, even when the bureaucracy has been politically neutral and well-respected.[40]

The organisation and the nature of the political controls over the bureaucracy are, therefore, important aspects of government structure, and it is to this side of the government machine that we will now turn our attention.

Notes and references

1. See J. D. Aberbach, R. D. Putnam and B. A. Rockman, *Bureaucrats and Politicians in Western Democracies* (Cambridge, MA: Harvard University Press, 1981) for the view of the bureaucrats themselves on their role. For critical views from politicians see Margaret Thatcher, *The Downing Street Years* (New York: Harper Collins, 1993).
2. See pp. 243–4.
3. See V. Wright, *The Government and Politics of France*, 3rd edn (London: Hutchinson, 1989) p. 112.
4. Luc Rouban, *The French Civil Service* (Paris: La Documentation Française, 1998).
5. R. Mayntz and H.-U. Derlien, 'Party Patronage and the Politicization of the West German Administrative Elite 1970–1987 – Toward Hybridization?', *Governance*, 2 (1989) pp. 381–481.
6. See J. Blondel, 'Ministerial Careers and the Nature of Parliamentary Government', *European Journal of Political Research*, 16 (1988) pp. 51–71.
7. See S. White, *Gorbachev and After*, 3rd edn (Cambridge: Cambridge University Press, 1992).
8. R. Rose, *The Problem of Party Government* (London: Macmillan, 1974) pp. 379–426. See also R. Rose, *Do Parties Make a Difference?*, 2nd edn (London: Macmillan, 1984).
9. There is a good deal of popular and academic work on the general theme of bureaucratic domination. For a summary see B. G. Peters, 'The Problem of Bureaucratic Government', *Journal of Politics*, 43 (1981).
10. See B. G. Peters, R. A. W. Rhodes and V. Wright, *Administering the Summit* (London: Macmillan, 1999).
11. That is, there was a president from one party (Socialist) and a premier from the other major grouping (Gaullist).

12. R. E. Neustadt, *Presidential Power*, rev. edn (New York: Free Press, 1980) p. 9.

13. See Kurt Von Mettenheim (ed.), *Presidential Institutions and Democratic Politics* (Baltimore: Johns Hopkins University Press, 1997).

14. For an account of the Nazi regime, see Robert Koehl, 'Feudal Aspects of National Socialism', *American Political Science Review*, 54, 4 (Dec. 1960) pp. 921–33.

15. David Mayhew argues that 'divided government' has had little discernible effect on the policy output of American government. See his *Divided We Govern* (New Haven: Yale University Press, 1994).

16. S. P. Huntington, 'Congressional Responses to the 20th Century', in *Congress and America's Future*, ed. D. B. Truman (Englewood Cliffs, NJ: Prentice-Hall, 1965) ch. 1.

17. See J. W. Riddlesperger and J. D. King, 'Presidential Appointments to the Cabinet. Executive Office, and the White House Staff', *Presidential Studies Quarterly*, 16, 4 (Fall, 1986) pp. 691–9.

18. See G. Marshall, *Ministerial Responsibility* (Oxford: Oxford University Press, 1989); D. Judge, *The Parliamentary State* (London: Sage, 1993).

19. See Antonio de Figueiredo, *Portugal: Fifty Years of Dictatorship* (New York: Holmes & Meier, 1975).

20. See Chapter 12. In Poland the Communist Party in effect abdicated power to the military authorities in December 1981. In a number of Communist systems the military, e.g. the PLA in China, is closely connected with power.

21. See L. Edinger, *West German Politics* (New York: HarperCollins, 1986) pp. 124–34.

22. The other major source of recent presidents has been the United States Senate, e.g. Harry S. Truman, John F. Kennedy, Lyndon B. Johnson.

23. See I. Deutscher, *Stalin* (Oxford: Oxford University Press, 1967) chs 7, 8, 9.

24. See N. Nugent, *At the Heart of the Union: The European Commission* (London: Macmillan, 1997).

25. M. Smith, 'Balance of Power: Parliament's Role of President Breaker', *Financial Times*, 17 March 1999.

26. James Bryce, *The American Commonwealth*, 3rd edn (New York: Macmillan, 1928) vol. 1, p. 72.

27. For the fall of Margaret Thatcher, see A. Watkins, *A Conservative Coup: The Fall of Margaret Thatcher* (London, 1992).

28. A. J. P. Taylor, *English History, 1914–1945* (Oxford University Press, 1965) p. 1.

29. G. T. Allison, *Essence of Decision* (Boston: Little, Brown, 1971).

30. The best account of the Suez operation and the power of Eden, the Prime Minister, is that by a member of the government at the time, Anthony Nutting, *No End of a Lesson* (London, 1967). On the 1982 Falklands War, see M. Hastings and S. Jenkins, *The Battle for the Falklands* (London: Pan, 1983).

31. See P. Dunleavy *et al.*, 'Prime Minister, Cabinet and Core Executive', *Public Administration*, 68, 1 (Spring 1990). Also P. Madgwick, *British*

Government: The Central Executive Territory (Hemel Hempstead: Harvester, 1991).

32. See B. G. Peters, R. A. W. Rhodes and V. Wright, *Administering the Summit* (London: Macmillan, forthcoming).

33. See D. T. Regan, *For the Record* (London, 1988). For Sununu, see C. Campbell, 'Presidential Leadership', in *Developments in American Politics*, ed. G. Peele *et al.* (Basingstoke: Macmillan, 1992) pp. 102–8.

34. R. E. Neustadt, '10 Downing Street', in Anthony King, ed. *The British Prime Minister*, 2nd edn (London: Macmillan, 1985) p. 150. Neustadt continues, however, to argue that the PM's control would be greater if the British developed the PM's Private Office on the lines of the American White House Office. See K Berrill, 'Strength at the Centre – The Case for a Prime Minister's Department', in *The British Prime Minister*, pp. 242–57. See also M. Holmes, *The First Thatcher Government, 1979–1983* (Brighton: Wheatsheaf, 1985) pp. 29–34.

35. For an unusually rich account of making and maintaining cabinets, see O. Ruin, *Tage Erlander: Serving the Welfare State, 1946–1969* (Pittsburgh: University of Pittsburgh Press, 1990).

36. This is true even though foreign policy issues are relatively low on the priority list of the Greens.

37. T. T. Mackie and B. W. Hogwood (eds), *Unlocking the Cabinet* (London: Sage, 1985).

38. D. J. Savoie, *Public Spending in Canada* (Toronto: University of Toronto Press, 1990).

39. In France this was designed in part to prevent governmental instability; if a government falls then the former minister is out of a job.

40. See D. J. Savoie, *Reagan, Thatcher, Mulroney: In Search of a New Bureaucracy* (Pittsburgh: University of Pittsburgh Press, 1994).

10

The Public Bureaucracy

Bureaucracy has negative connotations for most citizens. It implies inefficiency, rigidity, impersonal rules, unexplained decisions and a host of other forms of maladministration.[1] Despite the connotations, the exact meaning of bureaucracy is simply a formal structure of offices governed by authority and rules.[2] Further, despite its generally negative connotations, bureaucracy – or more generally public administration – is crucial to the success of government, and, certainly more than any other part of the public sector, has been involved in a process of reforming itself and of attempting to discover new ways to serve the public better.[3] Rather than dismissing the bureaucracy as a clumsy instrument of self-aggrandisement, we need to understand how it actually does its job.

Scope of government administration

We have seen that it is difficult to draw a hard-and-fast line between the policy-making of governments and the implementation of these policies by professional administrators,[4] and that the increased number of activities of modern states have emphasised the roles and the size of modern bureaucracies.[5] The social policy fields of public health and the 'social safety net' have joined traditional defining functions of the state (policing and tax collection) and activities concerned with economic regulation and control.[6] In some countries the increased level of control over large industries took the form of direct ownership of electricity, gas, railways, road and air transport, banking and other service and production industries, all of which has necessitated a large expansion of the public service.

The seemingly unstoppable expansion of government has been halted and even reversed in many countries. The post-communist states are attempting a massive withdrawal of the state from the economy. In the old system of central planning in communist regimes, political authorities determined the volume and methods of production and distribution. Now those states face the task of dismantling a governing system based largely on public ownership, and then introducing private ownership regulated by the market. In many West European systems there has also been large-scale privatisation of nationalised industries.[7] In some less-developed countries there has also been a reduction of the economic role of government as the appeal of markets has increased, and international organisations have stressed the need to make economies more competitive.[8]

This is not to seize on some new aspect of human organisation and relate it to modern political developments: public administration is a continuing feature of all political structures, but the size and the capabilities of modern bureaucracies present differences in degree (see Table 10.1). Even in the United States, where federal government interference in the economic field is relatively low compared with other liberal democracies, there are now almost two million federal civil servants, and new areas such as space exploration are naturally dominated by government agencies; state and local government in the United States employ another 17 million people.[9] In the United Kingdom there are now over 596,000 civil servants, and this does not include the (now relatively few) personnel still employed by the nationalised industries, nor does it count the uniformed military. This formal figure for public employment represents some juggling of figures, including moving National Health Service employment outside the public sector.

Professional administrators usually have a degree of permanence denied to the politicians in most political systems. Their expertise, career specialisation, ability to control sources of technical information, sometimes a group solidarity directed against their political masters or their clients, as well as hierarchical structures necessitated by their increased numbers and specialisation and division of labour, can create additional

Table 10.1   Relative size of public bureaucracies (public employees as a percentage of labour force)

United States	16.8
Switzerland	16.9
Australia	16.7
Germany	13.2
Spain	19.3
United Kingdom	20.4
New Zealand	17.6
France	22.8
Denmark	29.4
Sweden	31.1

obstacles to political control.[10] Although their political 'masters' may want to control the bureaucracy, the expertise of the bureaucracy is crucial for effective government and the success of any elected government.

In some political systems the bureaucracy provides the stability, coherence and continuity that is absent from other political structures: it is claimed that the economic strides made by France during the 1950s were largely the result of the excellence of the permanent administrators, in the face of numerous changes of prime ministers and general government instability in that system.[11] In Germany the public administration inspires greater trust than the politicians,[12] and as in France before 1958, bureaucratic continuity has bridged the gaps between the many political upheavals of the twentieth century. In many third world countries the bureaucracy, though perhaps less permanent than in liberal democracies, provides the stability and expertise needed to reach developmental goals.[13]

Structure

The degree of decentralisation is an important aspect of the administrative structure. As one would expect, in most federal systems the majority of civil servants are recruited and controlled by the state and provincial governments (see Table 10.1). However, decentralisation of this sort may vary: federal functions may be carried out by the state civil service under the supervision of the federal government, or there may be parallel structures with the federal civil servants operating at state level to implement the policies of the federal government. The constitutional division of functions between the central government and the smaller units may merely leave less important functions to the state or provincial governments, or that distinction may be a function of cultural and historical factors.[14]

Federalism is but one aspect of decentralisation or devolution; the federal system of the United States allows for many important functions to be performed at local and state levels, but the federal administrative structure itself is far from unified. It is less a hierarchy than it is a holding company.[15] In addition to the formal structure of fourteen cabinet level departments there are independent regulatory commissions such as the Interstate Commerce Commission or the Federal Communications Commission created by Congress, and a number of independent executive agencies responsible directly to the President. Further, the subdivisions of the cabinet departments tend to have a legal basis of their organisation and have their purposes defined in their statutes. Some agencies, such as the Federal Bureau of Investigation, have more political 'clout' than the departments within which they are housed.

There are two major reasons for this lack of unity. First, there is the division of powers between the president and the legislature: Congress creates most agencies and controls their funds, and therefore they tend to act not as part of a coherent executive machine but rather more independently of the presidency. These agencies tend to promote their own programmes, and they can play Congress and presidency off against each other to advance their own policy or organisational goals, in fact often behaving like other pressure groups in the American political system.[16] Secondly, the top appointments in the American administrative structure are given not to career civil servants but to political appointees of the president, and therefore there is less sense of unity within departments, agencies and bureaux, or between them. Over three thousand posts now may change hands with the change of presidents.[17]

The British and French administrative structures are far more hierarchical and centralised than the American model, in spite of their own problems of co-ordination and departmental rivalry.[18] This is not to say that there is necessarily more political control over the bureaucracy, or that there are not individual traditions and styles within different ministries. It does mean, however, that the absence of a political civil service at the top, and a more standardised system of recruitment, tends to create more consistent self-regulation within the administration, and the various departments do act less as independent, self-contained power centres.[19] In both countries subnational regions are less important components of the administrative system, although the socialist government of President Mitterrand decentralised public administration significantly, in part by weakening the role of the prefects, traditionally the agents of central government in the departments.[20]

In Britain, the most important functions remain the monopoly of the central government, and there is increasing use of non-elected government agencies, such as urban development corporations, to bypass elected and therefore less pliant local authorities.[21] The central government also has been imposing a number of constraints on the behaviour of local authorities – for example compulsory competitive tendering – that also restrict the capacity of those authorities to act autonomously.[22] That having been said, however, the devolution of powers to the Welsh parliament, and particularly to the Scottish parliament, will tend to introduce more decentralisation into the making and implementation of policy.

The structures of bureaucracies cannot be classified easily into liberal democratic and non-liberal democratic categories. All bureaucracies are organised largely along functional lines, almost regardless of the political system within which they function. Nevertheless, there are important differences between the various systems. Communist systems, whether federal, as was the case with the former Soviet Union, or unitary such as China, have always been characterised by two features:

centralisation and party control. Both factors have complicated the bureaucratic realities in these states. Functional and personnel overlap of party and state bureaucracy is an enduring feature of the remaining communist systems.[23]

Post-communist systems have not been able yet to free themselves from many of their former organisational problems. There is no longer party control but there is still the necessity to employ the old administrative personnel despite structures evolving on liberal democratic lines; there is often no other source of the expertise necessary to manage a complex political system.[24] In the remaining authoritarian political systems, especially those in the third world, the key characteristics are the relatively large size, corruption, and patronage of bureaucracies. This is true despite the nature of their formal structures, often inherited from colonial times, that appear very like those in more developed political systems.

In all systems, the bureaucratic structures exhibit a large degree of independence in practice – no matter how closely they may be controlled by the political élites in theory. The 1966 Cultural Revolution in China was partly an attempt to subordinate the bureaucracy to 'the people'. In spite of the official emphasis on unity in communist systems, like elsewhere there is competition between various sections of the administrative system and 'departmentalism' is continually being criticised by the higher party officials. In democratic political systems the perennial problem of political accountability points to the difficulties of exercising effective control over bureaucracies, especially as those governments become larger and seemingly more remote.[25]

Functions

We have already seen that a rigid distinction between rule-making and rule application is difficult, and that the policy-making process, even in liberal democracies where the division is possibly easier, has to be defined broadly. This blurring of functions is inevitable given the extent of governmental activity and the permanence and specialised skills of the civil servants. Yet it would be wrong to emphasise this policy-making function unduly: there are important external controls, and some bureaucratic systems develop traditions that inhibit the civil servants from straying too far into what is regarded as the political decision-making field. In other cases – many countries in the third world for example – the bureaucracy may be the only source of effective policy advice and policy-making.[26]

Besides, the degree of policy-making initiative left to top permanent administrators depends on the nature of the political leadership provided by the ministers. Some ministers and heads of departments are more pliable mouthpieces of their civil servants and may lack political support to challenge their own administrators. For example, the British Ministry of Energy, in the late 1970s, successfully fought for the installation of the American type of nuclear reactor despite the opposition of the Minister himself.[27] The French Ministry of Education has always attracted more 'leftist' anti-clericals than other departments; the American State Department has had important influences on presidential foreign policy-making since 1945, especially in regard to relations with the former USSR; this was true despite the presence of the National Security Council advising the President directly.[28] The American Central Intelligence Agency is credited with both a large degree of independence and a great deal of initiative in various fields of American defence and foreign policy, and was particularly saddled with the responsibility for the disastrous Bay of Pigs (the attempted invasion of Cuba) episode in 1961.[29]

Of course it is difficult always to distinguish political and civil service influences: a consistent departmental policy may reflect consensus amongst the political leaders as much as the ability of the civil service to impose its approach to certain policies. The consistency of British foreign policy, at least in its main outlines, reflects more a widely based agreement in this area of policy-making since 1945 than a developed policy imposed by the permanent administrators in the Foreign Office. There was, however, a degree of conflict between politicians and the Foreign Office over the future of the Falkland Islands before the Argentine invasion in April 1982, and the Department was heavily criticised when the crisis broke.

Policy implementation at all levels is one major task of bureaucracies. They also assist ministers in their relations with assemblies in such fields as briefing ministers for questions and parliamentary committees of investigation, and drafting legislation are functions of the civil service. We have already noted[30] the growth of initiative in legislative activities on the part of the executive even in systems that emphasise the separation of executive and legislative powers. The importance of these law-making functions has been enhanced with the increased powers of governments to frame rules and regulations with less reference to the legislature than the normal rule-making process requires. In Britain these are referred to as 'statutory instruments': the government, under wide powers previously granted by the legislature, may propose and implement rules and regulations which, although supervised by parliament through a select committee and possibly requiring formal parliamentary consent, in practice give the executive great freedom of action. The definition of a 'legislative' sphere in the French Fifth Republic, reserving some areas to the executive, is a more ambitious attempt in the exercise of delegated legislative functions.[31]

Administrators also take part in the process of bargaining, consulting and negotiating with pressure groups, and we have seen[32] the important obstacles that the civil service may present to the groups' bargaining power because of the fact that fewer political sanctions can be applied to the permanent administrators compared with the politicians. Often the permanent officials, backed by a traditional pride in their own impartiality, see themselves as the main protectors of what they define as the 'national interest' between the conflicting political demands of rival groups in the political system.

This pride in the professional competence of the permanent civil servants may sometimes amount to a degree of condescension to the politicians, who are subject to the winds of electoral change or intra-party rivalries, and may play an important part in the civil servants' attitudes to the political process. The permanent administrators may feel that only they can judge what is in the general interest, and that they are more competent in the fields of initiation, implementation and supervision of policy. This emphasis on the rationality and objectivity of bureaucracies is identified with Max Weber: his Ideal Type of bureaucracy is one in which there is a hierarchical structure, fixed rules and a clear division of labour. All is orderly, objective, rational and therefore efficient.[33]

The bureaucracy, given such pride and self-respect, may become an important stabilising force within the political system. We have referred to the roles of the civil service during the political upheavals in France and Germany in the last half-century, and this may sometimes be an even more important function of bureaucracies in developing societies with tribal or ethnic divisions, poverty, lack of industrialisation and a weakly structured party system without effective pressure group activity on the wider scale of more developed countries. Ralph Braibanti emphasised these functions with regard to Pakistan during the early days of its independence: 'It is assumed that in Pakistan for the foreseeable future the Bureaucracy will be the principal factor in determining, interpreting, and safeguarding the policy of the state'; and he speaks of the 'Platonic guardianship' dominant in the civil service.[34] This statement does not imply that bureaucracies always perform these functions in all political systems, but rather that there may be a stage of dominance of the bureaucracy during development in which the education and the commitment of civil servants will be crucial to the capacity to govern effectively.

This stabilising function may be linked to the conservative role of bureaucracies in more economically advanced liberal democracies. The British civil service has been criticised for its timidity and fear of innovation in the policy-making process. The stereotype of the British civil servant has been as an anonymous, impartial adviser and executor of ministerial policy; unlike the French civil servant, he or she is said to believe that the primary responsibility is not to plan for the future, but to administer the present. British higher civil servants may not take part in national politics (beyond voting and other limited involvement), and certainly cannot become parliamentary candidates. French (and many other Continental) civil servants have far more freedom, and if they are elected to parliament, they are placed on leave; if defeated, they simply return to their posts in the administration.

The bureaucracy in some systems may be an important source of patronage for parties and government leaders: posts in the civil service can provide rewards for political support.

The 1854 *Report on the Organisation of the Permanent Civil Service,* known as the Northcote–Trevelyan Report, advocated competitive entry to the British civil service supervised by the Civil Service Commission, which was to be an independent body. Some of the criticisms of the report were based on the fear that the end of the patronage system would result in the collapse of the British party system, although patronage was already in the process of disappearing before the report. The United States combined patronage and merit for the selection of its top civil servants, and the number of posts directly under the control of the president serve as rewards he can make to political supporters and backers in the electoral and party struggle for the presidency.

To some extent, however, these appointees are no longer completely patronage appointments and the appointees are members of the 'networks' or 'communities' that surround each policy area.[35]

A final important function of bureaucracies is their own internal management. This activity includes the improvement of the mechanisms for internal communication, administrative co-ordination within and between departments, and the important field of personnel management, training, and recruitment. There are degrees of independence in these areas, but the larger and more complex the bureaucracy becomes, the greater will be the trend towards more independent self-management of organisations.

Internal management has been a central concern for governments over the past several decades, with increasing pressures to make government management more like private sector management and also to empower members of the organisations.[36] The spate of administrative reforms that have been adopted during these years tend to substitute private sector ideas, such as pay for performance, for traditional civil service personnel management. Further, government organisations are being pressured to become more 'results oriented' and more concerned with quality, rather than to rely on more traditional forms of accountability for their actions.[37] Structurally, government organisations have become more decentralised and managers have been granted greater autonomy over individual 'agencies', sometimes with unfortunate results for both citizens and the concept of accountability.

Control of the bureaucracy

The need for controlling bureaucratic discretion and power is apparent in every political system. This necessity has been emphasised in liberal democratic systems because of the representative and responsible aspects of political leadership, but even in socialist regimes the party usually possesses more communication links with the mass of the governed than the bureaucracy does. In all systems it is the 'political' element within a system, such as the political leaders, assemblies and parties, that are the legitimising forces, not the permanent administrators. Therefore, there is a perennial quest to ensure that the permanent, expert components of government remain under political control.

However, there is a possible conflict between the need for more representative government and the administrative need for more efficient government. This clash is significant in systems with a strong established central administration and weak representative, participatory traditions. The demands for more extensive and standardised government services may gradually transform party government into more oligarchic patterns even in the more representative liberal democracies.

One form of protection is the development of a concept of public service, and it is the absence of this concept which presents difficulties in developing countries, particularly those where no effort was made by the colonial government before independence to encourage the development of an indigenous public service. There is a stronger consciousness of this spirit in British, French and German civil services than in the United States, partly due to the pattern of recruitment. Yet even where this tradition exists, there still remain some important obstacles to democratic control, such as the permanence of many public servants, their expertise, size, complexity and secretive nature of modern bureaucracies.

Supervision is necessary, not merely to ensure that the wishes of the governed, indirectly expressed with varying degrees of efficiency by parties and representative assemblies, are taken into account, but also to further efficiency, administrative co-ordination and the primacy of the political arm of government in the choice of political priorities. There are problems of protecting the individual from over-zealous public officials not accountable in the usual legal and political ways, and there is also the possibility of corruption within the administrative machine itself. The controls may be divided into three broad divisions: internal, political and legal.

The internal machinery for controlling bureaucracies con-, sists of the self-regulatory means within the administrative structure itself. These are aimed at internal co-ordination, self-discipline and a recognition of the hierarchical structure. In Britain, the Treasury regained the task of controlling the civil service in 1982, especially with regard to its size, pay and distribution; the Conservative government abolished the Civil Service Department, established in 1968 to co-ordinate the civil service. Recruitment, however, remains in the hands of the Civil Service Commission, which works closely with the Treasury in this area, but higher promotions rest heavily on the advice of the permanent secretary of the Treasury. Other departments, such as the various economic ministries, the former Department of Economic Affairs in Britain and the former Ministry of Economic Affairs in France, were also potential conflict-resolving institutions. The methods of re-cruitment and training and the social background of the civil servants are other factors.

In the United States the Office of Personnel Management is primarily responsible for personnel management. The Office of Management and Budget (OMB), a part of the Executive Office of the American president, exerts a substantial degree of influence similar to that exerted by the British Treasury, by virtue of the fact that all the American administrative agencies, no matter what their degree of independence, must clear their budgets with the Office before they are submitted to Congress. In particular OMB has used personnel controls as one part of its controls over other agencies, and also has had responsibility for legislative and regulatory clearance.[38]

In the second category of controls, the supply of money is also important. It is key to the supervision exercised over the administrative agencies by the American Congress, especially bearing in mind the rivalry between Congress and the pre-sidency. Yet even where assemblies lack the independence of the American Congress, they often have various opportunities to act as watchdog over the bureaucracy. The Public Accounts Committee of the British House of Commons seeks to investigate government expenditure with the assistance of the Comptroller and Auditor General. It is one of the most powerful and prestigious committees of the House but it does have the disadvantage of investigating only *past* expenditure.[39]

The power to appoint civil servants is an important means of executive control; this may have to be shared with the legislature, as it is for very senior officials in the United States. The Republican-dominated Senate was able to thwart the intentions of the Clinton administration by refusing to confirm many of its nominations for senior positions. In the United States, co-operation of the assembly may also be necessary to provide an increase in statutory powers of departments or to change the organisation of government, and in 1962 President Kennedy was frustrated by Congress in his attempt to create a new department of urban affairs. Generally, the 'political' executive, supported by the stronger political party or parties, and having the prestige that goes with possessing governmental authority, can exert greater controls over the bureaucracy than the assembly.

We have seen[40] that chief executives are furnished with some form of personal staff which is independent of the assembly and the rest of the administrative machine, and which is responsible to the president or prime minister. Yet if the administrative machine is fragmented, and if there is competition for control from the legislature, this provides opportunities for different parts of the bureaucracy to resist the controls of the government leader, and pressure groups are able to exploit this fragmentation. The American president has his Executive Office, which includes not only the White House Office, but the Office of Management and Budget, the Council of Economic Advisors and the National Security Council; but this machinery has to be co-ordinated and controlled by the president before he can use it for wider controls. Some presidents have preferred the regularity of formal meetings, as did President Eisenhower, whereas others, such as President Kennedy, opted for a more informal, personal means of supervision. President Nixon was in the process of reforming the administrative machine before his resignation.

Administrative subservience to political demands was most evident in Soviet-type systems. Control was exercised through the key Party Secretariat, which determined state structures and personnel and provided control through a vast network of party structures which ran parallel to those of the state administration. However, the bureaucracy developed interests of its own, both as an institution and as individual organisations. Further, internal conflicts in the bureaucracy, and its imperviousness to change, presented major obstacles to economic reform processes.[41]

The third area of control is legal/judicial. This includes the machinery and procedure for dealing with administrative corruption as well as controls to ensure impartial and efficient administration. These controls are also directed at administrators exceeding the authority that has been granted to them. These controls may be exercised through the ordinary legal channels, the civil servant being responsible to the criminal and civil courts for failure to carry out his proper functions and for the misuse of his authority. The Soviet Union in 1962 included capital punishment as a possible punishment for bribery by state officials. The highest official known to have been executed for bribery was the Deputy Fisheries Minister, in 1982.

However, the ordinary law courts may not provide an adequate degree of control of civil servants, since the dividing line between corrupt and inefficient administration is not a rigid one. A special commissioner, the ombudsman or parliamentary commissioner, has been introduced in many states, to examine complaints of maladministration. His functions and powers vary; in Britain he can report back to parliament, having no executive power of his own, while in some other countries he has substantial latitude to investigate and remedy wrongs. Some countries such as Germany provide separate ombudsmen for groups such as prisoners and soldiers. In Poland, the Civil Rights' Ombudsman, introduced in the late 1980s, has proved to be an impressive protector of the public against bureaucratic abuses of power.[42]

Some countries have gone further and have created a different code of administrative law, with separate administrative courts to adjudicate cases arising under that code. Both

Britain and the United States have a system of administrative tribunals, a halfway house between executive and judicial supervision,[43] but Germany and France have distinct administrative legal systems. At the apex of the French administrative courts is the Council of State, which as well as acting as a form of protection for civil servants against the political leaders, exercises general supervision over all forms of French administration. It can insist that civil servants justify particular actions they have taken and award damages if these have proved injurious to a citizen.[44] It also reviews the legality of most decrees being made by the state bureaucracy.[45]

Recruitment and training

Recruitment to the public bureaucracy is now chiefly based on merit, with selection being made through competitive exams. The German civil service, for both the federal and regional services, demands for the higher administrative posts a university degree, usually in law, an entry examination, a rigorous three-year training period, and a second state examination. The French National School of Administration (École National d'Administration – ENA), established in 1945, an outstanding feature of the French administrative system, recruits and trains for the higher posts in the French civil service. There is open competition for two-thirds of the places at ENA, and an examination for existing civil servants to ensure the promotion of only the most intellectually able candidates. Candidates for the open places must have qualifications amounting in practice to a second university degree. The training course lasts for nearly two years; the students do not specialise for a particular branch of the civil service, but the best students are able to choose posts in the ministries with the greatest prestige. The system produces highly professionalist élite members, and it is difficult to enter the higher civil service in France except at the start of one's career. The École Polytechnique, founded by Napoléon I, still produces top administrators with an engineering background.

Recruitment for the higher civil service in Britain is similarly based on a competitive examination and a good university degree. Unlike France, there is more promotion for the middle ranks of the civil service, but these recruits to the higher civil service rarely reach the top posts. Another difference as compared with the French system is that the British examination requires a general interview, which, it is often alleged, produces distortions in the meritocratic basis of selection.31 Recruitment is controlled by the Civil Service Commission established in 1855, but the selection on merit was only gradually extended to the whole service and was not complete until the early years of the twentieth century. The basis of selection may be said to be still largely grounded on Macaulay's observation in 1854, a result of his experience of the Indian civil service:

> We believe that men who have been engaged up to 21 or 22 in studies which have no immediate connection with the business of any profession and of which the effect is merely to open, to invigorate and to enrich the mind, will generally be found in the business of every profession superior to men who have at 18 or 19 devoted themselves to the special studies of their calling.[46]

Despite the reforms following the report of the Fulton Committee in 1968, elements of this amateur basis of the higher civil service remain unbalanced by the pre-entry training of the French National School of Administration. However, the specialist classes of the British civil service, lawyers, scientists and doctors, who are recruited on the basis of existing specialist qualifications, are declining more slowly than the other classes in the civil service. Further, the numerous reforms in administration during the Thatcher government and in the period thereafter have made the British civil service more open to outside talent; in particular the creation of specialised agencies is beginning to emphasise specialised skills even more.[47]

Entry to the United States civil service is distinguished not so much by political patronage at the top, as by the fact that the federal public service is recruited along functional lines, rather than as a part of a more general career structure. Most people going into the US civil service are selected because of particular skills, rather than a capacity to learn on the job. Recruitment is mainly through open competitive exams managed either by the Office of Personnel Management or increasingly by the individual departments.[48] The Pendleton Act of 1883 first introduced selection on merit and it now extends to nearly 90 per cent of federal civil service posts, but entry is further distinguished from the British example by the absence of division into classes, and more so by the fact that entry is possible at any age. There is less of a rigid demarcation of the political and administrative areas than in Britain, although the barriers between permanent officials and political partisans are becoming less precise with the widening opportunities for patronage for British governments in public posts.[49]

In the communist states control of recruitment through the *nomenklatura* system was a major instrument of party rule. The *nomenklatura* was a list of posts in all spheres (political, economic, social, cultural) which could not be filled without party approval. The senior *nomenklatura* jobs were the most important and responsible ones, and their occupants constituted a privileged élite. One of the main fears of the new post-communist leaders was that the entrenched officials of the *nomenklatura* would resist the change to a new type of system. Fortunately, perhaps, in some countries such as Poland and Hungary numerous former communist appointees left the state administration to pursue lucrative economic activities; they formed a group known as the new *nomenklatura* capitalists.

A career-structured higher civil service and a competitive entry procedure appear to be synonymous with a preponderance of higher social class membership. The middle and upper middle class provide the majority of the entrants to the higher public service in Germany, Britain and France. Two-thirds of the higher civil servants in Britain were born into the upper or middle classes, with only 19 per cent being born to working-class parents. Two-thirds of those with degrees attended Oxford or Cambridge Universities, and over half attended private as opposed to state schools. The Fulton Report observed that entry to the higher civil service in Britain is narrower than entry to most other professions and occupations, and that pattern has changed little in the thirty years since Fulton.[50]

In France over 70 per cent of senior civil servants come from the upper and middle classes, with only 10 per cent coming from the manual classes, and as in Britain, the upper- and middle-class bias is even greater in regard to direct entry recruits as opposed to civil servants who are promoted from lower ranks in the bureaucracy. There is less social exclusiveness in the American federal service: nearly 25 per cent come from the working class, and a higher proportion from the lower-middle classes than in Britain or France.[51]

The social background of higher civil servants is important for a number of reasons. First, an examination of administrative élites in comparison with other élites in the society is a vital indicator of the balance in prestige and power in the political process. We have noted the stability provided in German politics by the prestigious civil service, and the relative lack of respect for elected political leaders. Second, the composition of the higher bureaucracy is a useful reflector of social forces in society: recruiting organisations are rarely in control of the type of civil servants they are able to select. Recruitment rather is a process more dependent on the relationships of social class, education, and the prestige of the public service. Third, the existence and origin of common values and attitudes among higher administrators, given their importance in the policy-making process, may have important bearings on how society is governed. There is little evidence to substantiate this last assumption, but it does appear logical.[52]

Changing the bureaucracy

Bureaucracy has a negative connotation to most citizens, and governments have themselves been attempting to make public administration more service oriented. Beginning in the late 1970s there has been an immense amount of reform in the public sector. This reform has been concentrated in the developed democracies, but some of the same ideas are now being transported to the less-developed countries, often with less than positive results.[53] Further, the former socialist countries are now facing the need to convert administrative systems based on high levels of state power and political conformity into services that meet the needs of their people and that also meet the demands of democratic accountability, and to make these changes in a relatively brief period of time.

Although these changes are often all described as 'new Public Management', they actually contain several different ideas about how to make government work better. The dominant idea is the *market*, and the simple nostrum that government would perform better if it functioned more as if it were in the private sector. This style of reform has been especially evident in the United Kingdom and the Antipodes.[54] It has involved changes such as devolving administration from ministries to more or less autonomous agencies that are then placed under executives, often drawn from outside government, with clear performance targets for their actions. The market approach also involves using pay-for-performance rather than traditional civil service pay and grading systems for managing the people in government.[55] Finally, when possible, market mechanisms are substituted for bureaucracy in allocating of public resources, e.g. using vouchers for a variety of public programmes or developing internal markets in the health sector.[56]

Another approach to reform, one somewhat antithetical to the market concept, has stressed ideas of participation and empowerment.[57] In this approach both citizens and lower-level workers in public sector organisations are the subjects of programmes to enhance their involvement in government, and their influence over public policy.[58] Examples of empowerment include reducing the number of levels within organisations and eliminating layers of middle management in order to increase the discretion of people at the lower levels of those organisations, as well as creating consultative structures for the clients of programmes, and for citizens as a whole. While the market approach has been most evident in the UK and in the Antipodes, the empowerment perspective has been found primarily in North America and in Scandinavia.[59] For example, the National Performance Review (the Gore Commission) has removed a number of layers of control within public organisations and moved powers downward to the lower levels of bureaucracy.

While these reforms may make some sense in the developed democracies, they are very poorly suited for the less-developed world. In particular, the successful implementation of an idea such as empowerment assumes the existence of a set of values in bureaucracy that recognise the need to treat citizens without regard to family, religious or other social characteristics. That idea tends not to be well-institutionalised in much of the less-developed world, where patronage and particularistic criteria are considered not only acceptable but indeed as the most appropriate ways to allocate resources.[59] Likewise, market ideas depend upon the capacity and willingness to measure performance, something that may also be lacking.

In all these cases the 'New Public Management' is attempting to improve the quality of public services and to make the process of administering public policy more effective and more efficient. The available evaluations of these programmes question whether these goals have been achieved as fully as the advocates of reform have promised. In addition, the move away from traditional bureaucracy appears to have created some of the same problems in the industrialised democracies as are feared in the less-developed systems. In particular, removing controls over personnel, purchasing and budgeting may open government to greater corruption and the politicisation of the civil service.

Summary

The concept of bureaucracy implies a relatively high degree of similarity in the formal structures of public administration. In practice, however, there are as many or more differences as there are commonalities among these systems of administration. These differences appear in the formal structure of bureaucracies but even more in the behaviour of individuals within those systems. They are particularly evident in the way in which senior administrators are selected and rewarded, and in their relationships with political authority. The demands to create highly professionalised managers of public business appears to produce similar responses in a wide variety of countries with differing political traditions.

The continuing reforms of public administration are argued to be creating even greater homogeneity among public bureaucracies. While there are some common patterns in these reforms, e.g. the increased use of market-like mechanisms to deliver public services and to manage government personnel, these reforms also appear to be implemented within the context of national styles of administration. Further, reforms that are popular in some countries may be anathema in others; the market-based reforms are not widely accepted in France or in other countries with strong traditions of state-provided services. Public administration may well be changing, but it remains an activity shaped by national traditions and national priorities.

Notes and references

1. See James Q. Wilson, *Bureaucracy* (New York: Free Press, 1993).
2. Max Weber, *Theory of Social and Economic Organization* (Glencoe, IL: Free Press, 1947).
3. See B. Guy Peters and Donald J. Savoie, *Taking Stock: Assessing Public Sector Reforms* (Montreal: McGill/Queen's University Press, 1998).
4. See Chapter 9.
5. We are using 'bureaucracy' in the general 'institutional' sense of public administration, and will be mainly concerned with higher-level public administrators. The term 'bureaucracy' lacks a precise definition, but there are several alternative ones suggested in M. Albrow, *Bureaucracy* (London: Allen & Unwin) ch. 5.
6. For a discussion of this pattern of development, see Richard Rose, 'On the Priorities of Government', *European Journal of Political Research*, 4 (1976), pp. 247–89.
7. See Vincent Wright (ed.), *Privatization in Western Europe: Pressures, Problems and Paradoxes* (London: Pinter, 1994).
8. See O. C. White and A. Bhatia, *Privatization in Africa* (Washington, DC: The World Bank, 1995).
9. See Hans Ulrich Derlien and B. Guy Peters, *Who Works for Government and What Do They Do?* (Bamberg: Lehrstuhl für Verwaltungswissenschaft, Universität Bamberg, 1998).
10. See Paul Thomas, 'The Changing Nature of Accountability', in B. Guy Peters and Donald J. Savoie (eds), *Taking Stock* (Montreal: McGill/Queen's University Press, 1998).
11. See P. Avril, *Politics in France* (London, 1969) ch. 5. For a note of caution, see V. Wright, *The Government and Politics of France*, 3rd edn (London: Hutchinson, 1989) pp. 115–16.
12. See Chapter 4.
13. See J. D. Holm and P. P. Molutsi, 'State-Society Relations in Botswana: Beginning Liberalization', in G. Hyden and M. Bratton (eds), *Governance and Politics in Africa* (Boulder, CO: Lynne Rienner, 1992).

14. For example, in Germany, broadcasting is a *Land* function because of the fear of national centralisation such as that which occurred during the Nazi regime.

15. H. Seidman and R. Gilmour, *Politics, Position and Power*, 5th rev. edn (Oxford: Oxford University Press, 1997) ch. 9.

16. See Martin Laffin, 'Reinventing the Federal Government', in Gillian Peele *et al.* (eds), *Developments in American Politics 2* (London: Macmillan, 1995) pp. 185–90.

17. Some scholars argue that this number is continuing to increase rapidly. See Paul C. Light, *Thickening Government: Federal Hierarchy and the Diffusion of Accountability* (Washington, DC: The Brookings Institution, 1997).

18. See Keith Dowding, *The Civil Service* (London: Routledge, 1995).

19. For a contrary view on France, see Harvey Feigenbaum, *The Politics of Public Enterprise: Oil and the French State* (Princeton: Princeton University Press, 1985).

20. John Loughlin and Sonia Mazey, *The End of the French Unitary State?* (London: Frank Cass, 1995).

21. See G. Stoker, *The Politics of Local Government*, 2nd edn (London: Macmillan, 1991).

22. Kieron Walsh, 'Competition for White-Collar Services', *Public Money and Management*, 15 (1995) pp. 11–19.

23. See L. Holmes, *Politics in the Communist World* (Oxford: Basil Blackwell, 1986) pp. 174–5 for a discussion on the problem of separation of the party and the state.

24. See B. Guy Peters, 'Bureaucracy', in *Encyclopedia of Political Revolutions* (Washington, DC: CQ Press, 1998).

25. See Justice, *The Democratic Deficit: Democratic Accountability and the European Union* (London: Justice Society, 1996), for one interesting analysis of the issues involved.

26. Merilee S. Grindle, *Getting Good Government: Capacity Building in the Public Sectors of Developing Countries* (Cambridge, MA: Harvard University Press, 1997).

27. See B. Sedgemore, *The Secret Constitution* (London, 1980) pp. 108–25.

28. See G. Kennan, *Memoirs* (Boston: Little, Brown, 1968). Kennan was an influential career specialist in the State Department in the years after 1945.

29. See A. Schlesinger, *A Thousand Days* (Boston: Houghton Mifflin, 1965) chs 9 and 10.

30. See Chapter 8.

31. See E. C. Page, *Political Authority and Bureaucratic Power*, 2nd edn (Brighton: Wheatsheaf, 1992) pp. 68–73.

32. See Chapter 6.

33. Max Weber, *The Theory of Social and Economic Organisations*, trans. A. M. Henderson and T. Parsons (Glencoe, IL: Free Press, 1947).

34. R. Braibanti, 'The Civil Service of Pakistan', in *Comparative Politics*, ed. R. R. Macridis and B. E. Brown, 3rd edn (Boston: Little, Brown, 1968) p. 470.

35. Hugh Heclo, 'Issue Networks and the Executive Establishment', in A. King (ed.), *The New American Political System* (Washington, DC: AEI Press, 1978).

36. B. Guy Peters, *The Future of Governing* (Lawrence: University of Kansas Press, 1996); Christopher Pollitt, *Managerialism and the Public Services: Cuts or Cultural Changes in the 1990s?*, 2nd edn (Oxford: Blackwell, 1993).

37. Geert Bouckaert and Christopher Pollitt, *Quality in European Public Services* (London: Sage, 1996).

38. Bert A. Rockman, 'The United States', in B. G. Peters, R. A. W. Rhodes and V. Wright (eds), *Administering the Summit* (London: Macmillan, 1999).

39. See L. Chapman, *Your Disobedient Servant* (London: Chatto & Windus, 1978) chs 8 and 9, for two case studies of the Committee at work.

40. See Chapter 9.

41. Jan Winiecki, *Resistance to Change in the Soviet Economic System* (London: Routledge, 1991).

42. H. Elcock, 'Working for Socialist Legality: The Polish Commissioner for Citizen's Rights', *Public Policy and Administration*, 5, 3 (Winter, 1990) pp. 37–47.

43. D. Foulkes, *Introduction to Administrative Law,* 5th edn (London, 1982). These quasi-judicial venues handle many more cases than do the conventional courts, but do raise questions about rights and fairness since they may be operated within the very agency that is a party to the proceeding.

44. For a comparative discussion of judicial control, see Page, *Political Authority and Bureaucratic Power*, pp. 121–9.

45. Jean Massot and T. Giradot, *Le Conseil d'Etat* (Paris: La documentation Française, 1999).

46. Quoted in A. Sampson *Anatomy of Britain Today* (London: Routledge & Kegan Paul, 1965), pp. 222–3.

47. For the first round of post-Fulton reforms, see N. Johnson, 'Change in the Civil Service: Retrospect and Prospects', *Public Administration*, 63, 4 (Winter, 1985) pp. 415–33; for the later reforms see

48. Part of the deregulation of the federal civil service following the National Performance Review (the Gore Report) permits departments to make more of their own personnel decisions.

49. However, in Britain, since the election of 1979, this ideal is being undermined by the promotion of business values and private sector management methods. The *Next Steps* programme clearly challenges the notion of a centralised, integrated and co-ordinated civil service. L. Metcalfe and S. Richards, *Improving Public Management,* 2nd edn (London: Sage, 1990). Also N. Flynn *et al.*, 'Taking the Next Steps: The Changing Management of Government', *Parliamentary Affairs*, 43, 2 (April 1990) pp. 159–78.

49. For the background of higher civil servants in Britain, see Rose, 'The Political Status of Higher Civil Servants in Britain', pp. 144–5.

50. See B. G. Peters, *The Politics of Bureaucracy,* 4th edn (New York: Longman, 1994) ch. 3 for a discussion of civil service recruitment.

51. Robert D. Putnam argued that this hypothesis was 'plausible but ambiguous and unsubstantiated'. Robert D. Putnam, *The Study of Political Elites* (Englewood Cliffs, NJ: Prentice-Hall, 1967) p. 44.

52. See B. Guy Peters, *The Future of Governing* (Lawrence: University Press of Kansas, 1996); Also, Christopher Hood, *The Art of the State* (Oxford: Oxford University Press, 1999).

53. J. Boston *et al.*, *Reshaping the State* (Auckland: Oxford University Press, 1991).

54. P. W. Ingraham, 'Of Pigs and Pokes and Policy Diffusion: Pay for Performance', *Public Administration Review* 53 (1993), 348–56.

55. See Julian Le Grand, and Will Bartlett, *Quasi-markets and Social Policy* (London: Macmillan, 1993).

56. K. Kernaghan, 'Empowerment and Public Administration: Revolutionary Advance or Passing Fancy', *Canadian Public Administration* 55 (1994) pp. 194–214.

57. See J. Pierre and B. G. Peters, 'The Problems of Mutual Empowerment', *Administration and Society* (forthcoming).

58. Paul Tellier, 'Public Service 2000: Renewal of the Public Service', *Canadian Public Administration*, 33 (1991), pp. 123–32.

59. These values may also be lacking in many parts of the more economically developed countries. See William Tordoff, *Government and Politics of Africa*, 2nd edn (London: Macmillan, 1993).

11

The Courts and the Political Process

The discussion in the last chapter illustrated the difficulty of confining bureaucracies to the function of implementing policy as opposed to policy-making. Likewise, in a discussion of the courts in modern political systems, it is impossible rigidly to distinguish between interpreting rules and making them, between rule-making and rule adjudication. It is sometimes convenient to separate different political structures for analysis, but this separation can be artificial, and it is often dictated by political patterns characteristic of liberal democratic systems rather than a reflection of the reality of the contributions that the institutions make to governing.

Administrative courts and administrative tribunals have emerged as increasingly important in modern political systems,[1] and these institutions prevent an inflexible dividing line being drawn between administrative and judicial structures. Also, in a number of countries the judiciary may be used to implement certain policies. In the United States, for example, the courts may take control of government activities when they decide that the normal implementation institutions are not managing those functions according to legal standards.[2] School districts that were slow to desegregate and state prison systems troubled with over-crowding have been common examples.

This is also true of the whole legal system: judges and courts of law are significant aspects of the total political process, and a distorted view of that process would result if there were too crude a separation of functions. Robert Dahl has argued this point strongly:

To consider the Supreme Court of the United States as a legal institution is to under-estimate its significance in the American political system. For it is also a political institution, an institution, that is to say, for arriving at decisions on controversial questions of national policy.[3]

The American Supreme Court was the pace-setter in the 1950s, 1960s and into the 1970s on important political questions such as civil and defendants' rights, with the presidency and the Congress alternating between periods of inaction and reluctant acceptance of the political lead established by the Court in such controversial areas. Likewise, the European Court of Justice has taken the lead in many aspects of integration, and has made courts major players in countries such the United Kingdom where they have been less significant as lawmakers.[4]

This is not to imply that all courts of law have the political independence of the American Supreme Court. One main task facing post-Soviet reformers was how to generate judicial independence in a system long accustomed to Communist Party interference in legal matters. But it is important to recognise that legal adjudication is not a process far removed from the world of politics, and that there is an interplay between the legal structure, the political culture, and the political and social values of the judges. These political factors all bring the legal system firmly into the arena of choice, priorities and conflict. Legal arrangements that are effective in one cultural setting may not be acceptable in others, thereby reflecting the extent to which legal decisions are embedded in the remainder of political life.

There are two main reasons for emphasising that the judicial system is part of the political process. First, liberal democratic theory has traditionally placed a premium on the necessity of protecting the citizen from a too powerful state, and has therefore emphasised the impartiality of the judicial process, to increase the independence of the judiciary, and to deepen the respect and confidence with which judicial decisions are received.[5] This semi-fiction is therefore a necessary aspect of the stability of many political systems, and there is disquiet in some liberal democratic regimes over the growth of administrative courts and quasi-judicial administrative tribunals. If these institutions located within the state itself are accorded the same status as more independent bodies, it is feared that impartiality of other institutions will be undermined.

Second, the growth of quasi-judicial institutions has led to emphasising some aspects of the doctrine of the separation of powers, both to prevent too much concentration of political power in the hands of the government, and to guard against the 'excesses of democracy' or the tyranny of the majority.[6] The non-majoritarian institutions of the courts are crucial in providing a balance of democratic control and the preservation of the values that will preserve that democracy. Further, these institutions can make difficult decisions that institutions whose members must be concerned about re-election might find it difficult to make.

In communist political systems, no lip-service was paid to the doctrine of the separation of powers; the Party was considered the embodiment of the will of the people, and the courts are the servants of the people. It is not a difficult step to the conclusion that the courts, therefore, are subject to the directions of the Party, albeit not always in the form of explicit, case-by-case, instructions. This distinction between socialist and liberal democratic attitudes to the legal system has important repercussions on the role of the courts in their respective political systems, but it does not mean that the courts in liberal democracies are somehow divorced from the political process. There is a good deal of evidence that judges do have political attitudes and opinions that shape their decisions.[7] Further, the public appears to think of the courts much as they think of other political institutions.[8]

To examine the role of judiciaries in the political process we need to focus on the following topics: (1) the nature of the legal system, and its relationship to political decision-making; (2) the structures of the courts and the selection of their personnel; (3) the functions of the courts and the nature of the external controls from other political institutions; and (4) the relation of the citizen to the legal process, and the openness of the court system to challenges to the state.

The nature of law and the political process

In liberal democratic systems the legal system is said to be characterised by such concepts as impartiality, consistency, openness, predictability and stability. All citizens, in theory, are equal before the law; citizens have rights to counsel; the legal results of certain actions may be reasonably foreseen, and the legal procedures are known in advance and will follow predictable patterns. This is what is usually meant by the 'rule of law'. It is claimed that these aspects do not characterise the legal systems in socialist and autocratic states, and that the use of arbitrary powers by the police, absence of trials, secret trials, and failure to publicise procedures and verdicts are the antithesis of liberal democratic systems.

However, the distinctions may be more relative than absolute. Liberal democratic systems can grant extraordinary powers to governments during emergencies, whether war or internal unrest, resulting in the abrogation of normal judicial procedure, and in 'normal' times the definition of internal security may be wide enough to give the police extra powers and give special tribunals increased jurisdiction – the suspension of civil liberties in Northern Ireland is a clear example. We have already noted the impact of the administrative courts on the 'rule of law', and we also know that the more affluent have greater access to skilled legal defence, despite formal equality before the law. Also, it is possible to have predictable legal rules and due processes of law in autocratic systems: the legal theories of the Prussian state and liberal democratic systems in nineteenth-century Europe appear to underline the fact that the differences are of degree rather than of kind.

In communist systems the absence of such characteristics as impartiality and predictability may have been true only of certain areas. Criminal and civil cases, involving cases of theft, slander, debts and other common legal issues, may have been conducted in a manner common in liberal democratic systems, but the uncertainty, discretion and the degree of bias are more characteristic of what are termed 'political' cases. In the Soviet Union there was a marked move towards stabilising judicial procedures after 1956–7 and the end of the Stalinist regime.[9] But it is difficult to apply liberal democratic concepts to regimes whose dominant ideology is based on Marxist-Leninism. Socialists see the legal system of liberal democracies and non-Marxist totalitarian or autocratic states as instruments of class rule, and argue that the main functions of the courts in these systems are to legitimise and buttress the domination of the capitalist class. The Bolsheviks argued that the courts would have only a temporary role, before the 'withering away of the state'. The courts were not to be a check on the executive, nor a form of protection for minority rights, but only a means of enforcing the will of the majority as expressed through the ruling party.[10] There are various problems of this stage, in that all crime tends to become an ideological challenge and a possible indication of weakness of the political system. The few remaining communist states, such as China and North Korea, still use the death penalty for certain 'economic' crimes such as black-marketeering and corruption.[11]

However, many of the different attitudes to the legal system and the role of the courts that British and American jurists identify in communist states are not solely the result of ideological differences but emanate from a contrasting development of legal procedures. Many East European states had strong pre-war continental legal traditions which they have sought to revive in the post-communist period. Thus pre-trial procedures, committal proceedings, the power of the state prosecutors as compared with that of the defence counsel, the role of the judge as an investigator, not an umpire, and the absence of a jury system are common in many European legal systems. This is true irrespective of whether the regime can be described as liberal democratic, socialist or autocratic. These European procedures are termed 'inquisitorial' as contrasted with the Anglo-American 'accusatorial' or 'adversarial' procedures. This, of course, has important implications for the concept of 'the rule of law' which is essentially a product of British and American liberal democratic systems. This is not to imply that there are not important differences between the legal systems of socialist and liberal democratic regimes, but merely that departures from the Anglo-American legal pattern do not necessarily indicate the absence of legal concepts considered important in liberal democratic systems.

The West German Federal Constitutional Court provided an illustration of some of the difficulties of attempting to ideologically classify different legal systems. One observer said of this court:

> The constitutional courts are not, nor were ever intended to be neutral, 'nonpolitical' instruments of the state in the sense of the positive tradition in German jurisprudence. Their judges are supposed to be nonpartisan in interpreting the constitutional principles of the prevailing order, but biased in favor of the regime. In other words, the constitutional courts and particularly the Federal Constitutional Court are quite explicitly judicial structures for legitimizing and preserving the present political system.[12]

The Federal Constitutional Court did not hesitate to act in ways to preserve the West German political system. Article 21(2) of the 1949 Basic Law reads: 'Parties which according to their objectives or according to the behaviour of their members aim to threaten or to abolish the free democratic basic order, or to endanger the substance of the German Federal Republic, are unconstitutional. The Federal Constitutional Court shall decide on the question of unconstitutionality.' The Court, under the provisions of this article, accordingly declared a neo-Nazi party illegal in 1952 and outlawed the German Communist Party in 1956.

In other liberal democracies high courts do not have the status and powers of either the American or German courts, although they certainly are not powerless. For example, the Italian Court has limited jurisdiction and few powers to overturn cases. The French court must wait for a political leader to appeal to it before making a decision.

Although there is ample variation among the legal systems of the liberal democracies, and between those systems and communist systems, there is even more when we look more widely in the world. One of the more obvious examples of alternative forms of law is the increasing imposition of Koranic law in Islamic countries.[13] Also, in many African countries law often operates at two levels. At the national level there is a more formal system, generally derived from the former colonial power, while at the local level a more traditional form of justice, based on the powers of local élites, dominates.

Legal structure and recruitment

Legal structures vary according to several factors. Federalism may lead to a structure of parallel courts adjudicating on federal matters, on the one hand, with separate state or provincial courts. Yet this is not universal; in the United States, the jurisdiction of the federal courts extends into every state alongside the state system. On matters of a constitutional nature the Supreme Court is at the apex of both systems, while state supreme courts handle matters of state law. Yet Canada, likewise a federal state, has only a single system of courts. However, in spite of this difference, basically all judicial systems have a hierarchically structured court system, although communist systems do not have 'supreme courts' to decide on constitutional questions.

Some legal systems emphasise specialisation. In Germany there are regular courts for civil and criminal cases, separate administrative courts and distinct constitutional courts. There are separate federal and state courts, but at the top they are integrated into a single hierarchy. In Britain there are no separate administrative and constitutional courts, but above the lowest courts there are, as in France, separate civil and criminal courts with separate courts of appeal.[14] The highest court of appeal in the United Kingdom, the House of Lords, is unique. As well as constituting a part of the British legislature, it is the highest court of appeal, although by constitutional convention only members with the appropriate legal back-ground may participate in these appellate functions.[15] The Judicial Committee of the Privy Council still acts as a court of appeal for some Commonwealth countries.[16]

The structure of legal systems is important for some of the functions of the courts, such as those concerned with the increasing powers of the central governments, and for the protection of administrative and civil rights, but for the wider range of functions the principles underlying the selection of the judiciary have more significance. The procedures for selecting and dismissing judges, and the background of the recruits are perhaps more crucial factors in assessing the degree of independence and in evaluating the political behaviour of judges.

Judges may be appointed by the government, elected directly or indirectly, or co-opted by fellow judges. The extent of their legal training and the nature of their qualifications also vary. Germany and France provide the best examples of hierarchical career structures for judges. In both countries they are appointed by the government after acquiring a university degree in law, and having undergone a period of legal training culminating with a stiff competitive examination. They must choose a judicial career early in life, and are not recruited from among barristers as they are in Britain, and they have established security of tenure. The methods of recruitment and training mean that the recruits come from predominantly upper-middle-class backgrounds. In both countries they are imbued with a tradition similar to the civil service, that of impartial, dedicated service to their view of the state's interests.[17]

British judges, above magistrates, are selected from among barristers and likewise have a distinct upper-middle-class, conservative background. Also, as with other systems where some form of appointment by the government takes place, the legal profession itself has various formal and informal channels of access to influence the selection process. Security of tenure of judges is another important aspect of the British legal system: judges of the superiour courts may only be dismissed by both Houses of Parliament on the grounds of misbehaviour. Thus, as in France and Germany, legal training, method of selection, security of tenure and the consequent prestige and respect given to higher court judges make them a significant conservative stabilising force in the political system.

Election of judges may weaken this respect shown to them, but it may also make the judiciary more representative of the electorate, or of the particular groups that direct the election. The election of judges for the courts (especially lower courts) in some states of the USA may make them more responsive to current political feeling in particular states, and may lead to conflict with the federal courts, especially on such issues as the rights of minorities and women. In the Soviet Union all judges were elected, either directly or by the appropriate soviet; but in practice recruitment took place through the *nomenklatura*. One early task of the post-communist regimes was to introduce a process of 'verification' of judicial appointments, to weed out those who were professionally incompetent or ideologically suspect.

Constitutional courts and courts which have constitutional powers of adjudication as part of their functions are even more involved in overt political considerations as regards appointments. The Canadian Supreme Court, which was made the final court of appeal in 1949 in place of the Privy Council, must have at least three judges from Quebec to ensure ethnic and religious balance. The judges of the Federal Constitutional Court of Germany are elected by parliament, with six coming from the ranks of the career judges elected for life, and the other ten being elected from the most important groups in Germany, such as the political parties, administration and other élite groups; these are not elected for life but only for eight years. The Constitutional Court of France, which is difficult to classify really as a court in the strict sense, but which has the power to examine the constitutionality of laws, has a different source of recruits from the regular and administrative courts. Its members are not professional judges but are past presidents of the republic, with three appointed for nine years by the president, the National Assembly and the Senate.

The American Supreme Court is nominated by the president with the consent of the Senate, and the selection, which is for life, is even more involved in political considerations than other courts with constitutional functions, or at least this aspect receives more publicity and emphasis in the United States than in the more circumspect procedures elsewhere. But these political factors involved in the appointment of American Supreme Court justices only reflect issue conflict within the American political system, they do not challenge it. Class background in the appointment merit of American Supreme Court justices is important, 88 per cent coming from north-western European ethnic groups, which in American terms indicates roughly middle and upper-middle class. All nominations to the Court involve political considerations. In 1969 and 1970, President Nixon suffered two defeats, only the second and third rejections in the twentieth century, when his nominations of Haynesworth and Carswell were rejected by the Senate, partly on the grounds of incompetence, but chiefly because of racial attitudes. Reagan's nomination of Bork in 1988 was blocked after lengthy Senate hearings, mainly as a consequence of Bork's conservatism and views on abortion. Bush succeeded with the conservative black justice, Thomas, in 1991, after a very bruising battle; Thomas was accused of sexual harassment whilst his doubtful legal competence was ignored. The Court now has a firm right-of-centre majority, although the unpredictability of some justices has made many cases in the late 1990s decided by slim majorities.[18]

It should be remembered that security of tenure of judges may not necessarily indicate the independence of the judiciary from government or electoral pressures, but may be more of a sign of the underlying stability of the political system. It may also be an indication of the ability of the judiciary to underpin the authority of the more powerful élites in the political system. Robert Dahl has said of the American Supreme Court that it 'is inevitably a part of the dominant national alliance'.[19] This is a fact of all stable political systems, and the more obvious tampering with the judicial system in many developing countries is a sign of instability of the political system, not merely that the judiciary is more involved in the political process than in more-developed systems.

Functions of the judiciary

The courts will have various functions to perform in the political system depending on the degree of specialisation involved. We have already noted the work of the administrative courts, and the regular courts involved in criminal and civil cases do not concern us in so far as they do not involve overtly political areas such as civil liberties. We will therefore concentrate on the functions of the constitutional courts, or on the constitutional functions of courts in systems where legal specialisation has not developed in this way. To examine this area of judicial responsibility we can look at the following four fairly distinct groups of functions: (1) judicial review and interpretation of the constitution; (2) arbitration between separate institutions in the political process; (3) general support for the existing political system; (4) the protection of individual rights.

The power to review the constitutionality of decisions and legislation varies enormously. In Britain the legal sovereignty of parliament and the absence of a codified written constitution force the courts to construe acts of parliament with the intentions of the framers of the legislation as the paramount considerations. This is far from the judicial power of review that has gradually been acquired by the Supreme Court of the United States. The famous case of *Marbury* v. *Madison* in 1803 established the Court's right to declare a law void if it is in opposition to the American constitution as interpreted by the Court. Generally, the Court has reflected the dominant forces in the American political process, and the right of judicial review did not provoke serious contradictions within the system until the 1930s, when the Court declared unconstitutional several of the legislative enactments of President Roosevelt's New Deal. The president did attempt to interfere with the Court to make it responsive to what he regarded as the wishes of the majority of Americans, by expanding the membership of the court to make it more amenable to his programme. Although he was defeated in his attempts, the Court, after 1937, ceased to regard economic regulation by the federal government as a serious threat to the constitution, and this type of legislation has not been challenged since.

The Federal Constitutional Court of Germany is the nearest equivalent to the American model among European states. The wide powers of judicial review were written into the 1949 constitution to protect the Federal Republic from the fate of the Weimar Republic, which allowed the rise of Hitler to power without serious infringement of the constitution. We have seen how this power has been invoked in regard to extreme political parties of the right and left. Powers of judicial review have been granted to the Supreme Courts of Italy and Austria for similar historical reasons, but these courts lack the wide powers of the German court.[20] The strengthening of the

French Constitutional Council in 1958 (formerly the Constitutional Committee, established in 1946) marked a further move away from a republic dominated by the National Assembly, but its powers of judicial review are seriously limited by the necessity for another organ or official of government to take in appealing the constitutionality of legislation.

South Africa provides an interesting example of judicial review of legislation, and the government's reaction, which deserves some closer examination. In 1951 the Nationalist government introduced the Separate Representation of Voters Bill into the South African parliament; this was designed to remove coloured voters from the common electoral roll and put them on a separate roll which would elect white representatives to parliament. As the coloured voting clause was one of the entrenched clauses of the constitution, it needed a special parliamentary majority to become law: a two-thirds majority vote of the two Houses of Parliament sitting together.

This special majority was not attained and so the South African Appeal Court, in March 1952, declared the act invalid. The government attacked the courts for political interference, and by a special bill in 1952 set up a special committee of parliament called the High Court of Parliament which was to have power to review any Judgement of the Appeal Court which invalidated any act of parliament. This new Court reversed the decision previously reached by the Appeal Court. However, the Cape Provincial Division of the Supreme Court upheld the decision of the Appeal Court.

As the government could not gain the necessary two-thirds majority in parliament, it threatened various devices such as that of setting up a special Court of Constitutional Appeals. Finally, in 1955, the government, led by a new prime minister, J. G. Strijdom, won its long-drawn-out constitutional battle with the courts, firstly by appointing five new judges to the Appeal Court, and secondly by raising to eleven the number of judges required to sit on the Appeal Court when it is considering the validity of acts of parliament. The government also increased the size of the Senate to ensure the necessary two-thirds majority. New legislation was then passed, not only securing the coloured voters legislation which had initiated the constitutional conflict, but also reducing the entrenched clauses of the constitution and limiting the courts' rights to question the validity of any legislation other than the one remaining entrenched clause. The enlarged Appeal Court validated this legislation in 1956.[21]

All constitutional courts have the important function of arbitrating between various political institutions, whether between federal and provincial governments or between executives and assemblies. The early history of the American Supreme Court saw an insistence on the national government's rights as opposed to the powers of the states. In 1821 the Court ruled in *McCulloch* v. *Maryland* that the states had no authority to levy a tax which would challenge the right of Congress to establish a federal bank, and this continued insistence on the powers of the federal political institutions has been of great political importance in the growth of nationalising tendencies and the expansion of executive authority in spite of the economic liberalism of the Court before 1937.

Similar attempts to arbitrate between central and regional governments may be found in the short history of the West German Federal Constitutional Court. In a decision of 1958 the Court ruled that the Hamburg and Bremen atomic rearmament referenda cases violated the constitution, thus buttressing the power of the West German federal government.[22] Similarly, the European Court of Justice (ECJ) has tended to rule against the power of the member states to use their law-making powers to prevent the completion of the internal free market – Germany has not been able to protect its beer nor Italy its pasta under EU law. The ECJ has played a significant role in monitoring the implementation of European Union regulations in the member states, and has attempted to create common standards for those rules, in so far as possible given the differences among the member countries.[23]

However, the decisions of constitutional courts are not always directed towards strengthening the central government in federal cases, nor do they automatically decide in favour of the executive arm of government when this is in conflict with representative assemblies. The American Supreme Court severely limited the powers of the presidency in regard to the concept of 'executive privilege' in 1974, forcing President

Nixon to surrender the tape recordings of his White House conversations, and similar rulings were made during the Clinton administration. Yet because the movement in the twentieth century has been towards stronger and more complex functions being given to national governments, constitutional courts, as part of the political process, have tended to reflect this movement.

It may be seen that in this centralising tendency constitutional courts are performing one of their most important functions, that of stabilising and supporting the existing political system. The degree to which it is necessary for the courts to perform this task depends a great deal on the political culture within which the courts operate. In Germany and Italy there is less agreement both on the ends and on the structure of government than there is in Great Britain, and therefore the need for the role the courts play is of greater political significance. Thus in spite of the courts' involvement in political decision-making, it is necessary to stress their political impartiality and to increase the respect given to the decisions of the courts. To return to the 1937 example of President Roosevelt's attempt to change the composition of the Supreme Court, he was defeated in spite of his massive electoral majority gained in 1936 because of the belief that the Court was above politics and that it was politically dangerous to the stability of American politics to tamper with it in the way the president proposed. The Court showed its political sensitivity by changing the policy that had given rise to the conflict. We have already noted the underlying purpose of the West German Federal Constitutional Court implicit in the method of selecting its members.

The courts are an important aspect of legitimising the outputs of governments, and it is a necessary feature that they should reflect conservative opinion. This does not mean that the courts are still anti-democratic in that they will not reflect the aspirations of the majority, but that the courts tread carefully in reflecting majority opinions. Since 1966 the American Supreme Court has been more cautious on segregation issues, not as a result of sudden changes in the composition of the Court, but because of the underlying uneasiness in American politics as the issue remained no longer one for the minority southern states alone, but became more important in the industrial states outside the south. The blows the Court received over the disclosures of Justice Fortas's financial involvements in 1968, leading to his resignation shortly after President Johnson had nominated him as chief justice, illustrate the sensitivity of the Court's relationship to the total political process, and that its power is closely related to the respect it can engender.

For these reasons many constitutional courts tend to be cautious in the fourth category of functions, that of protecting individual civil rights. Lewis Edinger has noted that the West German Court 'has been more conservative than innovative, especially on socio-economic and civil liberty issues, and has sought to remain above partisan controversies'.[24] Donald Fouts has referred to the slightly anti-civil liberties tendencies of the Canadian Supreme Court,[25] although after the passage of the Charter of Rights and Freedoms the Court has changed direction.[26] Of course there are other means of protecting the civil rights of the citizen: in Britain there is no constitutional declaration of rights, and civil liberties have been established through judicial decisions interpreting the common law subject to the supremacy of statute law.[27] Communist courts play relatively little part in the protection of civil liberties, although it should be remembered that the communist concept of human rights is rather different from the liberal emphasis on individualism; communists stress the protection of the collective as opposed to the individual and place greater weight on social and economic rights. However, even in Poland, before the demise of the communist system, an Ombudsman for Civil Rights was established in 1987.

Civil rights have become one of the major areas of impact of American Supreme Court decisions since 1937. The Court has ruled on such issues as whether it infringes the constitutional rights of citizens for their children to have to salute the flag, and whether prayers should be said in state schools, and more recently on the rights of homosexuals under anti-discrimination statutes. There have been two major problems of civil liberties facing the Court: those of the concern for law and order – generally meaning the rights of the accused – and the issue of the separation of church and state. In the former area

the famous *Miranda* ruling has required the police to inform
suspects of their rights, and the courts have generally attempted to ensure fair treatment of defendants in the face of
substantial public opposition.[28] In the latter area issues such as
school prayer, abortion rights, and government support for
parochial education provide continuing sources of cases.

The aspect of civil liberties that has firmly brought the Court
into the political process has been that of race. In the famous
1954 *Brown* case the Court ruled that the Fourteenth Amendment, guaranteeing equal protection of the laws, would not
permit separate facilities for blacks, in this instance for education. The Court extended its rulings to cover other facilities,
including the important field of voting rights. The presidency
and the Congress have intermittently added their support to
the liberal decisions of the Court, but as Robert McCloskey has
remarked: 'In the decade 1953–63 the paramount innovations
in public policy can be traced more to the Supreme Court than
either the Congress or the President.[29]

There are other functions of constitutional courts in addition
to these four main areas, including those of ruling on disputed
elections and electoral boundaries and advising the executive
on the assumption of emergency powers. But these are clearly
related to those we have discussed and can quite easily be fitted
into our existing categories. The significant point that arises in
the context of these functions is that within all these areas the
courts function as important policy-makers. Their contribution
is made in different ways from those of the traditionally
identified policy-makers, but it is as crucial in understanding
how the political system works. It is to limitations on this role
that we must now turn our attention.

Control of the judiciary

Criticism directed at the degree of independence of the courts
often is based on misconceptions about the role of the courts in
the policy-making process, but it is sometimes, more realisti-
cally, directed at the political élite supporting anti-democratic
orientations of the judiciary. The mode of selection of the
judges, their socio-economic background, the anonymity of

their decision-making, and their relative immunity from dismissal and other political sanctions often make them appear as an aristocratic intrusion on representative governmental process.[30] Yet we have seen that the methods of their selection, their adherence to procedural norms, especially important in systems where case precedent (i.e. previous judicial decisions establishing a norm) is followed, and judicial sensitivity to political and societal pressures are important limitations on judicial independence. Moreover, legal professions themselves establish norms of behaviour that govern the relationship of judiciaries to the political process.

Beyond these are the more institutionalised forms of control. Legislatures may circumvent judicial opposition by new laws, and may share in the power to dismiss judges. Constitutions may be amended or rewritten. Specialisation of the courts may be developed to encourage greater sensitivity to political demands, as we have seen with constitutional and administrative courts, the development sometimes taking the form of quasi-judicial tribunals. Perhaps the most important controls are exercised through the executive. The party also performs this function in communist systems. After the death of Mao in China, in 1976, a procuratate was established to ensure the constitution was obeyed and the rights of the citizens were protected. Naturally, all appointments to the procuratate were governed by the *nomenklatura* system.[31] The new French constitution of 1958 gave the president increased disciplinary powers over the legal profession by decreasing the independence of the High Council (Conseil Supérieur de la Magistrature) in matters relating to discipline, promotion and selection. Ministers of Justice in most liberal democratic political systems are able to exercise considerable control over administrative matters relating to the behaviours of the judiciary, such as appropriations, initiating new laws, regulating punishments, as well as controlling appointments for the higher posts in the legal system.

The most important weapon in the hands of the executive is that without its co-operation judicial decisions cannot be implemented. In the 1954 *Brown* case the American Supreme Court ordered the desegregation of public schools, but given the hostility of the southern states, it needed enforcement by the federal government. President Eisenhower was reluctant to act, but, more important, the federal government had difficulties in enforcing such decisions on reluctant states. Several similar decisions by the Court followed, and although the federal government did intervene in some cases – e.g. Central High School in Little Rock – it was not until the 1964 Civil Rights Act provided sanctions, such as the withholding of federal funds, that a president had limited powers of ensuring compliance with the Court's rulings.[32]

These limitations on the power of the courts do not imply that the courts have little power in the policy-making process. This power will vary according to the political coalitions ranged for and against the courts on particular issues. The courts are part of the political process, and the analyst should stress co-operation between the branches of government as much as the conflict between them. They interact with other parts of the political system, not as illegitimate outsiders but as part of the stable ruling political alliance. If they are not part of the 'successful coalition', their subordination to other political groups will be apparent.

Conclusion

Judges and other participants in the legal system would like to have the public believe that they are above politics, and are deciding cases purely on the basis of the law. This is a useful myth for legitimating the actions of courts, and has been successful in having numerous unpopular decisions accepted. The above discussion should make it clear, however, that the courts are an integral part of the political process. Politicians have been willing to accept the political nature of courts when they view the actions of courts in communist or authoritarian systems, but have been much less willing to accept the point about their own systems.

Judicial politics is a distinctive form of politics. It depends in part upon the mystique of law and the courts to protect it from overt challenges being political. The courts also are often conservative institutions, even when their society is in the process of rapid change; law itself tends to be a conservative institution, preserving existing social arrangements until they are altered by legislation. But in other instances the courts have been far in front of the rest of society, protected in part by general respect for the law in most societies. The courts must, however, depend heavily upon other branches of government for enforcement and for resources, and hence must find a way to balance their own views with the views of other political institutions.

Notes and references

1. See Diana Woodhouse, *In Pursuit of Good Administration: Ministers, Civil Servants and Judges* (Oxford: Oxford University Press, 1997).
2. For example, federal judges have assumed management of state and local prison systems when the managers were deemed to have violated the rights of prisoners by over-crowding and inadequate facilities. See M. M. Feeley and E. L. Rubin, *Judicial Policy Making and the Modern State: How the Courts Reformed America's Prisons* (New York: Cambridge University Press, 1998).
3. R. A. Dahl, 'Decision Making in a Democracy: The Role of the Supreme Court as a National Policy Maker', *Journal of Public Law*, 6 (1958) p. 279. See also J. D. Casper, 'The Supreme Court and National Policy Making', *American Political Science Review*, 70, 1 (March 1976) pp. 50–63.
4. J. H. H. Weiler, 'The Transformation of Europe', *Yale Law Review*, 100 (1991) pp. 2403–83; I. Loveland. 'Incorporating the European Convention on Human Rights into UK Law', *Parliamentary Affairs*, 52, 1 (1999), pp. 113–27.
5. See A. Hamilton, 'Federalist 78 – Judges as Guardians of the Constitution', in B. Wright (ed.), *The Federalist* (Cambridge, MA: Belknap, 1961).
6. See Chapter 7 on representation.
7. H. J. Spaeth, *Studies in Supreme Court Behavior* (New York: Garland, 1990).
8. G. A. Caldeira and J. L. Gibson, 'The Etiology of Public Support for the Supreme Court', *American Journal of Political Science*, 36 (1992), pp. 635–64.
9. See F. C. Barghoorn, *Politics in the USSR*, 2nd edn (Boston: Little, Brown, 1972), ch. x.
10. For a fuller study of the basis of the Soviet legal system, see J. N. Hazard, *The Soviet Legal System* (New York: Columbia University Press, 1984).
11. On practice in China, see T. V. Lee, *Law, the State and Society in China* (New York: Garland Press, 1997).
12. L. J. Edinger, *Politics in Germany* (Boston: Little, Brown, 1986) pp. 322–3.

13. See D.J. Stewart, B. Johnson and A. Singer, *Law and Society in Islam* (Princeton, NJ: Markus Wiener, 1996).
14. There are, however, specialised quasi-judicial structures.
15. The mixture of legislative judicial roles became evident during the Pinochet case in 1998–9.
16. For an outline of the English legal system, see D. Keenan, *Smith and Keenan's English Law*, 10th edn (London: Pitman, 1992) chs 1–3; also A. Patterson, *The Law Lords* (London, 1982).
17. For a comparison of the French and German legal systems, see Y. Meny, *Government and Politics in Western Europe* (Oxford: Oxford University Press, 1990) pp. 296–327.
18. See L. H. Tribe, *God Save This Honorable Court: How the Choice of Supreme Court Justices Shapes Our History* (New York: Random House, 1985). R. Hodder-Williams, 'Constitutional Legitimacy and the Supreme Court', in *Developments in American Politics*, ed. G. Peele *et al.* (London: Macmillan, 1992).
19. See R. A. Dahl, *Democracy in the United States*, 4th edn (Boston, 1981) p. 160.
20. See Meny, *Government and Politics*.
21. See B. Bunting, *The Rise of the South African Reich* (London, 1964) pp. 125–9. In 1987 South African courts continued their partial opposition to executive decisions by declaring aspects of the State of Emergency illegal, for example the banning of public reporting of clashes between demonstrators and police.
22. See G. Smith, *Democracy in Western Germany*, 3rd edn (London: Dartmouth, 1986) pp. 201–11.
23. See A.-M. Slaughter, A. Stone Sweet and J. H. H. Weiler, *The European Court and National Courts – Doctrine and Jurisprudence* (Oxford: Hart, 1998).
24. Edinger, *Politics in Germany*, p. 324. See also S. Cobler, *Law, Order, and Politics in West Germany* (London, 1978).
25. See D. E. Fouts, 'Policy Making in the Supreme Court of Canada, 1950–60', in *Comparative Judicial Behavior*, ed. G. Schubert and D.J. Danielski (Oxford: Oxford University Press, 1969) ch. 10.
26. See the essays in P. Bryden, S. Davis and J. Russell (eds), *Protecting Rights and Freedoms: Essays on the Charter's Place in Canada's Political, Legal and Intellectual Life* (Toronto: University of Toronto Press, 1994).
27. K. D. Ewing and C. A. Gearty, *Freedom under Thatcher: Civil Liberties in Modern Britain* (Oxford: Clarendon Press, 1990).
28. The various provisions of the Bill of Rights, the first ten amendments to the Constitution, form the basis of these rulings. See D.J. Bodenhamer and J. W. Ely (eds), *The Bill of Rights in America: After 200 Years* (Bloomington: Indiana University Press, 1993).
29. R.G. McCloskey, 'Reflections on the Warren Court', *Virginia Law Review* (Nov. 1965) pp. 1250–1.
30. This immunity is far from absolute. In the United States several federal judges have been impeached, along with numerous state judges. Further, there are even options in some states for recalling judges by the public directly through elections.

31. See S. White *et al.*, *Communist and Postcommunist Political Systems*, 3rd edn (London: Macmillan, 1990) pp. 295–6.
32. For a general discussion of the problems of federal enforcement of Supreme Court decisions, see D. McKay, *American Politics and Society*, 2nd edn (Oxford: Martin Robertson, 1989) pp. 264–5.

12
The Military and Politics

Readers fortunate enough to live in stable democratic countries will probably not think much about the role of the military in political life. In the (larger) remainder of the world in which democracy is far from assured, however, the military is often an active component of political life. The lengthy list of successful and unsuccessful direct interventions by the military in Central and South America, the Middle East, the new African states, Asia and several European countries since 1945 creates the impression that seizure of political control by the armed forces, or the military ensuring the replacement of one civilian government by another, has been the norm rather than the exception in modern political systems.[1] Between 1960 and 1982 there were 25 coups in Africa, fifteen in Latin America, twenty in the Far East and fourteen in the Middle East (including Turkey); the number of military take-overs has been dropping during the recent wave of democratisation (see Chapter 13), but they are still frequent in many parts of the world. Latin America has been a particularly fruitful area for military intervention since the beginning of the nineteenth century, although Africa has had at least as many coups since its countries began to gain independence in the 1950s.[2]

The political influence of the military stretches from direct assumptions of complete political control to complete subservience of the military to other political structures. However, the military may be able to control the political process by more subtle means that simply seizing control of political power directly. In fact, this overt type of intervention may sometimes indicate the inability of the armed forces to achieve their political goals through other means, and may be an indication of the rigidities in the nature of the political system that has given rise to such interventions. Given the poor international image of military coups, and the possible effects on international assistance, it is generally in the national interest for the military to exert influence indirectly.

There are intermediate stages between these two extremes of military power, such as the option of the military being involved in replacing one civilian government by another civilian government, or simply acting as the main political support for a civilian government – Rouquie refers to these systems as supervised democracies.[3] Examples might be the Fujimori government in Peru and Jordan both before and after the death of King Hussein. In other instances the military behaves as one of the many pressure groups within the political system, using the methods of influence, and applying the sanctions acceptable within that system. This may be true of the United States where, especially during the cold war, the military was a powerful institutional interest group.

Characteristics of the military

The armed forces have several characteristic features that distinguish them from other groups in all political systems, and these characteristics would lead one to expect that the military would intervene more frequently than it does: they raise the question of what prevents direct military intervention, rather than the question of why it happens at all.[4] The structure of the armed forces is hierarchical and centralised, placing a premium on rapid communications. Discipline and obedience to higher commands are considered of fundamental importance, and here one should note the bureaucratic obedience, in Weber's sense, to the rank and not to the individual who holds that rank. This obedience to authority means that officers can often get the (relatively) unthinking co-operation of the rank and file.

The armed forces in varying degrees emphasise their separation from civilian society by living in separate barracks and wearing distinctive uniforms and by the indoctrination of recruits in the history and traditions of that particular branch of the armed forces, resulting in a pride in that tradition and a distinct *esprit de corps*. Sometimes the military ensures for potential recruits a different type of education from an early age from that of civilian society. The consequent values inculcated into members of the armed forces, especially the officers, may distinguish them from the remainder of society in a way that is not true of other comparable groups such as police forces. Above all, the military monopolises the chief instruments of legitimate violence in the political system.

Yet these values and attitudes may not be such that they inevitably lead to a belief in right-wing solutions for the ills that may face society. There are many examples of military intervention to support radical policies of both the right-wing and left-wing varieties. But generally such values imply that the military may be above the sectional, vested interest conflicts in politics, and that the military is the embodiment of the national interest, albeit an authoritarian, disciplined conception of the national interest. That having been said, in some cases the military, or at least the officer corps, is dominated by one ethnic group or another and may be the centre of conflict in society. The strife in Rwanda was in part a result of a clear case of an army perceived as representing one contending ethnic group.

Military influence may be used to protect the armed forces from civilian mismanagement, such as a failure to expand them or equip them with the necessary modern weapons to carry out the important functions of protecting national territory from foreign aggression. Also, in some instances military pressure may result from junior officers being dissatisfied with their promotion prospects. None the less, these distinctive features lead the military to the belief that it is the only body aware of what constitutes the true national interest, and that only the military is capable of implementing policies to protect that interest given the fractiousness of the remainder of society.

This belief is partly the consequence of the role that the military plays in war and the threat of foreign invasion, and it is often immaterial whether it has been successful and provided countless heroes, or whether it has been humiliated. Defeats can be blamed on convenient scapegoats such as ethnic or political minorities. Defeat in the Arab–Israeli war of 1948 led, with other factors, to a weakening of the Egyptian regime of Farouk, but it left the army with its reputation almost intact, as the military defeats could be blamed on governmental incompetence, the equivalent of the 'stab in the back' by German socialists and Jews in 1918. The poor showing of American forces during Vietnam was blamed more on the absence of support at home than on problems in the military establishment itself.

These political attitudes of the military, and indeed the total role of the military in politics, depend on two variables. Firstly, there is the nature of the military itself. Some armed forces are more professionalised than others, and this will affect the prestige of the military in society and will affect the degree of pride and feeling of separateness with which the military reflects its distinctive values and attitudes.[5] Conscript armies differ from volunteer armies, though few match the level of military conscription of the Swiss, with their conception of a citizen army with intermittent military service for all males from twenty to fifty years. The social background of recruits varies from the emphasis on élite recruitment in some armed forces to reliance on peasant and lower-middle-class recruits in others. For example, one explanation offered for the relatively slight involvement of the Mexican military in politics, as compared with other armies in Latin America, is that the Mexican army is a popular, as opposed to an élite, force. In contrast, the Brazilian officer corps is rather similar in background to the political élite and has been more involved in politics.

The degree of specialisation and technical and administrative competence also differs, and can have profound effects on the ability of the military to influence and control decision-making processes in government. It may be that the leanings to violence, the lack of political experience and the attempt to apply military values and procedures to the process of government are disabilities of all armed forces, whether they are trying to influence or actually seize control of the government. The absolute level of technical ability in the military is important, but it is perhaps more relevant when the society and economy of the country in question does not have the abilities that can match those within the military.

The second variable explaining the role of the military in politics is the nature of the political system. Direct military intervention is less likely in industrialised liberal democracies or in socialist systems controlled by one party. Conversely, in states in which civilian governments lack prestige and have not succeeded in winning the allegiance of the people, the ability of the military to intervene directly is enhanced.[6] The military lacks the basis of legitimacy that civilian governments have, with their right to rule often based on traditions and conceptions of popular sovereignty, and therefore there must be serious weaknesses in the structure of the civilian government for military intervention to be successful. This political stability is not always based on the level of socio-economic development – a comparison of Germany between 1918 and 1933 and India since 1947 is sufficient to cast doubts on the certainty of that relationship – but the lower the level of economic development, the greater the likelihood of a weaker basis of legitimacy for the civilian governments. Even successful civilian governments are not proof against coups; the Gambia survived as a successful democracy for thirty years after independence but then succumbed to a military coup.[7]

The interaction of these two variables, the nature of the military and the strength of the civilian government, does not submit to any simple pattern. The cleavages between the values of civil and military authorities, the intensity with which these values are held, and the complexity of the government process itself, all complicate the nature of the relationship. To examine the role of the military in politics more closely and to emphasise these variables, we shall look at examples of: (1) limited interference by the military; (2) direct interference; (3) interference leading to military rule.

Limited interference in the political process

Direct military intervention in the political process is the exception rather than the rule in liberal democracies, as well as in the communist states such as the former Soviet Union.[8]

While the armed forces attempt to influence governmental policy, especially in the fields of foreign policy and defence, and try to win concessions for themselves, the frequency of attempts to threaten the displacement of the civilian government or of refusals to carry out its commands is low. The histories of such liberal democracies as the United States, Canada, Britain, the Scandinavian countries, the Netherlands, Belgium and Switzerland, to give a few examples, have been relatively untroubled by military challenges to the legitimacy of the civilian government, in spite of the martial past and imperial glories that some of these states have enjoyed. The United States, one of the first states to win independence from European domination by force of arms, provides an outstanding example of this subordination of the military. Only once, at the birth of the republic, was there a serious danger of active, direct military intervention against the civilian government, but Washington refused to lead the army on such a speculative venture. The paramountcy of civilian legitimacy survived the bloody civil war of 1861–5 and remains a cardinal feature of American government in the present period of American ascendancy in international politics. The willingness of President Truman to dismiss General Douglas MacArthur, a popular leader who appeared ready to defy civilian control during the Korean conflict, demonstrated the centrality of this principle.[9]

Likewise, since the experience of army control under Cromwell in the seventeenth century, Britain has escaped the problem of overt military involvement in the processes of government. The Curragh mutiny of 1914 provides an inconclusive exception. Several officers in the British army in Ireland resigned because of the possibility of their being sent to fight the Ulster Volunteers. Three points should be noted in respect of this incident. Firstly, the period 1910–14 was an exceptional period in British politics, and the Irish Home Rule issue was but one aspect of an unusual breakdown of the consensus among the British ruling élites. Secondly, the resigning officers were from the northern part of Ireland and objected to forcing Protestant Ulster into self-governing union with the Catholic south. Thirdly, the officers did not disobey orders, but merely resigned when given this option by their commanding officer.

Perhaps more relevant to the role of the military in British politics were the relations that 1914–18 war prime ministers had with their generals. These problems did not recur in the Second World War, and it should be noted that war can produce exceptional strains on civilian–military relationships, even in the most stable political system.

Liberal democracies are characterised by a long history of independence, national unity, a relatively stable process of industrialisation, and an orderly and accepted means of transferring political power. These factors, allied to the notion of popular sovereignty developed with the liberal theories of the state in the nineteenth century, provide a strong basis of legitimacy for civilian governments. Other groups in the political process, such as political parties, can effectively challenge the moral authority of the military to intervene directly in politics. Moreover, the military in these societies lacks the prestige it receives in other political systems, and there is less emphasis on separateness from civilian society. In Britain the higher ranks are drawn from the upper classes in society, thus, to a degree, sharing the values of civilian élites, reflecting a balance that exists in society as a whole. The effect of the long British influence on the Indian army and to a lesser extent on the Malaysian armed forces may be a factor in the avoidance in these states of direct military intervention since independence, although the history, economic development and social structure offer sharp contrasts with the more industrialised liberal democracies.

Yet within liberal democracies the military, while respecting the legitimate supremacy of the civilian government, does play an important role in the political process. President Eisenhower, in his farewell message in 1961, warned of a 'military-industrial complex' that could dominate the government of the United States. The size of the American military budget, the complexity of the military machine and the overlap between foreign policy and military strategy have given rise to fears that the armed forces are exercising too great an influence on political decision-making.[10] Yet civilian supremacy is a fundamental principle of American government. As one writer has pointed out:

Not only is meaningful civilian supremacy accepted in principle by military and civilians alike, but military officers are essentially willing to accept the actions and decisions that flow from it (however much they may deplore specific ones). The leadership of the Department of State in foreign policy is accepted in the same spirit. Similarly, the State Department accepts military participation in foreign policy.[11]

The military thus accepted decisions that they did not like in the least during the Korean conflict, the Vietnam War, and at the end of the Gulf War.

It follows from this that the military is one group among many attempting to influence decision-making, and the controls are essentially similar to those exercised over other groups in the American system of government. The American military shares the fundamental values of American society as a whole, and the degree of control rests on the efficiency of the civilian organisations, such as the Department of Defense, in imposing their own more detailed directives. The military and its civilian allies do lobby for new weapons systems (for example the 'Star Wars' initiative during the Reagan administration), and to some degree also lobby within official circles for the adoption of strategic perspectives.[12]

In communist states such as the Soviet Union, civilian supremacy over the armed forces was as marked as in most liberal democracies. For periods before 1942 the Soviet army had a dual system of control in which the orders of the military commander had to be countersigned by a political commissar appointed by, and responsible to, the Communist Party. Efficiency demanded the abolition of this system several times, but in periods of political uncertainty it was restored. Trotsky had magnificently created the Red Army to defend the Bolshevik revolution of 1917, but it never achieved the independence of civilian control of other revolutionary armies in history. The most complete period of political subjugation of the armed forces occurred during the Stalinist period, and his great purges of 1937–8 ensured that there would be no political threat from the military.

With Stalin's death in 1953, and the lengthy struggle over his succession, the Soviet military appeared to acquire more direct political influence. Army units ensured the fall of Beria, the feared and hated chief of police, and the support of the Soviet leaders was important in the triumph of Khrushchev in his defeat of Malenkov in 1955, and the routing of his remaining political opponents in 1957. The army was suspicious of Malenkov's emphasis on consumer goods and decreases in the military budgets. It was rewarded for its support by an increase in military spending and the appointment of Marshal Zhukov as minister of defence.

However, this increased independent role for the army was short-lived. Khrushchev, aware of the dangers, counterattacked: Zhukov was demoted in 1957, and full civilian supremacy was restored. This civilian control was not threatened again until the abortive coup of August 1991, when conservative elements within the Party, the military and the KGB attempted to seize power.

China since 1949 displays the same characteristics that typified the USSR between 1917 and 1991, and which make communist regimes little different from liberal democracies in terms of civilian–military relationships: the ultimate control lies with the civilians. It is true that for a short period the communist leadership in China abolished the distinctions between officers and the rank and file, but these were soon restored. The Chinese People's Liberation Army was and is controlled as in other communist systems by the interpenetration of élites; the military leadership has close links with the Communist Party élites and are almost indistinguishable. The role of the military in supporting the communist leadership can be illustrated by two events. In the mid-1960s, the radicals in China were gaining the upper hand during the Cultural Revolution; the army played a key role in 1967–8 in defeating the radicals and restoring the authority of the more conservative elements within the Chinese communist leadership.[13] Secondly, in June 1989, the army was crucial in defeating disaffected elements, particularly amongst the students, and the unrest culminated in the brutal crushing of the opposition by the army, typified by the massacre of dissidents in Tiananmen Square, in Peking.

Post-communist regimes have attempted to follow closely the liberal democratic model in terms of civilian–military relationships and since the revolutions in those states many leading personnel have been replaced by officers with fewer loyalties to the old systems. So far the military has adhered to the model of limited interference, in spite of various rumours in some states to the contrary. However, given the seriousness of economic and social problems that these regimes face in varying degrees with the resultant threat to political stability, there is less assurance that direct interference by the military in the future may not become a feature of some of these political systems.

Direct interference

Direct interference by the military in politics, but falling short of the assumption of power by the military, may occur in any type of political system. The military may merely exert direct pressure to attempt to achieve a particular political goal, may create the conditions for a change of government or even dictate what type of civilian government achieves power. The army mutinies in Kenya, Tanzania and Uganda in 1964, which led to the respective governments calling for British military assistance to put them down, had their roots in dissatisfaction with army pay and conditions, and the rate of Africanisation of senior ranks; they were not consciously aimed at overthrowing the existing governments, and were certainly not a step towards establishing military governments.[14] It is difficult to find general reasons underlying the military interventions in other African states with similar problems of development, and with British influences in the military and political structures. The Ghanaian coups of 1966, 1972 and 1979, the Nigerian coups of 1966, 1975 and 1983, the Sudanese coups of 1985 and 1989, and that in Sierra Leone in 1992, partly represented clashes between different élites, protests against corruption, and the protection of military vested interests.

Nevertheless, in spite of these difficulties in finding common denominators for different levels of military intervention, there are some factors which tend to inhibit full military control. The

triumph of liberal democracy in France after 1870 was sufficient to survive several military crises in the early years of the
Third Republic. The McMahon scare of 1877, the Boulanger
crisis of 1886 and the Dreyfus scandal at the turn of the century
were overcome and it appeared that France had finally secured
the subordination of the military to the civilian government.[15]
Yet the intervention of the military was crucial in the collapse
of the Fourth Republic in 1958. An explanation lies in the
reverses of French foreign policy and the contraction of her
overseas empire since 1945. The disastrous reverses in Indo-
China, the military success followed by the political defeat in
the Suez crisis of 1956, and the clash of European settlers and
north African nationalists, especially in Algeria, had weakened
the army's faith in the governments' policies. French civilian
institutions were highly developed, but the instability of the
successive governments and the 'immobilisme' of the politics of
the Fourth Republic allowed the army, and especially the
army in Algeria, to challenge the legitimacy, the right to rule,
of the French government. Before 1958 the army had controlled Algeria and directed the war there with increasingly
little reference to the government in Paris, and flagrant acts of
insubordination were only lightly punished by the civilian
authorities. A significant factor in the 1958 crisis was that no
important sector of French society was willing to defend the
regime. Also, once the army had reached the position of open
defiance of the government, de Gaulle provided an alternative
source of authority to which civilians as well as the army could
appeal. If the events of 1958 are compared with the army
revolt of 1961, it can be seen that in the second crisis the army
did not confront a weakened civilian government. Moreover
the attempted coup was confined to the army in Algeria, and
was not supported by army units in France or those stationed
in Germany. President de Gaulle was able to rally all important sections of French society in opposition to the rebellious
generals, and the revolt which had achieved success in Algeria
soon crumbled in the face of this united civilian hostility.[16]

Two examples expose the limitations of the military's role in
the political process. The German army enjoyed unparalleled
prestige in the German Empire after 1871; responsible only to
the Emperor, bound by rigid professional loyalties which were

reinforced by the upper-class background of its officers, it supported the political system but was not the government. After 1918, the size of the army was limited and the country threatened by internal political upheavals with the army drawn more firmly into the political arena to restore its previous independence and prestige. The army leaders intrigued against the governments of the Weimar Republic, not to achieve absolute power, but to ensure the independence of the army. Thus, the army welcomed the authoritarian Nazi government of 1933 in the belief that Hitler's aims coincided with those of the army and that Hitler's mass movement would legitimise the stronger foreign policy which the army desired. However, by 1938 Hitler had succeeded in crushing the last vestiges of military independence and had established complete civilian – read personal and Nazi party – control.

The Spanish army had been one of the main props of the Franco regime after the civil war in the 1930s. This conservative loyalty was reinforced by the overwhelming upper-class background of the officer corps and the willingness of Franco to expand military strength. It was not surprising that the armed forces viewed developments after the dictator's death in 1975 with some suspicion. It opposed, with some success, military reforms to limit the size of the army and was completely opposed to the legalisation of left-wing parties such as the Communist Party. The reduced political importance of the military was instrumental in leading to the unsuccessful military coup of February 1981. The failure of the abortive coup forced the army reluctantly to recognise the legitimacy of the Socialist accession to power in 1982, while the Spanish membership of NATO and then the European Union, and greater democratisation of the officer corps. has almost totally removed the likelihood of direct military intervention.[17]

The French, German and Spanish examples illustrate the relationship between the strength and legitimacy of the civilian government and the political power of the military. When the civilian government is attempting to establish its legitimacy, as with France during the Fourth Republic, Germany under Weimar, and Spain in the post-Franco period of 1975 and 1982, the military will act with a degree of independence and either oppose the government or not seek to actively defend it.

However with the installation of civilian legitimacy with the election of a de Gaulle, the accession to power of a Hitler or the popular election of a Socialist government, the independence of the military was reduced. Further, although citizens of liberal democracies assume that civilian control is necessarily positive, the German case in particular demonstrates that the military value system may be preferable in some cases.

Military control

There are difficulties in measuring the exact degree of military interference short of direct military control, and arriving at a broad classification of the reasons why this particular level is reached in particular regimes. The same problems are present in an examination of regimes that endure direct military control. Some states may be described as being controlled by military–civilian coalitions: Finer gave the examples of Jordan, Morocco, Bahrain and the Sultanate of Oman,[18] while Peru and several African countries could now be added to that list. Also many countries that perceive themselves to be under constant threat, e.g. Israel and South Korea, may have a closer alliance between civilian and military powers than is usually found in a liberal political system.

Military governments may become more civilianised after the passage of time without any dramatic political changes taking place. This has happened in Egypt since the military coup of 1952; Spain offers an illustration of the army seizing power after a prolonged civil war, but gradually becoming an important, not dominant, prop of the existing regime, and then ceding power to civilian rulers. Some military dictatorships are camouflaged by presidential elections and representative assemblies, with the military leaders assuming civilian status in order to perpetuate army control, as in Brazil. Army control may be distinguishable from the continual replacement of one civilian government by another, a persistent factor in Syrian politics since 1945.[19]

There are examples of the military relinquishing control – direct political control, that is – for short periods in some cases. The Burmese army, seizing control in 1958, surrendered it partly after eighteen months, but returned to assume full control again in 1962. In Ghana, the army seized power in 1966 with a return to civilian rule in 1969 for a short period. Since 1979, there has been continuous military rule, despite several promises of free elections. Further moves towards civilian rule were again interrupted by the military coup of 1981. The Greek army surrendered control in 1974 after a period of military dictatorship lasting from 1967, a change that soon opened EU membership to Greece.

Thus the degrees of control make any system of rigid classification difficult. Nevertheless, the frequency of military takeovers in Latin America, the Middle East, the new nations of north and sub-Saharan Africa and South-East Asia does indicate the links between military dictatorship and the level of socio-economic development, the strength of civilian institutions and the nature of the military response to the problems that face these states.[20]

In the states that experience direct military control the legitimacy of the existing political institutions and of the ruling élites is disputed. The regime has not acquired the respect that puts it beyond the challenge of the armed forces. Thus, far from meeting widespread opposition to its intervention, the army may be welcomed as a means of ridding the state of the old corrupt and inefficient politicians. The colonels' seizure of power in Egypt in 1952 took place against a backcloth of a discredited political system that concentrated power in the hands of a narrow oligarchy which appeared to be manipulated by British imperial interests and was symbolised by an ineffectual, pleasure-loving hereditary ruler. This government had taken the country to the humiliating defeat at the hands of the Israelis in the 1948 war, and had lost what popular support it may have had. The cautious colonels were pushed on from their original intention of replacing one civilian government by another to seizing complete political control by the hollowness of the existing political system and the lack of support it received.[21] A similar selfish ruling group provided easy opposition for the Iraqi army's seizure of power in 1958. The prime minister, Nuries-Said, who was murdered with the king during the coup, had long resorted to emergency laws to ensure his political survival, but the government's failure to implement social reforms, its seeming rejection of the Arab cause against Israel, and the claims that it was assisting the aims of British foreign policy in the area, left it without serious support.

The failure of the existing political institutions to establish a legitimate base and to win the respect and support of powerful groups within the state is a particular problem for new nations that have recently emerged from colonial domination. These difficulties are increased if the level of socio-economic development has not allowed the emergence of strong political parties, trade unions and a business and professional class to rival the military's influence. In other words, there is no civil society to form the social foundation for less authoritarian governments.[22] The gap between rich and poor may preclude the development of a stable consensus within the country, and if the state is in a sensitive area of international politics, such as the Middle East, there is great emphasis on large military budgets assisted by the outside interference of the great powers.

The complexity of these variables is illustrated by Argentina's recent history. Long independent with a relatively high level of economic development and strong trade union and party organisation, the country's instability led to a military coup in 1976. The Falklands defeat in 1982 paved the way for the restoration of civilian government, but Alfonsin and his 1989 successor, Menem, have constantly been forced, in the face of military threats and abortive coups, to make compromises with the armed forces.[23]

However, the low level of economic development may lead the army to intervene on the part of radical forces in the country aiming at a more egalitarian social structure, as was the case with the Egyptian coup. Generally, however, the military tends to support conservative groups, as the Brazilian army did when it overthrew the left-wing president Goulart in 1964 and established a right-wing dictatorship. There are often tensions between senior and junior officers in regard to right and left political orientations. An added complication is that of external military aid. The United States is a lavish provider of aid in the forms of technical assistance, training, money and weapons to armies in underdeveloped countries to counter any possible threats to pro-western governments, and other western countries also spend ample quantities of money on military aid, especially to their former colonies. This assistance not only strengthens the military inside the state, but it is also designed to encourage anti-radical tendencies. The American government encouraged the Chilean army to overthrow the radical Allende government in September 1973, and the ensuing military dictatorship brutally suppressed any form of left-wing political activity.

Regional differences inside the state may be so acute as to precipitate crises leading to direct assumption of power by the military. This can occur in states with a long history of independence and unity such as Spain, but is particularly a problem facing new states and those states in which tribal loyalties take precedence over loyalty to the central government. Nigeria since independence is a clear example of regional divisions leading to military dictatorship. The state was a federal structure based on regions loosely adhering to the main tribal divisions, with political power being mainly controlled by the conservative, Muslim, feudal north in alliance with either of the two more advanced, sophisticated, mainly Christian coastal regions, the Yoruba west and the Ibo east. The army failed to overcome the tribal tensions within its own ranks, but the predominance of the Ibo officers, who had joined the army to advance the interests of their own region, led to a military coup in 1966 in which the northern and western military officers were the chief victims. General Ironsi, while trying to promote the 'one Nigeria' concept, was identified with eastern Ibo interests, which led to a tribal counter-coup in the same year. This time the Ibo tribe suffered the most, and a series of massacres of Ibo in the northern region led to a split in the military dictatorship of General Gowan and General Ojukwu; a civil war saw the end of Ibo secessionist aims with the victory for the federal military government in 1969.

The nature of the armed forces is a factor of great significance in the establishment of a military government. In some states the army is identified with nationalism, the protection of the general interest, and embodies the values of order and efficiency. Thus, when the heady wine of independence has evaporated and the unity of the groups that have fought for independence is cracking, the army is resorted to in order to support national as opposed to sectional interest; that is, if the army has maintained its own unity. This is true even when the army did not win prestige in the struggle for national independence. Certainly in new and underdeveloped countries the military may monopolise certain administrative skills and possess most of the trained manpower of engineers, surveyors, etc. The military is often the most 'westernised' or 'modern' structure in a traditional, rural, tribal and hierarchical society. Even where tribal and other differences exist, the army provides a structure where they are most likely to be minimised. The impact of rival training schemes in America, the Soviet Union, Britain and China may produce tensions within the military of a particular state that could destroy its unity and professional image. It was fear of Nkrumah's mistrust of the army, his spies and his proposals to train more officers in Soviet Russia that finally induced the army to bring down his regime in 1966 and establish a period of military dictatorship.

The degree of professionalisation of the army is important, but a factor that may cut across it and have important consequences itself is the area of recruitment. Armies in the Middle East have tended to draw their officers from the lower-middle classes, and these groups have joined because there was no other organisation capable of effecting the reforms in the political system that they thought necessary, and they have implemented important social reforms after the military has achieved power. Political leaders in northern Nigeria looked upon military careers with disdain, as being below their feudal dignity, with the consequent domination by the coastal tribes. Armies, in fact, may lack a monolithic structure. The Portuguese army that seized control in April 1974 divided into several political groups ranging from the conservative General Spinola to the more radical General Gonçalves. The political ferment in Portugal in the years after the coup tended to reflect the political conflicts within the armed forces more than the competition between the political parties.[24]

The existence of both institutional and economic crises has led to the relatively rare examples of military intervention in socialist states. In Poland the military came to play the dominant role after December 1981, not only through its administration of martial law and direct supervision of certain sectors of the economy, such as mining, but also through the increased participation of military personnel in the leading institutions of the Communist Party (PZPR). In Romania, in December 1989, the military proved the decisive force in the anti-communist revolution. Given the repressive nature of the regime, there was no organised popular opposition to Ceausescu; rather the revolution took the form of spontaneous popular protest. Military leaders resisted orders to fire on demonstrators and later transferred their support to the protesters, while the notorious, vicious Securitate, or secret police, fought doggedly on the side of the discredited government.

August 1991 saw unprecedented military intervention in the USSR. The Soviet military at that time had good cause to perceive threats to its major interests. The economy was in crisis and the military was increasingly being used for domestic law-and-order functions for which it was ill-equipped and untrained. Nationalism fuelled desertion and draft dodging in the non-Russian republics. New agreements with the United States meant not only radical cuts in weaponry but also severe reductions in the defence budget. Furthermore, Gorbachev had 'lost' Eastern Europe and had betrayed erstwhile allies such as Iraq in the Gulf War. A new draft treaty of union was about to be signed, transferring considerable power from the centre to the republics.

However, August 1991 was hardly a classic military coup; the coup was an attempt by one element of the Soviet leadership (party, government, military, KGB) to remove another. The Minister of Defence was among the plotters. None the less, there were reformist elements in both the military and the KGB and it is these divisions which above all explain the ignominious failure of the coup attempt. The Russian President, Boris Yeltsin, and the Mayor of Leningrad, Anatoly Sobchak, remained at large, and both had help from senior military officials. A number of commanders absented themselves or delayed or even refused obedience to commands (which were in any case confused). The conspirators lacked clear aims or a programme for their avowed intention to slow the reform process; their unity was short-lived. Instead of 'saving' the USSR the abortive coup simply precipitated its disintegration.

Conclusion

In all political systems the military possesses certain advantageous characteristics which allow it to intervene in the political process. But these advantages are marked by some corresponding deficits which tend to inhibit certain types of intervention. The type of intervention, whether merely seeking influence or that of establishing a military dictatorship, will vary according to several criteria: the nature of the political system, the stability of the political institutions, and the level of socio-economic development. There are also the factors of the organisation, recruitment and degree of professionalisation of the armed forces, and the extent to which military values correspond to the values of civilian society. However, both these groups of variables will depend, to some extent, on the particular circumstances that occur at particular times; in other words, historical accidents. External pressures are increasingly important in the twentieth century, with the improvement of communications, the importance of international ideological alignments, and a concern for human rights. Above all there is the need to base the various types of intervention on popular support, and the military is often reluctant to act unless it believes that it has some degree of popular support.

The problems facing the military do not end when the intervention is accomplished. The difficulties of retreating from a given level of interference are almost as great as effecting the intervention in the first place: we have already noted the example of the Argentinian military surrendering supreme political power in 1983, but continuing to threaten the civilian government for some time thereafter. Moreover, the assumption of a high level of interference begins to change the military's relationship with the governmental processes. It becomes responsible for unpopular decisions, it risks losing the belief that it puts the wider national interest before narrower sectional interests, and the unity of the armed forces may be impaired when it decides to rule. The military finds it difficult to restore its former relationship with civilian governments, and its leaders may risk being penalised – the precedent of Nuremberg and prosecution of crimes against humanity must now concern any prospective strong-man. Often the very act of intervention may lose the army its most important asset, that of potential intervention. The factors that determine the level of military interference are seldom removed by the subsequent intervention and are usually a consistent feature of the political system.

Notes and references

1. See R. Pinkney, *Right-Wing Military Government* (London: Pinter, 1990).
2. For example, since the military took over in the Sudan in 1989, there have been at least five attempted counter-coups by military groups. Somalia has basically disintegrated as a result of fighting between different military groups. Rival military groups have fought for control in a number of other African states.
3. R. Rouquie, *Demilitarization and the Institutionalization of Military-Dominated Politics in Latin America* (Washington, DC: Woodrow Wilson Center, 1982).
4. S. E. Finer, *The Man on Horseback,* 2nd edn (London: Routledge, 1988) p. 4.
5. For a classic study, see S. P. Huntington, *The Soldier and the State* (Cambridge, MA: Harvard University Press, 1957).
6. C. Cruz and R. Diamant, 'The New Military Autonomy in Latin America', *Journal of Democracy*, 9, 4 (1998), pp. 115–28.
7. J. A. Wiseman, 'The Gambia: From Coup to Election', *Journal of Democracy*, 9, 2 (1998) pp. 64–75.
8. See A. R. Ball and F. Millard, *Pressure Politics in Industrial Societies* (London: Macmillan, 1986) pp. 243–80.
9. R. Lowitt, *The Truman-MacArthur Controversy* (Chicago: Rand-McNally, 1967).
10. See C. Wright Mills, *The Power Elite* (Oxford: Oxford University Press, 1956) ch. 8, for a different emphasis on the role of the military in American politics.
11. B. M. Sapin, *The Making of United States Foreign Policy* (New York: Praeger, 1966) p. 171.
12. E. Reiss, *The Strategic Defense Initiative* (Cambridge: Cambridge University Press, 1992).
13. See J. Gray, *Rebellions and Revolutions: China from the 1800s to the 1980s* (Oxford University Press, 1990) pp. 354–5.
14. See W. F. Gutteridge, *Military Regimes in Africa* (London, 1975). However, while Uganda has suffered civil war and a series of military coups since the overthrow of Milton Obote by Idi Amin, Kenya and Tanzania have escaped direct military rule although there was an abortive coup by air force officers in Kenya in August 1982. Mugabe in Zimbabwe, in spite of the guerrilla war background to independence and the military activities of his opponents, has kept civilian government intact since independence in 1980.

15. See D. Thompson, *Democracy in France,* 2nd edn (Oxford: Oxford University Press, 1952) pp. 147–63, for an outline of these crises in the Third Republic.

16. See Finer, *The Man on Horseback,* pp. 85–8.

17. See J. Hooper, *The Spaniards: A Portrait of New Spain* (London: Penguin, 1987) pp. 61–79.

18. See S. E. Finer, 'The Morphology of Military Regimes', in *Soldiers, Peasants and Bureaucrats,* ed. R. Kolkowicz and A. Korbonski (London: Allen & Unwin, 1982) pp. 280–309.

19. See N. Van Dam, *The Struggle for Power in Syria* (London: I. B. Tauris, 1995). Also P. Scale, *Assad of Syria* (Berkeley: University of California Press 1989).

20. See C. P. Danopoulos (ed.), *Military Disengagement from Politics* (London, 1988). Also A. Rouguie, *The Military and State in Latin America* (London, 1987).

21. See P. Mansfield, *A History of the Middle East* (London: Penguin, 1992) pp. 240–4.

22. See Chapter 13.

23. See P. Cammack and P. O'Brien, 'Conclusion: The Retreat of the Generals', in *Generals in Retreat: The Crisis of Military Rule in Latin America* (Manchester: University of Manchester Press, 1985) pp. 184–203.

24. See Antonio de Figueiredo, *Portugal: Fifty Years of Dictatorship* (New York: Holmes & Meier, 1975).

PART FOUR

Political Change

13

Change in Political Systems

Throughout the analysis of political institutions, political actors and policy processes, we have noted the impact of political change. We have seen, for example, that party systems are substantially affected by alterations in the electoral system; executive power *vis-à-vis* the assembly may be weakened or strengthened by changes in the formal rules, i.e. the constitution, and as a result of changing information technology. Change is inherent in politics; no political system is immune. It is most common to discuss change in the context of developing countries, but the industrial democracies also undergo constant change. New challenges and new answers to those challenges result in the gradual continued evolution of these political systems.

Problems of analysis

However, merely to claim that all political systems are subject to change adds little to our knowledge. We need to know what type of change has occurred in the past or is occurring now. Does it affect all aspects of the political system? Is it enduring, and, importantly, what are its causes? The most widely studied aspects of contemporary political change are democratisation and transition in the former communist countries of central and eastern Europe, as well as in Latin America, Asia and parts of Africa. But the increasing globalisation of political, economic and social life has accelerated change in the indus-

287

trialised democracies also. This is especially evident in Europe where the European Union is altering political identities and policy-making in systems that have seemed 'stable' for years.[1]

It may be easy to recognise change and establish its causes. Thus, the rewriting of the French constitutional rules in 1958 clearly led to a more powerful French executive, namely the presidency; the poor performance of the Russian armies during the 1914–18 war against Germany directly contributed to the Russian revolutions of 1917. Yet these two examples are of clearly defined and dramatic events. Most instances of political change are not so clear-cut. Britain at the beginning of the twenty-first century is a liberal democracy but at the beginning of the nineteenth century this was not the case. Change had occurred but there had been no manifest 'revolution' since the end of the seventeenth century. This makes it more difficult and complex to establish the sequence of events that led the British political system to evolve from an aristocratic élite system to the present liberal democratic one than it is to identify the events in France or Germany.

Obviously, there is a difference between 'evolutionary' change and 'revolutionary' change. Even this distinction, however, bristles with difficulties. Barrington Moore has stressed the pertinent point that all systems, even liberal democracies, have followed a 'revolutionary' path to their present status.[2] The United States, France and Britain all experienced revolutionary upheavals in their historical transition to democracy. The revolutionary commercialisation of agricultural production with the disappearance of the peasant class, the winning of autonomy by certain groups from state control, and the waning of the power of organised religion were all factors leading to the watersheds represented by 1776, 1789 and 1688 respectively. These were revolutions comparable in many respects to the Bolshevik Revolution in 1917, the Chinese Revolution of 1949, that of Cuba in 1959 and certainly the largely non-violent Eastern European revolutions of 1989.[3]

As well as forming the basis of the political transformations of countries such as the United Kingdom and France the changes mentioned by Moore also formed the basis of subsequent change, especially the development of the Welfare State.[4] For example, industrialisation was associated with movement of people away from their extended families and other sources of social support, and this in turn created a need for old-age pensions, social assistance and all the other programmes we now associate with modern social policy. Subsequent social change, such as increasing female participation in the labour force and the aging of populations, have continued the development of social programmes to meet changing needs and demands.

Political change is rarely the consequence of a single cause. For example, President Gorbachev began in 1985 to reform the communist system in the Soviet Union from within; within six years he had not only contributed to the demise of the CPSU in the Soviet Union, but to the disintegration of the state itself, as well as to immense changes in the former Soviet empire in Eastern Europe. His evolutionary reforms led to perhaps the most far-reaching revolutionary changes in the twentieth century. Yet he neither planned these changes, nor were they solely the result of his initial reforms.

The experience of 'third world' states in the second half of the twentieth century offers a cautionary tale of the pitfalls of political analysis. The mainstream view of political scientists in the 1950s and 1960s (generally presented as being value-free and 'scientific') tended to assume that there was a 'natural path' for development in the direction of liberal democracy, much like that found in European and North American democracies. The reality proved far more complex and differentiated than the modernisation theorists or their radical critics had predicted.[5]

The recent concern with successful democratisation in post-communist and post-authoritarian systems (including relatively affluent systems such as South Korea) has produced a new set of theories about political change. This can be broken down roughly into those which focus on institutional factors, those which focus on political élites, and societal theories. Scholars in the first camp argue that the best way to create successful democracies is to build and invigorate democratic institutions.[6] This may not be a simple task, but the proponents of this approach argue that it is faster, and probably more likely to succeed, than waiting for society to develop to a point that democracy becomes more feasible. Further, this approach can build up legitimacy for government through non-major-itarian institutions (central banks, courts, etc.) and then build the democracy to sustain that legitimacy.[7] Political élites are important in this process but the more important factor is the institutional structure.

For proponents of the second approach political élites are the crucial force in producing political change. With particular reference to democratisation it has been argued that successful cases such as Spain are the product of élite 'pacts', or agree-ments among potentially hostile groups that some form of peaceful transition is more important than their particular political advantages.[8] While successful democratisation almost inevitably involves some element of élite acquiescence, this approach places élites at the centre of the process of change and assumes that their agreement is sufficient for peaceful transformation of the political system.

The third alternative assumes that the only way to create political democracy is to build the social structures and values that support democracy.[9] Following Robert Putnam, this approach focuses on the need for 'social capital' and building an infrastructure of groups that creates social trust and fosters amity within the society.[10] Its adherents argue that attempting to build the institutions of democracy without first creating social and political trust among the population is doomed to fail, as can be seen in the breakdown of many multi-ethnic societies. Even more homogenous societies, it is argued, may not be able to construct effective democracies if there is inadequate social trust at lower levels of the society.

Political stability

Change is the obverse of stability, yet 'evolutionary' change may represent stability; stability and change are not necessarily opposites. The American political system has, since 1789, been an extremely stable one in spite of the mid-nineteenth-century civil war, with a few dozen amendments to the Constitution but no more basic changes. Despite that, the Founding Fathers would be utterly confused by the contemporary political system which has emerged from their reforms at the end of the eighteenth century. Stability is a relative term and it needs careful use. We have seen that governments in Italy since the end of the Second World War have been extremely unstable in terms of tenure, with a new government on average every six months. Yet the Italian political system actually has been very stable, i.e. the same social and political élites continue to rule despite numerous changes in office; regime stability is not the same as government stability.[11]

Obviously, political systems regarded as 'stable' display certain common characteristics. Thus if we look at systems in Western Europe, Australasia and North America, we find that in all these systems the political institutions and political processes are regarded as 'legitimate'. Governments have political power, but in the main their decisions are accepted because the governments are regarded as having the legitimate authority to make these decisions. In liberal democracies the authority of the government is based on their being elected periodically; the fact that the people have chosen the government through the process of free elections confers legitimacy on the government.

Furthermore, stable, liberal democratic systems have another distinctive characteristic; there is agreement on the 'rules of the game' by which the political system operates.[12] Political scientists employ the term 'consensus' to describe the nature of this agreement.[13] The term itself is open both to abuse and different interpretations,[14] but generally, it implies that while there is not complete agreement on system goals by the contending groups within the political system, these goals will not be sufficiently divergent to threaten other groups. Also, it implies there is basic agreement on the means by which the goals will be sought. Thus, in the liberal democracies of Western Europe, no matter how wide the disagreement on aims, all sides will abide by the existing rules of the game and essentially observe the wishes of the people as expressed through the ballot box. Further, there will be a limited range of acceptable means through which government can pursue its policy goals.

There is, however, never complete agreement on either ends or means; a system can be regarded as consensual even though groups exist which wish to destroy the state by violent means.

Neither the activities of the IRA in the British system nor the Basque separatist groups in Spain, with their violent opposition to the policies of the state, mean that the British and Spanish systems are not characterised by a high degree of consensus. Most stable, consensual systems are also able to accommodate various small groups that, while not wishing to overthrow the system, use relatively violent means to achieve their political ends; examples would include farming groups in France, some anti-abortion groups in the United States, and animal rights groups in Britain.

However, both the terms 'consensus' and 'legitimacy' cause many problems in political analysis. There is the constant danger of a circular argument: a political system is legitimate because it is stable and it is stable because it is legitimate. Both legitimacy and consensus are concepts which depend heavily on the distribution of power within the political system. It may be important for regime stability that there is agreement or consensus between the political élites and that the majority of people simply accept the values of the élites without necessarily agreeing with them. The American pluralist tradition has certainly viewed with disfavour 'too much' mass political participation within the political system and suggests that it may even be evidence of instability.[15]

To understand the process of change and stability better, one needs to ask various questions in discussing the relationship between consensus and political stability: Between whom is there a consensus? To what does the consensus relate: How deep and enduring is that consensus? For example, there may be general agreement among political élites about the nature of the system and the desirability of the existing political order, but if that is not shared by the public then there is danger of instability. Likewise, the consensus may be a function of good economic performance rather than basic political agreement, so that consensus is extremely fragile.

Political change

As with political stability, the nature and causes of political change cause disagreements among political scientists. Thus, groups may seize power within the political system and maintain the existing political institutions, yet change the previous pattern of power distribution radically; here the political change, because of the superficial continuity of institutions, does not appear to have been a radical one. The Sudanese army coup of 1989 is an example of this type; the system as previously constituted continued but its actual operations were fundamentally altered by the military and the attempts to create a more Islamic state.[16]

Other types of change are far more radical in every respect. The Bolshevik seizure of power in Russia, in 1917, not only entailed a redistribution of political power in favour of previously illegitimate groups, but a complete change in political institutions and decision-making processes, radical alterations in social relationships and a completely new economic system. All these changes were underpinned by a new ideology which owed little to previous dominant ideologies in Russia. Political change may be violent, as in China in 1949, or relatively peaceful as illustrated by Czechoslovakia in 1989. There may be organised violence by well-organised groups, such as those in Iran in 1979, or the groups may attain power through a relatively peaceful coup, as seen in Portugal in 1974. Change may be assisted significantly by spontaneous outbreaks of popular dissatisfaction, as in 1989 in East Germany, or the popular rising may he more of a cover for a coup on the part of sections of the armed forces, as was the case in Romania in 1989. Radical political change may be a consequence of foreign invasions, as in France in 1940 or Tibet in 1949.

Whatever the nature of these changes, revolutionary, as opposed to evolutionary, change is characterised by its speed and intensity, and by the extent to which it changes the political system. Evolutionary change involves the gradual replacement of existing political institutions and processes while maintaining the fundamental characteristics of the system.

Causes of political change

Historians, seeking to offer explanations for the collapse of the Austro-Hungarian Empire during the 1914–18 war, while not in full agreement, have tentatively offered the following explanations for this momentous change:

1. The multinational empire, containing Germans, Poles, Czechs, Hungarians, Italians and Serbs could not withstand the growing forces of nationalism.
2. The Hapsburg government was over-centralised, inefficient and unable to cope administratively with the demands within this huge, 'ramshackle' empire.
3. In a period when there was increasing emphasis on democratic government, the Imperial system was both conservative and unrepresentative, opposed by both liberals and socialists.
4. The Emperor, controlling this vast empire, was personally inadequate for the task.
5. The economic problems of the system were immense and with few raw materials compared to its political competitors, the empire was failing to match their level of economic development.
6. The impact of war on this system was devastating. As the Austrian foreign minister observed at the outbreak of war in 1914: 'We were bound to die. We were at liberty to choose the manner of our death, and we chose the most terrible.'[17]

There is little doubt that all these six factors are relevant to any discussion of political change in central Europe in 1918. However, the problem for political scientists in discussing the causal factors relating to change is basically twofold: what weight should be given in particular circumstances to one or other of these factors and what are the relationships between the variables? In addition, there is the danger of arguing in a circular fashion. Thus, to claim that weak and inefficient governments are causal factors in political change comes very close to claiming that weak systems collapse because they are weak and those that survive without revolutionary or radical change are, by definition, strong. This would not advance the argument very far. Finally, this list of six causes may be useful for the Austro-Hungarian Empire, but does it have any general utility? Are multi-ethnic countries – Yugoslavia or Burundi, for example – more likely to change in dramatic fashions than more homogenous countries?

The problem of demonstrating causality, however, should not deter political scientists from seeking to identify fundamental factors promoting political change and attempting to apply those variables to examples of change such as the largely bloodless revolutions in Eastern Europe in 1989. For example, what role do counter-élites play in producing change, and are there cases of effective change in systems in which there were no autonomous organisations to provide the new leadership? This question and numerous others can be addressed through the rich body of evidence that has emerged from political changes in the late twentieth century.

Economic and social factors

There is little doubt that economic and social factors are both a consequence and cause of political change. Marxists have developed a whole theory of political change within these parameters; in general, they argue that political structures and processes are a consequence of economic relationships. The Marxist view of political change rests on what is often called 'the materialist conception of history'. Marx saw human beings as essentially social beings moulded by particular stages of economic and social development; the values and attitudes of individuals are, in particular, a product of the economic class to which the individual belongs, while the class itself is defined by relationships within the society to the means of production. As the division of labour developed in history, so did class differences, and the classes with economic power also wielded political power.

According to Marxists, contemporary capitalism, the economic system characterising present liberal democracies, witnesses a struggle between two opposing classes, the bourgeoisie, the capitalist class which owns the means of production, and the proletariat which possesses nothing but its own labour power. The contradictions within capitalism give rise to ever deepening economic crises, the proletariat becomes an agent of revolutionary change and a communist society is the final result. Of course, there are many differences between Marxists yet it is important to remember that Marxism has also been one of the most significant legitimising agents of revolutionary change in the twentieth century.

Even without accepting Marxist interpretations of political change, it is clear that economic and social relationships within a society are significant. Race may replace or lie alongside class as the catalyst, as illustrated by the rapidly changing political map of South Africa. Population migrations have had important repercussions in the United States throughout the history of the republic. Since 1945, internal movements of people within American boundaries have given more political power within the American political system to the southern and south-western states. Carter, in 1976, was the first southerner to be elected president since the American civil war, if one discounts the abnormal accession of Johnson in 1963; and in 1992 the Democratic presidential ticket was led by two southerners, while Bush on the Republican ticket claimed Texan allegiance. Just as the movement of non-European Jews into Israel after 1947 gradually weakened the Labour Party's dominance, so the massive influx of Russian Jews constituted a major factor in the Labour Party's victory in 1992, with important implications for Israeli foreign policy.

War and foreign intervention

Marx once observed: 'The redeeming feature of war is that it puts a nation to the test. As exposure to the atmosphere reduces all mummies to instant dissolution, so war passes extreme judgement on social systems that have outlived their vitality.'[18] Defeat in armed conflict often has serious consequences for political systems. German and Japanese defeats in 1945 ushered in stable liberal democratic systems to replace the dictatorial, authoritarian systems of the pre-war period. War may hasten economic decline even among the victors; after 1945, the British, French and Dutch empires collapsed, and their economies had been weakened by war, with manifold consequences for the successor states in Africa and Asia.

The use of force may also create and sustain political systems. East European communist systems were largely a result of Soviet occupation after 1945; the USSR maintained the communist systems in Hungary in 1956 and in Czechoslovakia in 1968 by the use of the Soviet army. The United States has a long history of intervention in Latin America.[19] The fall of the democratically elected Marxist leader Allende in Chile, in 1973, was partly engineered by the American government. and this in turn ushered in a long period of right-wing, repressive dictatorship led by General Pinochet. Guatemala, Nicaragua, Panama and the small island of Grenada all provide examples of political change following armed American intervention.

Foreign intervention may be more indirect yet no less crucial as an agent of political change. The collapse of the USSR has made American sanctions against Cuba far more significant and may eventually lead to political change there, although perhaps only after Castro leaves office. Economic sanctions against South Africa were instrumental in introducing the possibility of evolution to a more liberal, representative system of government there.[20] International economic sanctions have not caused the downfall of strongmen in Libya and Iraq, but they do place strains on those regimes that ultimately may produce fundamental change in these governments.

Effectiveness of government

Historically there has been a close relationship between the performance of a political regime and its survival. At the extreme there have been cases such as the overthrow of the Tsarist government in Russia when it could not cope with the problems thrown up by the 1914–18 war. It could neither manage the conduct of the war with Germany to ward off humiliating defeats, nor could it deal with the internal dislocation that the war imposed.[21] The Chinese revolution, with the communists finally triumphant in 1949, was partly a consequence of the Nationalist regime's inability to cope with the various crises of the 1930s and 1940s. The collapse of the Weimar Republic and the Nazi take-over in 1933 is adequate testimony to the failures of the government in the face of the economic crises created by the Great Depression. The Depression also struck the liberal democracies of Europe and North America, but those regimes proved to be more resilient.

Ironically, a system may respond too vigorously to challenges and the effective response may set in motion a chain of events that the government was seeking to avoid. An armed insurrection in Dublin, in 1916, offered little direct threat to British rule in Ireland; it was poorly supported and easily crushed. However, such was the ferocity of the British government's response, especially the execution of some of the captured rebels, that opposition to British rule increased enormously and helped pave the way for the creation of an independent Irish state by 1922.[22] More recently, the over-response of the Indonesian government to students in 1998 led to the eventual downfall of that regime.

Individuals, groups and political élites

One does not have to subscribe to the 'great men of history' thesis to appreciate the important role played by individuals in the process of political change. It is an area of some controversy, yet whilst individuals are not independent of the society in which they live, it is difficult to regard them as helpless pawns of impersonal forces. The historian Christopher Hill, writing of one of the most significant men in English history, Oliver Cromwell, says: 'Oliver was no conscious revolutionary like Robespierre or Lenin: the achievements of the English Revolution were not the result of his deliberate design. But it would not have astonished Oliver or his contemporaries to be told that the consequences of men's actions were not always those which the protagonists intended.[23]

Other revolutionaries, such as Lenin, Hitler or Mao, would be more confident in claiming paternity of their respective revolutions; and clearly any examination of radical political change would be forced to incorporate these individuals. Yet the individuals are not always clearly separable from the groups they lead and on which they become to a large degree dependent. All revolutions are characterised by the existence of groups willing and competent to seize power given the existence of favourable circumstances. An American historian has called the making of the new American Constitution in the 1780s a type of coup organised by a group of extremely talented politicians.[24] In contemporary Peru, a well-established coastal political élite has long been challenged by a formidable revolutionary group, Sendero Luminoso, or Shining Path. Based ideologically on a mixture of Maoism and Stalinism, Shining Path formed itself into a highly disciplined and effective revolutionary threat to the Peruvian regime; although weakened by the arrest of its top leadership in autumn 1992 and by a failed hostage-taking in 199x, it continued to undermine the legitimacy and effectiveness of the government.[25] Shining Path has been stronger in the mountains and also reflects some of the interests of the Indian and *mestizo* populations.

Barrington Moore in his assessment of the revolutionary movements that have produced modern political systems and of the paths to liberal democracy stressed the importance of the existence of groups independent of the state that were willing and able ultimately to seize power. They could then use suitable liberal democratic ideology to legitimise their political power.[26] In non-liberal democratic states, the role of the military is crucial, as we have seen in Chapter 12. Thus although the military generally plays a conservative role, there are many examples of its revolutionary potential, as Egypt in 1952 or Sudan in 1989 illustrate.

The role of political élites in revolutionary situations is crucial. The unity of the élites underlines stability; thus studies of British history show that since the eighteenth century élite unity has been an important and consistent feature of the British political system. Only once, over Irish Home Rule, on the eve of the 1914–18 war, was that unity threatened, with some danger to British political stability. A similar picture characterises the United States since 1789, with the civil war as a major exception. Amongst the liberal democracies, France and Germany have not enjoyed the same political fortune; the history of the French Third Republic until its collapse in 1940 is littered with examples of serious conflicts within the élites, and the rise of Hitler during the collapse of the Weimar Republic is a good example of élite disunity contributing to political change. The disintegration of the Soviet Union in 1991 underlines the lack of collective resolution on the part of the ruling Soviet élites to crush the opposition, which the Chinese communists had done so effectively in Tiananmen

Square in 1989.[27] Plato's words are pertinent here: 'revolution always starts from the outbreak of internal dissension in the ruling class. The constitution cannot be upset so long as that class is of one mind, however small it may be.[28]

Political ideologies

Ideologies are an important factor in the process of political change. These systems of thought can explain, justify, accommodate and encourage change; they are also universal and can be effective in a variety of settings. They are action-related, normative systems of ideas that are coherently articulated and are used to defend or attack the existing distribution of power within and between political systems.[29] To the extent that they are fully developed, they provide overall guides to political action, and perhaps also for other types of social behavior. The German term *Weltanschaung*, or 'world outlook', is a useful way to describe and understand political ideologies.

All political change, whether evolutionary or revolutionary, and likewise resistance to change, is equally justified by ideological principles. The 1789 French Revolution summed up its ideological aims with the powerful slogan of 'Liberty, Equality, Fraternity' and the Bolshevik Revolution carried the same ideological message, albeit with important qualifications. Liberalism has been and remains a significant ingredient of most revolutionary changes; the American Declaration of Independence of 1775 constitutes one of the most powerful ideological statements in modern history. The revolutionary changes in Europe, Latin America and southern Africa of the 1980s and 1990s have all been accompanied by liberal democratic justifications.

Some ideologies are more coherent than others. Marxism is far more coherent than fascism, irrespective of the political influence of these ideologies in the modern world. Populism, despite its drawing power, defies systematic conceptualisation, or attempts to apply the label of either 'right' or 'left'.[30] Ideologies are often historically and intellectually linked. Thus since the nineteenth century, liberalism has gone hand in hand with democracy; in the twentieth century, fascism has been closely identified with nationalism.

Nationalism is now one of the most powerful motors of political change, yet it is one of the most difficult of all contemporary ideologies to analyse.[31] The post-1989 events in the former Soviet Union and the political disintegration of the former Yugoslavia are powerful examples of the role of nationalism in contemporary political change. Nationalism is even more potent when it is allied to other ideologies, such as liberalism or fascism. Nationalism also indicates the problem of separating ideologies from other systems of belief and from political culture.[32] Thus modern Islam cannot be defined solely as an ideology. It is far more comprehensive because of its religious essence and cultural dimensions, yet it is currently a powerful agent of political change, particularly when allied to forms of nationalism. The changes in the Middle East since 1945 are impossible to analyse without reference to these twin forces, and the Iranian Revolution of 1979 and the success of the Taliban in Afghanistan are recent relevant examples.[33]

Of course, not all political scientists and historians have accepted either the universality or political relevance of political ideologies; it was once fashionable to speak of the 'end of ideology'.[34] One problem is that ideological consensus can be mistaken for an absence of ideology. The underlying ideological language of the United States is liberalism, inherited from the eighteenth-century revolution and reinforced by the capitalist system. Because of the underlying ideological consensus in America, it is often wrongly assumed that ideology plays no part in the politics of that system. In Europe there was discussion of a 'post-war consensus' around the mixed-economy welfare state. Individual countries may have somewhat different versions of that political and economic arrangement,[35] but there were some fundamental commonalities. Again it was argued that ideology had ended, given that both left and right accepted the appropriateness of the political and economic arrangements. If indeed ideology had ever ended, it was certainly revived by ideological regimes with values coming from the political right such as those of Mrs Thatcher and Ronald Reagan.[36]

A separate (but related) notion from the 'end of ideology' thesis is that introduced by Francis Fukuyama in 1989, in an article entitled 'The End of History?'[37] His argument is that the revolutions of 1989 marked the end of a particular stage of historical development; liberal democracy had triumphed at the expense of rival ideologies and that period of history characterised by conflicts between powerful rival ideologies is at an end. The thesis invoked a storm of intellectual of protest[38] but it is clearly relevant to the discussion of political change and to the significance of the revolutions in Eastern Europe in 1989.

The East European revolutions, 1989

The revolutions in Eastern and Central Europe were remarkable for many reasons. They had important consequences for the post-1945 Cold War and international relations and for the international status of communist ideology. The changes in Eastern Europe were immense. Poland, Hungary, Romania, Czechoslovakia, Bulgaria and East Germany saw the end of Soviet domination, the collapse of one-party communist rule, the introduction of competitive elections, the creation of more representative assemblies and the often rather brutal transitions to free-market economics. These changes intensified the rate of change in Albania. They changed the political map of Europe by hastening the break-up of the Soviet Union into states based on its constituent republics; they also produce the unification of the two Germanies and also the separation of Czechs and Slovak republics.

For the political scientist, the process of revolutionary change and its political, economic and social consequences are of tremendous importance. There is, however, not a great deal of systematic evidence linked with the theories about rapid change in politics. The events in Russia and Eastern Europe since 1989 provide a good source of data about political change and the creation of new governments. Let us now look at the various reasons why these momentous events of 1989 took place and whether they match the generalisations already discussed. However, it is important to bear in mind that the various factors hastening political change are interdependent and that some factors are more relevant than others in the context of particular political systems, and therefore any generalisations must be considered with some scepticism.

External factors were of obvious importance in Eastern Europe. The progressive disintegration of the Soviet Union not only provided a spur, but as soon as Gorbachev came to power in the Soviet Union in 1985, he began to urge major changes on the East European satellite states. Moreover, Gorbachev had redefined the USSR's strategic interests, and besides being unable to interfere in the internal affairs of these states in their transitions in 1989, he did not wish to. Thus the Soviet and Warsaw Pact armed forces that had intervened or threatened to intervene to stifle change before, remained in their barracks. Changes in Poland and Hungary showed the populations elsewhere that communism could be toppled and each successive revolution was more rapid than its predecessor. Another important external factor was the willingness of first Hungary and later Czechoslovakia to permit East German refugees to cross their borders in the late summer of 1989, thus fatally undermining the DDR regime.

A second set of relevant factors in the 1989 upheavals was the economic and social problems of the East European states. These problems were both serious and worsening. Poland by 1989 was suffering from extreme food shortages with the resulting economic hardships for the population. The situation in Romania was even more desperate. Even the relatively successful East German economy, dependent as it was on West German economic assistance, was in serious difficulties. All countries suffered energy problems, labour shortages and obvious technological backwardness, especially in areas such as information technology. Social problems also were acute throughout Eastern Europe, with profound environmental devastation, rising death rates and frightening infant mortality rates.[39]

These problems were not sufficient to spark off the 1989 revolutions, but they were allied to two other interrelated variables: the weaknesses and ineptitude of the respective governments in the face of these problems and splits within and loss of confidence by the political élites of Eastern Europe. The erosion of confidence was exacerbated by the knowledge that the Soviet Union was no longer willing or capable of coming to their aid. They were unable to deal with the huge problems such as the shortages of essential goods, food ration-

ing and fuel shortages. Political divisions appeared, of which
the most dramatic was the split between the military and the
Securitate, the secret police, during the Romanian revolution.

The importance of these divisions within the former political
élites is emphasised by the relative absence of opposition by
existing organised groups within these political systems. It is
true that Solidarity played a key role in Poland and the
Protestant Churches became a focus of opposition to the
communist regime in East Germany, but these were exceptions. A major problem of analysis concerns the role of the mass
of people. It has been argued that these were not spontaneous
revolutions, but there is little doubt that, particularly in
Czechoslovakia and East Germany, the label 'popular uprising' may be applied. On the other hand, it is clearer that in the
élite-led Polish and Hungarian revolutions reform communists
played a vital part. Certainly, with the exception of Romania,
there was little of the bloodshed usually associated with mass
revolutions.[40]

The role of ideology in these revolutions is more problema-
tical. Certainly there were no outstanding ideas such as
characterised the 1789 French or 1917 Russian revolutions.
Intellectuals played a major role in all the revolutions but not
all wanted to embrace the liberal democratic political and
economic models of Western Europe. Nationalism, liberalism
and populism embroidered the ideological claims of the new
revolutionaries, but the main foundation of unity was simply a
rejection of communism. The 1989 revolutions were, in one
sense, the most non-ideological revolutions in modern history.

This lack of clear ideological foundations raises serious
problems for the post-communist regimes and indicates that
the revolutions are not yet finished. All the political systems of
Eastern Europe face huge political, economic and social problems and only East Germany, as a result of unification with
an economic giant, may escape a lengthy period of turmoil. In
many respects the successor states resemble the political systems of the area between 1918 and 1939; they must all be
viewed, at present, as unstable political systems with uncertain
futures. Certainly ideology is not dead. These political systems
may undergo future changes and develop into stable liberal
democracies on the West European model, or some may, given

the economic and social uncertainties, worsened by the crude application of fashionable market economics, develop into varying types of authoritarian populist regimes.

It seems that there are no simple generalisations that can be made from this set of major changes in Eastern Europe. In some instances the revolutions may have been élite dominated, while in others there was a more significant popular element. Likewise, in at least one case there was a readily apparent ideological alternative to the dominant communist system, but what does come through all the possible explanations is that when there is widespread pressume for change there will be some change. It may be delayed by force, but it will come.

Retrograde political change?

We have already noted that there was widespread democratisation of the countries of South America and the former socialist countries during the 1980s and early 1990s. This was an extremely hopeful occurrence and fostered a good deal of academic debate and theorising. In some accounts democratisation appeared almost inevitable, and irreversible. Unfortunately, that does not appear to be the case and there have been some turning back toward more authoritarian regimes. Interestingly, however, these retrograde steps have been chosen at the ballot-box in several cases. For example, the Peruvian people selected President Fujimoro in 1990, and he has created a close alliance with the military to preserve his power. Likewise, in several Central American countries the allies of former autocratic leaders are doing well in open elections.

To some extent any assumption about the inevitability of democracy could have been questioned from the outset. As much as most people in western democracies value that form of government, the economic and social strains in most of the developing countries may make the use of greater coercion appealing to political leaders. Many practical politicians conceive of the goals of democratisation and socio-economic development to be somewhat inconsistent, despite strong academic evidence to the contrary.[41] Further, the military in many poorer countries continues to enjoy a great deal of technical expertise that is crucial for development of these regimes. Creating closer alliances with the military may, therefore, be a means for accelerating the development process.

Change in industrialised democracies

We have been discussing political change primarily in terms of democratisation and political development. That certainly is a pervasive topic of concern, but as we noted at the beginning of the chapter there is also on-going change in the more affluent democracies. We have documented those changes in a number of the earlier chapters. Party systems have been changing as voter allegiances to older parties have declined and new issues have arisen. Parliaments have tended to wane in power as executives have increased their impacts on policy. Administrative systems have changed perhaps the most dramatically, and have come to resemble private sector management almost as much as they do civil service systems. These systems may be developed, but they are far from stagnant.

Perhaps the most important change has been the creation of the European Union and the potential creation of a quasi-federal state in Europe. In the forty-plus years since the signing of the Treaty of Rome the (then) European Economic Community has progressed from little more than a customs union toward a state with its own currency and with the beginnings of a foreign policy.[42] It still lacks its own military and depends upon the member states for implementation of most policies,[43] but in many ways has the appearance of a developed state. In addition, the political identification of citizens has been shifting from the individual nation states to Europe as a political entity (Table 13.1). In the context of the European nation states from which the European Union has been formed, the major problem may be the apparent 'democratic deficit' and the absence of direct connections of voters, particularly with the executive.

The Europeanisaton of countries in Europe can be seen as occurring at the same time as a downward movement of political power and authority. Even in countries such as France and Spain with long histories of centralised control there is a

Table 13.1   Changing support for European Union membership
(percentage of survey respondents in favour)

	1975	1980	1985	1990	1993
Belgium	70	67	68	76	64
Denmark	43	35	36	55	61
France	70	56	70	68	56
Germany	63	71	63	69	59
Greece	–	44	47	80	68
Ireland	61	53	57	79	75
Italy	77	78	79	81	71
Netherlands	78	80	84	86	83
Portugal	–	–	61	73	64
Spain	–	–	67	72	56
UK	55	25	39	56	48

Source: European Commission, *Eurobarometer* (Brussels: annual).

process of decentralisation, with increasing powers of regional governments.[44] In Spain this has produced an incipient, if asymmetrical, federalism, with some regions with longer histories of opposition to the centre – Catalonia, Galicia and the Basque country – gaining more powers than the other regions. The United Kingdom held out against these decentralising pressures longer than the other countries, but the creation of Scottish and Welsh assemblies in 1999 marks the beginning of a more regionalised Britain as well.

The simultaneous growth of the European and regional levels of government is producing a system of 'multi-level governance' in Europe in which the nation state can be seen as losing powers upward to Brussels and downward to regions.[45] These changes may produce a very different style of governing than in the past, and also may appear to change the way in which political life is conceptualised, and the ultimate sources of power and authority. The shift to a multi-level pattern of governing has not been completely achieved, however, and nation states do remain at the heart of most governing, but European states are now different and face a different set of constraints than in the past.

As well as the constraints within Europe, the industrialised democracies are also facing even more extensive changes in the international political economy. Globalisation is primarily a threat to the governance capacity of the less developed countries, but even the most affluent governments must take somewhat into account the increased influence of international markets and international organisations.[46] These international pressures may drive governments toward more common patterns of economic and social policy, and reduce their capacity to tax mobile industries, for fear that the companies will simply leave and relocate in a more hospitable environment.[47] The mobility of capital may be exaggerated, but it is clear that governments no longer can ignore the international economy as they might once have been able to do.

Summary

Political change is an enduring phenomenon. No matter how wealthy, democratic and effective a political system may be, there appears to be a human need to attempt to improve. The political process may also drive the change process, with the opposition (whether in a democratic or non-democratic system) having to advocate new programmes that can appeal to the public. If they are elected to office, the former opposition may actually try to make their proposals work, although the rate of success should not encourage the average citizen. Indeed, many of the 'new' programmes implemented may simply be swings of a pendulum, going from centralisation to decentralisation, or regulation to deregulation, and back again.

Notes and references

1. The literature on the European Union has been mushrooming. For one useful collection, see J. Redmond and G. Rosenthal (eds), *The Expanding European Union* (Boulder, CO: Lynne Rienner, 1998).
2. B. Moore, *Social Origins of Dictatorship and Democracy* (London: Faber, 1967) part 1; see also T. Skocpol, *States and Social Revolutions* (Cambridge: Cambridge University Press, 1979).
3. For a comparative analysis of revolutions, see K. Kumar, 'The Revolutions of 1989: Socialism, Capitalism and Democracy', *Theory and Society*, 21 (1992) pp. 309–56.

4. See, for example, K. Polanyi, *The Great Transformation* (New York: Farrar & Rinehart, 1944); also, see H. L. Wilensky and C. N. Lebeaux, Industrial Society and Social Welfare (New York: Russell Sage, 1958).

5. For a good review of the development literature up to the present, see M. Palmer, *Political Development: Dilemmas and Challenges* (Itasca, IL: F. E. Peacock, 1997).

6. See S. P. Huntington, *The Third Wave: Democratization in the Twentieth Century* (Norman: University of Oklahoma Press, 1991).

7. G. Majone makes an analogous argument for building the political community in the European Union. See his 'Coasian Analysis and Non-Majoritarian Institutions in Europe', unpublished paper, European University Institute, Florence, Italy.

8. J. Higley and M. Burton, 'Elite Settlements and the Taming of Democracy', *Government and Opposition,* 33 (Winter, 1998) pp. 98–115.

9. See, for example, P. Gibbon, 'Some Reflections of Civil Society and Political Change', in L. Rudebeck, O. Tornquist and V. Rojas (eds), *Democratization in the Third World* (London: Macmillan, 1998).

10. R. D. Putnam, *Making Democracy Work: Civic Traditions in Modern Italy* (Princeton: Princeton University Press, 1993).

11. When asked how many governments Italy had had since the Second World War, one commentator answered wryly, 'One'.

12. This was one of the basic ideas of pluralist theory. See R. A. Dahl, *Who Governs?: Democracy and Power in an American City* (New Haven: Yale University Press, 1961).

13. Two interesting attempts to deal with the issue of consensus are M. Mills and F. King, *The Promise of Liberalism: A Comparative Analysis of Consensus Politics* (Aldershot: Dartmouth, 1996); P. Birnbaum, J. Lively and G. Parry, *Democracy, Consensus and Social Contract* (London: Sage, 1978).

14. See Arend Lijphart, *Democracies: Patterns of Majoritarian and Consensus Government* (New Haven: Yale University Press, 1984).

15. See S. M. Lipset, *Political Man* (London: John Hopkins University Press, 1981) pp. 226–9.

16. J. O. Voll, *Sudan: State and Society in Crisis* (Bloomington: Indiana University Press, 1991).

17. Quoted in A. J. P. Taylor, *The Habsburg Monarchy, 1808–1918* (London: Penguin, 1964, 1951) p. 232.

18. Quoted in A. Marwick, *Britain in the Century of Total War* (London: Bodley Head, 1968, 1970) p. 13.

19. L. Shoulz, *Beneath the United States: A History of U.S. Policy Toward Latin America* (Cambridge, MA: Harvard University Press, 1998).

20. See A. Lemon, *Apartheid in Transition* (Aldershot: Dartmouth, 1987) pp. 355–63; also, J. Blumenfeld, 'Economy under Siege', in *South Africa in Crisis,* ed. J. Blumenfeld (London: Croom Helm, 1987) pp. 17–33.

21. See L. Schapiro, *1917: The Russian Revolutions and the Origins of Present Day Communism* (London, 1984) pp. 1–19.

22. See J.J. Lee, *Ireland, 1912–1985* (Cambridge: Cambridge University Press, 1989) pp. 24–38, for a discussion of the political significance of the Easter Rising of 1916.

23. C. Hill, *God's Englishman: Oliver Cromwell and the English Revolution* (London, 1970) p. 263.

24. J.P. Roche, 'The Founding Fathers: A Reform Caucus in Action', *American Political Science Review*, 55, 4 (December 1961) pp. 799–816.

25. See M. Radu and V. Tismaneanu, *Latin American Revolutionaries* (London: Brassey, 1990); D.M. Masterson, *Militarism and Politics in Latin America* (New York: Greenwood, 1991); G. Tarazona-Sevillani, *Sendero Luminoso and the Threat of Narcoterrorism* (New York: Praeger, 1990).

26. See Moore, *Social Origins of Dictatorship and Democracy*, pp. 413–32.

27. See S. White *et al.*, *Developments in Soviet and Post-Soviet Politics*, 2nd edn (Basingstoke: Macmillan, 1992) pp. 2–21. For China, see S. White *et al.*, *Communist and Postcommunist Political Systems*, 3rd edn (London: Macmillan, 1990) pp. 304–7.

28. Quoted in Kumar, 'The Revolutions of 1989', p. 321.

29. For a discussion of ideology, see David McLellan, *Ideology* (Minneapolis: University of Minesota Press, 1986).

30. But see M. Kazin, *The Populist Persuasion: An American History* (Ithaca, NY: Cornell University Press, 1998); P.A. Taggart, *The New Populism and the New Politics: New Protest Parties in Sweden in Comparative Perspective* (New York: St. Martin's, 1996).

31. There is an excellent discussion of nationalism in E.J. Hobsbawm, *Nations and Nationalism since 1780* (Cambridge: Cambridge University Press, 1990). See also A.D. Smith, *National Identity* (Reno: University of Nevada Press, 1991).

32. There is some argument about the distinction between political culture and ideology. See W.T. Bluhm, *Ideologies and Attitudes* (Englewood Cliffs, NJ: Prentice-Hall, 1974); see also Chapter 6.

33. For the links between Islam and nationalism, see A. Heywood, *Political Ideologies* (London: Macmillan, 1992) pp. 163–70.

34. 'For the radical intellectual who has articulated the revolutionary impulses of the past century and a half, all this has meant an end to the chiliastic hopes, to millenarianism, to apocalyptic thinking – and to ideology. For ideology, which was once a road to action, has come to a dead end.' D. Bell, *The End of Ideology* (New York, 1960) pp. 369–70. A different, but still hostile approach to ideology is provided by a British Conservative: 'Ideology seems inseparable from class; hence the Tories can only remain a national party if they remain free from ideological infection.' I. Gilmour, *Inside Right: A Study of Conservatism* (London: Hutchinson, 1977) p. 132.

35. D. Kavanagh and P. Morris, *Consensus Politics from Atlee to Major* (Oxford: Blackwell, 1994); J.-E. Lane, 'The Decline of the Swedish Model', *Governance* 8 (1995), 579–90.

36. D.J. Savoie, *Reagan, Thatcher, Mulroney: In Search of a New Bureaucracy* (Pittsburgh: University of Pittsburgh Press, 1994).

37. Francis Fukuyama, 'The End of History?', *The National Interest*, 16 (Summer 1989) pp. 3–18.
38. See Kumar, 'The Revolutions of 1989', pp. 313–17.
39. One branch of the literature argues that economic problems *per se* are insufficient to produce revolutionary change. What appears more relevant is a sharp downturn after a period of economic progress. See J. C. Davis, 'Toward a Theory of Revolution', *American Sociological Review*, 27 (1962), 5–18.
40. See J. Eyal, 'Why Romania Could Not Avoid Bloodshed', in *Spring in Winter: The 1989 Revolutions*, ed. G. Prins (Manchester: University of Manchester Press, 1990) pp. 139–62.
41. Seymour Martin Lipset made one of the earliest, and still largely valid analysis. See his 'Economic Development and Political Development', *American Political Science Review* 53 (1959), 69–105.
42. See A. Sbragia, *Euro-Politics* (Washington, DC: The Brookings Institution, 1992).
43. The same is true for many federal systems such as Germany , where the central government implements almost all of its programmes through state and local governments.
44. S. Loughln and S. Mazey, *The End of the French Unitary State?* (London: Frank Cass, 1995).
45. G. Marks, L. Hooge and K. Blank, 'European Integration since the 1980s: State-Centric vs. Multi-Level Governance', *Journal of Common Market Studies*, 34 (1996), 341–78.
46. See Susan Strange, *The Retreat of the State* (Cambridge: Cambridge University Press, 1996); Jon Pierre and B. Guy Peters, *Globalization, Politics and the State* (Basingstoke: Macmillan, 2000).
47. Fritz Scharpf, 'Globalization: The Limitations of State Capacity', *Swiss Political Science Review* 4, (1998), 323–29.

Index